Lost in the Wild

T0151431

Lost in the Wild

Danger and Survival in the North Woods

CARY J. GRIFFITH

BOREALIS
BOOKS

Borealis Books is an imprint of the
Minnesota Historical Society Press.

www.borealisbooks.org

The Minnesota Historical Society
Press is a member of the Association
of American University Presses.

Manufactured in the
United States of America

11

∞ The paper used in this publication
meets the minimum requirements of
the American National Standard for
Information Sciences—Permanence
for Printed Library Materials, ANSI
Z39.48-1984.

ISBN-13: 978-0-87351-589-4 (paper)
ISBN-10: 0-87351-589-7 (paper)

Library of Congress
Cataloging-in-Publication Data

Griffith, Cary.
Lost in the wild : danger and survival
in the North woods / Cary J. Griffith.
    p.   cm.
  ISBN 0-87351-561-7
  (cloth : alk. paper)
  1. Wilderness survival—
      Minnesota—Boundary Waters
      Canoe Area.
  2. Search and rescue operations—
      Minnesota—Boundary Waters
      Canoe Area.
  3. Boundary Waters Canoe Area
      (Minn.)—Description and
      travel.
  I. Title.

GV200.5.G75 2006
613.6'9097767—dc22
                              2005029863

For Anna, Nick, Noah, and Jess—who have always shared my love for wild places. There are many more wilderness trails in our future.

And for my Mom, who tried to teach me piano before she ever suspected I might have a future with a pen.

And for my Dad, whose love of language infected us all.

Lost in the Wild

Lost in the Wild

PROLOGUE

Wilderness is a word we use very carelessly. The bogs of the Gunflint region . . . are the only true wilderness in this area: undisturbed, obscure, and a little otherworldly. . . . Bogs are mossy grottos of silence.

JOHN HENRICKSSON
Gunflint: The Trail, the People, the Stories

Bogs

There are still two hours of sunlight, more than enough time to make it back to camp—providing he can find it. Jason Rasmussen pushes through another section of brush, searching for his tent and supplies. He should have crossed his camp hours ago. Instead, he has been hiking since just before noon. It's almost four.

At least the rain hasn't restarted, he thinks. He slogs through yet another thick patch of forest, hoping he will find the long stretch of water, the narrow lake at whose north end he was camped. If he can find it, he can find his tent. If he can locate his tent, he can light a fire, get out of these wet clothes, and have something to eat. At this point he knows the food will make him feel better. He can already taste the freeze-dried, gourmet teriyaki chicken.

And what if I don't find the tent?

He doesn't let himself contemplate the devastation. He knows it is foolish to castigate himself for *not packing matches* in his waist pack, along with the crackers, tuna, whistle, and knife. *Idiot,* he thinks, before he can choke the thought. He pauses, opens his waist pack, and again rummages through its contents. He pats his coat and pants pockets—just to be sure. *No matches.* Bushwhacking in wet woods has left him soaked and cold. But if he finds the lake. . . .

Twenty yards ahead he sees light. There's a break in the tree line! He has finally found that hidden stretch of water. He allows himself one brief moment of hope. He pushes through the edge of brush. A sense of divine intervention, of deliverance starts to wash over him. He can practically feel his fire's warmth.

He bursts out of the forest wall and sees it: *another bog.* He is stunned. He stares at it, wondering if it is only a dream. A nightmare. His third bog in two days! He looks across its surface. This one appears more solid than the two he crossed yesterday. And it's narrower. He looks to his left, but the bog's treeless, flat surface stretches as far as he can see. He looks to the right and sees the same interminable gap. There is no way he can walk around it. Yet he feels certain that just beyond this bog he'll encounter the lake—his lake—stretching in front of his camp like a broad clear boulevard.

But bogs are dangerous. Jason Rasmussen is not a seasoned wilderness hiker, but this much he knows. Bogs are masses of floating vegetation, rivers and islands of floating grass hummocks. They can be anchored in spots, making the ground appear firm. You can place your foot on what appears to be solid ground. And it can feel solid. But when you give it your full weight, the thin vegetal surface can suddenly yawn and disintegrate, and you can drop like a rock into whatever depth of water lies beneath.

Jason envisions the sudden break, the plunge, the weightless feel of his body as it falls into freezing water—not touching bottom—kicking to the surface as he watches the last glint of sunlight disappear between closing sphagnum lips.

Come on, he catches himself. *Get hold of yourself. What's up with all the negativity?* He reminds himself of yesterday's bog-crossing success. And Jason knows he has to cross this one. There is no other way. He knows his lake, camp, and supplies rest just beyond that next rise. He can feel it. And the afternoon is getting on. He is cold, wet, tired, and hungry. The Tootsie Rolls he ate over an hour ago have done little to quiet his stomach's growl.

He searches for a test stick. He picks up a long tamarack bough and trims it down to a sturdy five-foot pole. He takes his first step, prodding the bog's grass and fern surface. It gives, but just barely. He steps onto it. It holds.

Across the twenty-foot gap he can see plenty of foot-wide pockmarks filled with black water. But he can also see several probable footholds through the honeycombed maze. He pushes his test pole forward. He finds another firm hummock and steps onto it. It gives, but holds.

He continues crossing the bog, first testing with his long pole. Twice the heavy staff breaks through the grassy surface. Both times he backtracks, chooses alternative routes to the left and then right, searching for more solid ground. Both times he moves forward.

Finally, he comes to within seven feet of the far edge. Too far to jump. He pushes the pole forward, testing, probing the tangled surface. It holds. He realizes he can jump from his current position, plant a foot on the solid patch, and close the distance between that hummock and the bog's edge with one strong leap.

That is just what he tries. He leaps forward five feet, feels the hard bottom of his hiking boot hitting solid turf —and then it starts to give. With sickening panic he feels his foot sink. The cold water envelopes his boot top, clams around his ankle and shin. His other foot is moving forward, searching for solid ground. He lurches forward. His first foot plunges into the hummock. His other foot searches in vain for something solid, and then it, too, disappears beneath the widening black water. For one brief moment, while the momentum of his body carries him across the bog's edge, he is knee-deep in mucky swamp. And then he falls in a shattered heap on the opposite shore.

A groan squeezes out of him as though someone has slammed him hard in the center of his stomach. He gets up stamping his feet, trying to shake them free of the freezing water. He looks down at his soaking pant legs. They cling to the contour of his calves. Water runnels off them, pooling in his boots.

Goddammit, he swears. Darkness is coming fast. The thought rises unbidden.

In one hour you're going to be wandering in the dark. And it could get cold. It could get very cold. You could freeze to death.

He exhales and notices his breath cloud in front of his face. He looks back over the bog, then forward. He is wet, tired, plenty cold already. The bog water feels as though it has soaked into much more than the bottoms of his shoes. Its icy fingers pull at the inside of his body, at his heart, at his spirit. He collapses on the side of the boggy bank. He doesn't want to push forward through another stand of low-hung tamarack, alder, and stunted, leafless black ash. It looks like a wall behind him, an impenetrable wall of wilderness brush.

Suddenly he's claustrophobic, barely able to breathe. He begins to wonder if he will ever find his way out of these woods. Tears start rimming his eyes. His vision blurs. He can't see anything. He cannot see the bog in front of him, the forest through which he came, even the ground in front of his face. He feels disoriented. He knows he should have long ago recovered his camp. He feels the panic he has kept at bay for the last two hours starting to rise. The huge body of an invisible wilderness weighs on him. He can feel its heaviness on his chest. He can feel his temples pound. He slumps on the edge of the bog and tears spill from his eyes, creasing his haggard face.

He came to the woods for solace. He wanted respite and wilderness solitude. He cannot believe it has come to this. He can't believe anything. He tries to get hold of himself, tries to calm his hiccupping desolation, to recover his reason, but there is nothing. A huge emptiness settles over his heart, over his entire self, a final desperation, and wrenching words surface from this depth: *What am I going to do? What in God's name am I going to do now?*

Bell Lake environs, Quetico Provincial Park, Ontario, Wednesday afternoon, August 5, 1998

Dan Stephens stumbles south all afternoon, penetrating deeper into remote bush. When he remembers his friends, he calls out, but the sudden vibration coming up from his throat intensifies his head throb. And besides—no one ever responds. An interminable insect whine follows him. He hears occasional bird songs. He walks deeper into the wilderness, wondering if there's a lake. He crosses more small creeks in stagnant bogs. He pushes through the marshy region.

He has trouble recalling that just five hours earlier he was leading a group of Scouts from Chattanooga, Tennessee, down the Quetico's Man Chain of lakes. He can barely remember who he is: Dan Stephens, an Eagle Scout from Georgia, spending the summer of his twenty-second year leading Scout groups out of the Northern Tier High Adventure Camp in Ely, Minnesota.

He remembers this much about his Chattanooga group: there are two fathers and six kids. Until this trip none of them had ever set foot in the North Woods. One of the fathers had been on other scouting trips, but he moved like an aging bear and was ill-suited—at least by current health—to spend a week paddling and portaging. The other father was a reasonable hand with a paddle, but he had spent little time in the wilderness.

In spite of their inexperience, the Chattanooga group had been his summer's best. From their first day out they felt as comfortable as old friends, though Dan could see they would be lost without him.

Dan remembers he was with the group. He remembers some of their names and faces. He recalls the Man Chain and their ultimate destination: Prairie Portage on the Canadian border. But there are still thirty miles of hard paddling in front of them and it will be at least two more days before they reach it.

What he can't quite figure out is why he now stumbles alone through lowland bush and swamp creased by waterways and bogs, waving away bugs.

Near late afternoon he comes to a U-shaped lake. He is

tired and hungry and not entirely clear-headed about where he is or how he got here. He pauses at the shore, hoping to regain his bearings. He sits for an hour, trying to rationalize his position. He knows he is not thinking clearly. He needs to get an unfettered look, from someplace high enough to give him a reasonable vista.

Near the lake an old-growth white pine stretches skyward, offering a panoramic view of the area—Dan assumes—if he can climb it. He considers the lower branches. This one has enough hand- and footholds to make climbing a possibility. He walks around the tree in the shade, locates the most viable route upwards, and starts to climb.

Fifteen minutes later he is almost fifty feet off the ground. From his aerie he has a wide view of the surrounding country. He can see a medium-sized lake, with a longer, larger lake beyond it. By dead reckoning he surmises the lakes lie west or southwest. He guesses the longer lake is Other Man, and is comforted by finding a lake he remembers from the map. He thinks it is probably the best place to turn. If he can make it to Other Man, a common route for those traversing the Man Chain, he might encounter his group, or some other group paddling down the chain.

He descends the tree, takes his bearings, and stumbles ahead, pushing through more swamp. In a few places he has to turn to avoid boggy patches or open water, and in this lowland area the brush is particularly thick, but he tries to maintain his direction.

It is heavy slogging for another forty-five minutes, maybe an hour. He loses track of time. He hasn't checked his watch, but at the very least he thinks he should have run into, or rounded, the smaller lake before Other Man.

He should be close. But after he has been hiking for what seems like well over an hour, all he sees in front of him is more swamp and bog.

He approaches the edge of an old beaver pond. The area is boggy and stunted with low-hung willow, cattails, and thick marsh grass. The tall grass surrounds a large pond-bog complex. Another white pine rises over the pond's edge. It has a scraggly head but otherwise angles out over an outcropping of rock and appears scaleable. Dan climbs up to have another look, trying to discern his position.

When he looks west he sees the larger lake farther south. He realizes he has angled in the wrong direction, probably north-northwest. He is stunned. He has *increased* the distance between himself and Other Man. He cannot believe it. He castigates himself, cursing. *Idiot!* He can hardly believe he angled through the swamp until he was walking in almost the exact opposite direction from the way he should have been heading. He was sure he was hiking west-northwest. Instead he has slogged through at least a half mile of swamp, hiking almost due north. He looks down, shaken by the realization, and curses again.

He climbs out of the tree. It doesn't feel like the right place to reconnoiter, but reason has at least reasserted itself enough to convince him he should stay put until he figures out some kind of plan.

He comes down to the edge of the old beaver pond. It looks clear in the late afternoon sun. His head still hurts. He kneels beside the water to fill his collapsible canteen. When he leans over, his head aches and a brief bout of vertigo threatens to relieve him of this morning's oatmeal and gorp.

He sits and waits for the nausea to pass. He is beginning to realize his predicament. He is in the middle of a swamp with not much of an idea where to turn. He had not considered it, but now he looks around in the late afternoon—and it dawns on him. He may have to spend the night in darkness, in wilderness, alone under the stars.

As if in answer, a small cloud of bugs rises like a fist to his face. He waves them away and turns to be rid of them. His head is still splitting, with a knot on his forehead the size of a loon's egg. He knows he is not thinking clearly. But he also knows the sun is going down and dusk brings out the bugs. He recalls stories of moose and deer driven to frenzy by swarms of black flies and mosquitoes. Seeking relief, they would swim into the middle of lakes where some of them, rather than return to shore and the swarms, would tread water until they finally weakened and drowned.

He peers around the edge of the pond and wonders what he will do when dusk settles. He knows the end of the day ushers in one good hour of bugs, maybe more. And he knows this night there will be no netting or nylon or rim of firelight and smoke or bug juice to keep them in abeyance. People who have not lived through pestilential swarms do not know they can separate a person from sanity and reason. And it is this knowledge that focuses Dan's eyes over his lowland swamp, searching for some kind of shelter, some place to hide.

FIRST STEPS

Hiking here is like going back in time to the Stone Age—at least that is the feeling I got hiking among the harsh bedrock lakes with intriguing names like Superstition and Rock of Ages.

JOHN PUKITE
Hiking Minnesota

If it had not been for my care in protecting my eyes . . . these fierce creatures would have blinded me many times. . . . It had happened so to others, who lost the use of their eyes for several days, so poisonous is their stinging and biting to those who have not yet become acclimatized.

GABRIEL SAGARD-THÉODAT
The Long Journey to the Country of the Hurons

1

Preparation

Twin Cities REI, Sunday, October 21, 2001

Jason Rasmussen walks under REI's pine bole and iron beam archway separating the parking lot from the store near the Mall of America. For the second time this week he passes a large sign on his left proclaiming:

> Gunflint Lake
> Elevation 470 m.
> BWCAW–Quetico
> Minnesota–Ontario

Like everything else in this place, it reminds him of outdoor adventure. He continues across the narrow courtyard and steps over a footbridge. An artificial waterfall cascades over stones into a small pool. On this late fall day the water is littered with yellow birch leaves, giving the place a North Woods feel, reminding Jason why he has come.

As it had for so many others, the catastrophe of September 11, 2001 altered his travel plans. For over a year, the third-year medical student from the Medical College of Wisconsin–Milwaukee had been training for a trek in Nepal. His REI Adventures tour was scheduled to leave in October, his rotation month off. Now that his tour has been canceled, he has unexpected time on his hands and a yearning to walk in wild places.

He needs to get away. He needs to go someplace where he won't smell antiseptics or see fluorescent lighting or classrooms. The Nepalese trek, for which he had trained so assiduously, was going to satisfy his thirst for remote adventure, for someplace entirely different. Now more than ever he needs wilderness and the solace it has provided him in the past.

He had lived in Minnesota until he was ten. Then his family moved to California, where he finished high school and attended community college before returning to attend the University of Minnesota, and then the Medical College. And in all that time he never once had a chance to set foot in the North Woods. It is an absence he has regretted. He thinks his visit to REI can help him sort out a destination and a plan.

He grabs hold of the canoe-paddle handles and opens the massive doors, looks up at the fifty-five-foot climbing wall. It's difficult not to admire the glass-enclosed wall; on the outside, large beams stick out of the roof—the REI landmark. From either side down a considerable stretch of Interstate 494, the protruding spikes beckon like half of the Statue of Liberty's crown. And for many, including Jason Rasmussen, that's what this store means: freedom, the special call of wild places, and twenty-first century technology that will take you there in style and bring you back safe.

Jason enters the store. He admires the colorful resin-based kayaks and Kevlar canoes hanging from ceiling rafters. Old Town, Shadow, Perception, Wilderness. Even the names convey adventure. Racks of the finest outdoor merchandise in the world line store aisles. He sees paddle gear, winter sportswear in vibrant primary colors, waterproof duffels, pullovers, pants, and socks that wick away sweat. There are boots lined with Thinsulate — small layers of light and warm hyperinsulation surrounded by Gore-Tex, a semipermeable layer that breathes out, but prevents water from penetrating.

REI's layout forces you to amble through much of the store; around the corner to accessories, a small display of wristwatches, sunglasses, high-end compasses, GPS devices, Leatherman and Swiss army knives, windproof lighters, compact digital cameras with built-in binoculars. Down the aisle he sees yellow, light green, and orange tents pitched on the cement floor. Across from them hang camping stoves and several racks of bottled gas. Beyond the tents are mittens, gloves, hats, gaiters, and still further down, backpacks. Gore-Tex, nylon, polypropylene . . . Camelback, Valhalla, The North Face. The latest gear made from the best stuff man can cultivate or conjure, and named by someone with a flare for merchandising the wild.

Winter is coming on, and Jason knows he'll have to dress warmly. But with equipment like this, much of which he has already accumulated in anticipation of his Nepalese trek, his only concern is which freeze-dried gourmet meal he'll cook for dinner.

In the camping section he talks to one of REI's helpful attendants. This one he knows: an old algebra teacher from his hiatus year at Normandale Community College, when he was establishing residency before enrolling at the University. Like many of REI's attendants, his former instructor is moonlighting, not so much for money, but for the love of wild places and the conversation it engenders—and a discount on REI goods.

REI doesn't have sales people; it has consultants. Jason tells him he is thinking about heading up north, preferably to the Boundary Waters, for a three-day hike, and his old prof takes him to a rack of books. He pulls down John Pukite's *Hiking Minnesota* and shows Jason the Pow Wow Trail, a twenty-six-mile-long circular hike that puts in near Isabella Lake and immediately crosses into the Boundary Waters. It meanders through spruce, pine, poplar, and—as the book describes—"remote bedrock lakes, beaver dams, and cascading creeks."

That's it. He can tell just from the description and the way the trail-line curves over the page in a wobbly circle, crossing small lines of creeks, edging along pine symbols, with plenty of small tents signifying campsites. He glances over the section describing the terrain. "Difficult. Western side composed of rough and tumble trails."

Jason has hiked in woods before and knows what to expect. He has a good map and compass and knows how to use them. But Pukite's book was published in 1998, a full year before the July 4 blowdown storm that altered large tracts of BWCAW forest, making some of it impassable. In fact, three years later, areas around the Pow Wow Trail had grown up so dense you would need a machete and a chainsaw to get through.

Pukite's text identifies some of the trail's complicated background and significant challenges. The Pow Wow was developed in 1977 by the Youth Conservation Corps. Rather

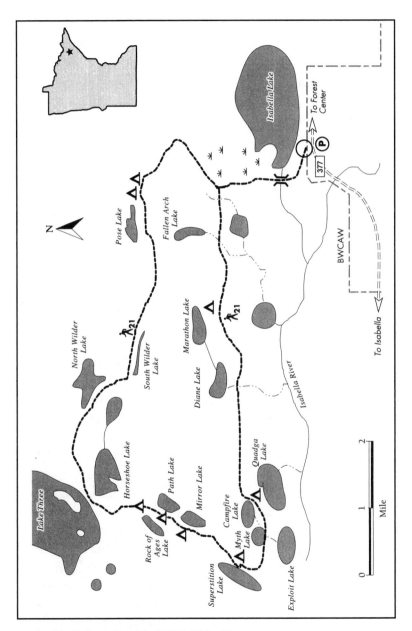

Pow Wow Trail map from John Pukite's *Hiking Minnesota*

than plot and cut an entirely new path, they made use of a maze of old logging roads that crisscrossed the boggy country east of what was then the small town of Forest Center. But the bogs finally prevailed, forcing them to move the entire trail system west, where the country was for the most part drier and better suited to hiking and backcountry camping. There are still plenty of places where the path is questionable, marked by fallen trees and rugged country. The wise, Pukite advises, will rely on a good compass, map, and serious orienteering skills.

Jason doesn't ignore these lines, but he skims over them, feeling a greater appreciation for trail descriptions that speak to the kind of hike he imagines: "If you go, you will be treated to special lakes that you have nearly all to yourself." He is left with a vague notion of hiking through quiet woods and finding the solitude he desires.

He notes the book, and another entitled *Wilderness Survival.* This one is a small pamphlet, light enough to carry, and with enough information so that the entire text is worthwhile. He places it with his other items.

He walks over to REI's map section, where the consultant shows him the yellow-and-blue Fisher maps, familiar to anyone who hikes or fishes the wild places in northern Minnesota. They find the one containing the detail of the Pow Wow Trail and surrounding area. Map F-4: *Lake One, Lake Two, Lake Three, Lake Four, Bald Eagle Lake, Lake Insula.* Spreading the map out on a table nearby, he can clearly see the entire area, including elevations and streams. He smiles, contemplating the fall hike through cool woods—the air crisp, the sky a perfect blue. In the Cities the week has been one of those easy transitions from season to season, when the days are warm and the leaves hang on, lulled by the false promise of Indian summer.

Beside the Fisher maps are McKenzie maps. Number 19, *Isabella Lake,* depicts the Pow Wow Trail in much the same detail as the Fisher map, with one notable exception. If you hike along the circular portion of the trail counterclockwise, the first two miles move north-northeast in a near-straight line. Then the trail angles sharply left almost ninety degrees, moving north-northwest. A small dotted line continues along the north-northeast route, indicating the path of the old trail, the one the Pukite text described as originally forged along old logging roads east of Forest Center. That part of the trail was later abandoned and moved to the western half, drier region.

The Fisher map shows the same ninety-degree turn to the left, but not the faded continuation of the line depicting the original Pow Wow Trail. But Jason Rasmussen doesn't look at the McKenzie map.

He rolls up the familiar yellow-and-blue map, and on his way out gathers a few more items for his trip. At the last minute he fingers a small orange whistle, the kind you can hang around your neck on a colorful lanyard. He thinks about it—wondering if he really needs it. Like most things in this store, it is expensive: $4.95 for a little piece of plastic. Jason peers at the product description, smiling while he wades through the marketing hype that will tell him why an orange plastic whistle costs almost five bucks. It was rated at 118 decibels. "Exceeds U.S. Coast Guard and SOLAS regulations," he reads.

"SOLAS regulations?" He flips the package over: "Safety of life at sea."

But he is not going to sea; he is walking into the woods.

Surrounded by so much high-tech equipment—all designed to bring us closer to the wilderness, but make our journeys comfortable and safe—it is easy to forget that people still hike into woods, get lost, and die. Jason conjures an image of the one-million-acre wilderness as one vast undulating sea of forest and lake. He pauses over the orange whistle, finally tossing it into his basket with its accompanying orange lanyard. Then he turns and walks toward the checkout.

He has been camping before, he reminds himself. Plenty of times. His family has camped in California, and he has been camping with friends in local parks and in Wisconsin. He knows how to use a compass and a map. And though he has never seen the North Woods, he has always wanted to get up there. This is his perfect chance.

He continues toward the checkout, content with his purchases, excited about his trip. The other effect of touring REI, among so many people bent in similar pursuit and among so much gear and merchandising, is to heighten Jason's enthusiasm for his adventure. As he waits in line he picks up a disposable camera—something to record his adventure—and then moves to the open cashier.

On Quinn Road in West Bloomington, a suburb south of Minneapolis, his parents' wide sloping redwood house backs up to a small stand of trees. There are Berber carpets, tiled floors, stairs to the left, stairs to the right, and plenty of windows in the front and back, opening onto trees. His mom, Linda, sits in her kitchen and listens to his directions.

"Here's where I'm headed," he says, looking into her clear, penetrating eyes, just like those he sees in the mirror. He opens Pukite's book and shows her the Pow Wow Trail.

"Looks beautiful," she says. She is only slightly worried. This isn't the first time Jason has walked into the woods alone. He knows it is dangerous. Most camping and instructional guides advise against it. But sometimes—particularly at this time of year, when no one else is available—the only alternative is going solo.

And besides, she knows her son. Jason is a driven, determined kid. Once he sets his mind on something, he pursues it with a remarkable degree of focus and single-mindedness. When he was young, he attended high school in southern California, where Lee, his dad, was working for the Mennen Company. At the time, California schools had few rules and fewer expectations. Like most kids who were preoccupied with everything but what they planned to do with their lives, Jason skated. He coasted through his high school career, uncertain of his future and what he wanted to do with it. Then in his two years at Orange County Community College he met a professor who turned his head toward the compelling world of science. It was a moment of epiphany. He became absorbed in his classes. He began to study. At the end of his two years at Orange County he did well enough to have the audacity to contemplate a career in medicine.

When he shared the idea with his parents and his younger sister, Heidi, they smiled, somewhat incredulous. But they supported his efforts. His newfound ambition was in marked contrast to his high school drifting, and as unlikely as a career in medicine sounded, his parents welcomed the change.

And then he shocked everyone by his sustained, unremitting effort. He struggled with math and science, but gradually absorbed them. By the time he entered the University of Minnesota in his junior year, he was an academic sponge. And he did well. He enrolled in all the math and science allowed, he remained focused, and his efforts were rewarded.

But the MCATS, the medical school entrance exams, are difficult. It took Jason three years to finish his coursework and score high enough to be admitted to med school. Linda and Lee had always been impressed by their son's ambition and perseverance. He had worked damn hard to overcome a mediocre secondary education, and he succeeded—largely by the sweat of his own brow. Lee, who has run in over twenty marathons, knows plenty about hard work. At this point, Linda knows Jason does, too.

She's not too concerned about his solo adventure into the cold North Woods.

"It's only three days," he reminds her.

"It's a shame about Nepal," she muses.

"It will be beautiful up north. This time of year I'll have the woods to myself."

"Just be careful, Jason. It could get cold."

"I've got it covered," he says. And he does. He has the compass, the Fisher map, the trail description and map from the Pukite text—and plenty of the right gear. He has a polypropylene pullover, a red flannel shirt, a sweater, a light Gore-Tex North Face windbreaker with a pullover hood. He has nylon hiking pants with an insulated layer and water-resistant polyurethane coating. He has good boots, a down bag rated for temperatures as cold as ten degrees below zero, an air mattress, a waterproof tent with a bright orange tent fly, wool socks, plenty of food, a camp stove, two canisters of white gas, the charcoal lighter from his parents' grill, his orange whistle with the lanyard he can hang around his neck. He packs Tootsie Rolls, crackers, canned tuna, and enough freeze-dried food to last a week.

His mom glances at the Pukite map again, sees the twenty-six-mile circle with plenty of campsites. The trail meanders through a string of small lakes: Pose, South Wilder, North Wilder, Horseshoe. She imagines glades sloping down into clear, still water—park-like conditions.

"Here's where I plan to hike," Jason explains, pointing to the start of the trail on the map. "It's over two miles to the circular part of the trail. Then I'll walk counterclockwise for another couple of miles and camp the first night near Pose Lake." He points to it on the map. He traces the wobbly line along the north side of the circle, ending at a tent symbol near Rock of Ages Lake.

"Here the second night," he says. "That's a pretty good hike, but I should be able to do it."

He will camp near Marathon Lake the third night, and then exit the next day. If he has time, he'll explore the Superstition Trail spur, a one-mile, round-trip side trail that's supposed to be scenic and haunting.

And this is important, he thinks, figuring the time it will take to hike out. "I should be out Thursday afternoon. I'll call you."

"Okay," she nods, comforted by his plan and the places she can see on the map. It looks like a good itinerary, and she knows her son's determination and strength. She looks forward to his Thursday afternoon call.

He considers the trail and the time he's given himself. Plenty. He'll be out well before noon on Thursday, so calling shouldn't be a problem. "If you don't hear from me by Thursday evening," he says, knowing his mom will appreciate his care, "call the Lake County sheriff's office." He doesn't write down the phone number, because he doesn't really believe the need will arise. He mentions it to her as a minor precaution, something more to comfort his parents than from his own genuine concern.

"I'm sure everything will be fine," he says. "But if you don't hear from me by Thursday evening," he repeats emphatically, "call the sheriff."

Jason knows the likelihood of anything going wrong is remote. But things do happen. The history of North Woods travel is littered with stories of those who walked into wilderness to find satisfaction for their yearning for wild places, solace, scenery, or replenishment, and found something else entirely.

2

Hidden Portage

A nameless lake, between Fran and Bell, Quetico Provincial Park, Wednesday, August 5, 1998

Well before noon, Dan Stephens and the group of eight Scouts he is leading carry their canoes down the slope into the northeast end of a lake with no name. They are glad to have the portage behind them. Fran Lake had been crystalline in the mid-morning sun. In the faint breeze it had been like crossing mottled blue lapis. But the seventy-six-rod portage out of Fran was difficult to find, overgrown, uphill, and bug infested. The morning left the group hungry and ready for lunch.

These remote crossings are tough, Stephens thinks. Doug Hirdler from the Sommers Canoe Base had told him the next one—from no-name lake into Bell—was well concealed and might take some time to find. Now Dan squints across the azure sparkle, trying to discern its whereabouts.

The Scouts blow and wave away the bugs. The pests are thick and persistent, and the paddlers are anxious to get onto the water and be rid of them. Aside from the bugs, it is practically paradise. The lake ripples under a light breeze. Occasional pillows of high cumulus clouds float like gauzy cotton across an azure dome. The wide, diamond-shaped waterway stretches out in front of them, bordered by cedars and pines that grow in thick profusion to the lake's edge. In a few places there are tiny gaps in the green where giant slabs of igneous rock drop into aquiline. It is typical terrain for this part of the Quetico, haunting and resplendent, where everything but the water has a sharp edge.

At twenty-two, Dan Stephens is spending his summer up from Athens, Georgia, as a group leader for the Charles L. Sommers Canoe Base/Northern Tier High Adventure Scout Camp near Ely, Minnesota. It is not Stephens's first time guiding. Six foot two, 165 pounds, he is lean and tall, with a serious, quiet look that conveys intelligence, a core of inner strength, and an abiding love for wild places. His long, unkempt hair hangs over his collar. His chin sports a ragged length of beard that makes him look more Amish than Eagle Scout. He wears a black T-shirt under his blue and black PFD vest. The high-tech personal flotation device is a constant requirement for the group—one of Dan's few absolute rules. He wears green khaki nylon hiking shorts and lightweight shoes. He doesn't have the look of an Eagle from Athens, but he is one.

This group of eight from Chattanooga have appreciated both his expertise and his Georgia drawl. When they arrived in northern Minnesota, none of them expected to find a southern boy in the Canadian woods. Instead of a Yankee, their guide has a disarming southern smile and more skill with a paddle than any of them have ever seen. He can canoe all day, find and set up camp, catch, clean, and cook some of the best-tasting fish they have ever eaten, and he's a leader. His abilities, appearance, quiet demeanor, and habit of journaling toward the end of the day haven't gone unnoticed. There is admiration in the young Scouts' eyes. They appreciate their Georgian guide and depend on him more than they realize.

But the morning of portaging and paddling has tired his crew and he can tell they're getting edgy. Before reaching Fran they had crossed a shallow lake that in places was only six inches deep. Dan and his group leaders—Jerry Wills and Tim Jones, the only two fathers—had to get out and slog their canoes through moose muck. The fathers didn't say it, but Dan could see the pull had wearied them.

Since leaving Sommers Canoe Base on Sunday he had pushed them. The group's entry permit into Canada was for Tuesday, August 4. They had to be at the Cache Bay Ranger Station their third day out, so they had paddled seventeen miles the first day, crossing Moose, Sucker, Birch, and Carp lakes, and then camped that first night on Robbins Island in Knife Lake. The next day they paddled fifteen miles along the international border, up the thick length of Knife, entering Ottertrack at the Little Knife portage and leaving it at the Monument Portage, where the group took photos of the marker at the U.S.–Canadian border. That evening they camped on a small peninsula at the southwestern end of Saganaga. The next morning they paddled twelve miles up the southwestern end of Saganaga and into huge Cache Bay, finally making the ranger station in the early afternoon.

They were thankful for reaching the station with plenty of day still before them. They enjoyed visiting the outpost, where the Scouts could buy souvenirs and where Doug and Janice Matichuk, the husband-and-wife ranger team, were friendly and informative.

Dan shared their route with the rangers as the two fathers listened in. Janice said it was a beautiful string of lakes. But she warned them about sticking to the portages, some of which were well concealed.

"A few weeks back a kayaker couldn't find a trail and decided to bushwhack it," she said. "Disappeared."

She waited for the words to penetrate.

"The others came back and got us. We went out and found him, but it reminded me how thick these woods can be, particularly this year with so much rain."

From the looks of the sky northwest of the station there was more rain coming their way. Their next stop was Silver Falls portage, over a mile across open water in Cache Bay. Dan didn't want to get caught in the open, and it was going to be a rough paddle across the bay.

They said their goodbyes and started out over the lake. The wind came up ahead of the storm, and their narrow crafts struggled across the whitecaps. If they didn't paddle, the blow pushed them backwards or whipped their canoes sideways and threatened to capsize them. They dug in hard against the wind, with no alternative but to muscle their way across, their limbs burning from the effort. Thankfully, the heavy rains passed north of them, showering the portage but leaving them dry.

The Silver Falls portage was a breath-stealing 130 rods from Saganaga Lake to Saganagons. It was never an easy portage, and now it was muddy. At its start they had to scale some large slippery boulders. Then there were plenty of ups and downs, ferrying packs, gear, and the canoes down the muddy trail. The cataract thundered beside them. The trail was difficult and long, all of it picturesque, but none of it a cakewalk. By the time they reached its end they had descended over 500 vertical feet from the trail's start back on Saganaga.

The fathers more than carried their load. But at five feet, six inches, and 210 pounds, Jerry Wills was struggling. The barrel-chested Tim Jones, six feet, four inches, was more than equal to the task, though he, too, slipped and slid for much of the descent, balancing a canoe over his head, his heart pumping and his lungs working hard. The kids—seventeen-year-olds Shawn Jones (Tim's son), Matthew Thomson, and Jake Span, eighteen-year-old Justin White, and the younger Jesse Cates and David Shellabarger—pitched in as if they were born to the task.

Stephens considers it his best group this summer. But no doubt about it, the Cache Bay crossing and Silver Falls portage had taken a lot out of them. After pushing hard for three days, they were ready for a break.

At the bottom of the falls, Jerry Wills rested near the entrance to Saganagons Lake, entirely spent. He lay down near the outlook, appreciating the open vista, thankful for the momentary respite. He was glad to have that portage behind him and glad to know they wouldn't be returning this way. There wasn't a snowball's chance in hell he could scale back over those rocks—even without equipment.

Jerry spent the vast majority of his days settled in a desk job at the Oak Ridge National Laboratories. Before the trip, he had mild indications that he might have been in better shape. Now the rigorous paddling and exhausting hauls were taking their toll.

In a little less than a week he would return home and complain to his wife about chest pains and tiredness. He would finally acquiesce to a doctor's visit. A week after that he would undergo emergency open-heart surgery. But today, he lay down and rested, thankful for a chance to doze.

Dan took the kids to the bottom of the waterfall, and they waded into the torrent. They gripped each others' hands for support while Tim Jones held a rope ready on the nearby shore, should anyone be swept away. The kids loved feeling the power of the white water. The rush and foam was like an ablution, for the moment washing away their fatigue.

From the side of the falls, Tim Jones worried. He had noted that Dan was pushing them incredibly hard, but this was the first time he had thought Dan was unnecessarily risking the safety of their kids. Watching the boys wade through the foaming spray, he saw plenty of potential pitfalls. The water was riled and unclear. The boys staggered through the torrent across underwater rocks. It didn't take much imagination to see how one of them might be swept away by the current.

Tim Jones remembered the collective prayer they had shared with parents and friends before their Chattanooga departure. They had gathered together and asked the Lord to guide them and watch over them on their long journey north and into the woods. Now the recollected prayer beside the Quetico cataract calmed him, though he still held vigil with his rope.

Once they were back in the canoes and onto Saganagons, everyone eased up and reveled in the amazing scenery. They had found the most beautiful campsite they'd yet encountered, and after they set up camp, Dan let the kids do some fishing. For this part of the trip, they were luckless. But they were fortunate in scenery, location, and their perspective on the western sky. The sunset that evening had been a florid red wonder.

When they got up this morning, Dan knew he was going to drive them hard across Saganogons, Slate, Fran, and an unnamed lake. Then they would ease up at Bell Lake, set up camp, and relax for the rest of the day. He could tell they were ready for some serious R&R. It was going to be another perfect day in the Quetico woods.

Somewhere near the southeastern end of this lake lies their next portage, a twenty-one-rod distance into Bell. They have crossed enough portages to know by sweat and effort the length of a rod—16.5 feet, or about one canoe length. From what Doug Hirdler told them, the portage is flat. That would make this a reasonable, short carry, once they find it.

This is Stephens's first time paddling the Man Chain of lakes. Over ten miles north of the border, deep into the heart of the Quetico, it is not a well-traveled place. He has been warned about this particular portage.

"It's near the southeast side of the lake," Hirdler told him. "There's some downed trees and a dead one with a big fork. Look for those. And then you have to take a very middle waterway kind of route," Hirdler explained, in language only a guide could follow. "If you go right through the middle you can find it. It's the kind of portage we've waded through, tying a rope on and bringing the canoes across shallow connecting water." Stephens knows some of these trails are often little more than overgrown foot paths, but he's developed a method for locating concealed portages, and he has a knack for orienteering in woods.

It is their fourth day out. From the start it seemed as though they were old friends—close enough, at least, to allow young David in the middle of Stephens's canoe to lead them across no-name lake to the portage into Bell.

Dan calls to the young Scout. "Hey, David, want to guide us?"

"Sure," Dave agrees, excited by the prospect.

Dan tosses up his compass and the yellow-and-blue Fisher map. He likes to give his Scouts a chance to guide. It builds orienteering skills. And all summer his groups have been constant in their requests to have Stephens show them their map coordinates, where they've been and where they are going. It is a persistence that wearies him.

All of his groups have a maniacal hunger for map reading, as though the small outline of lakes, swamps, rivers, portages, and topographic lines with numbers might somehow explain wilderness, or articulate their experience of wild places. If he can teach David to identify their coordinates, maybe the young man can answer the questions about where they are and where they're headed. Besides, Dan is hungry and wants to get down to the end of the lake. Giving up the map and compass frees his hands for paddling. Once they cross over the portage into Bell it will be time for lunch.

Dan looks around. The other two canoes are twenty yards behind but gliding up fast. He turns to his own canoe and sees Tim Jones in the bow, ready with his paddle. David sits in the middle, perusing the map. He leans toward them and whispers, "Get your bearings and we'll race 'em."

"Yeah," they respond, eager for the contest.

"Just a second," David adds, returning to the map. The young Scout hesitates, then points the way to where the end of the lake narrows in the distance. "See that point down there?" David says, squinting across the blue water, looking down to take another reading from the map. The others have paddled up beside them. "That's where we're headed."

Dan turns and considers the other canoes. In one, he watches Shawn Jones, Matt Thompson, and Jake Span paddling up beside them. In the other, he sees Justin White, Jerry Wills, and Jess Cates coming up behind. The struggling Jerry is not a strong paddler. The canoe full of seventeen-year-olds will be the competition. But with Tim's whitewater experience and his own strong paddle they should be more than equal to the task.

"Okay," Dan says, grinning. He waits until his point man has paddle in hand. Then he lunges with his own flat blade, surges forward, and declares, "Last one there has to fix lunch!"

Suddenly all three canoes are leaping toward the distant shore.

It's not much of a contest. The leader's canoe prevails. The three seventeen-year-olds aren't far behind. Jerry Wills rests in the middle of the third canoe, making slow progress across the water. They lag more than a football field behind.

As the far side comes into view Dan is sure he sees the portage opening, a path of rocks so clear and level they look like cobblestones. He doesn't see the dead tree fork Hirdler described, but woods change. It could have toppled.

This far into the Quetico, finding an infrequently traveled portage on your first try is more luck than skill. They're often marked by nothing more than foot-wide openings in brush or trees or a few extra rocks running into water. On occasion, apparent openings turn into moose trails that dissipate into wilderness after twenty yards. And this year, with the plentiful rain, the lakes, ponds, and rivers have all risen, further obscuring the portages.

Dan feels lucky today. The path looks clear, and he can already taste the gorp (a trail mix of nuts, chocolate chips, and dried fruit), Kool-Aid, bannock bread with peanut butter, and granola bar. He tells his two canoe mates to unload their gear and get ready to portage.

As soon as they land, the bugs start in. Near the water, out in the open, the slight breeze makes it tolerable, but once on the trail it will be difficult to breathe without inhaling the dark pests. The Scouts have already smeared on Deet. Dan Stephens doesn't use bug goop. In his summer of guiding he's learned about the sweet smell of new groups. It takes a while for shampoo and soap to wear off hair and skin, and until it does his new recruits are beacons for the bugs. If he stays upwind, he won't be bothered.

He hikes twenty yards up the path and it disappears. "Damn," he mutters. "Another moose trail."

He returns and with a group sigh they reload their canoe. Dan glances up the shoreline and sees what appears to be the portage opening at the edge of a cedar swamp. They cross the distance, beach their canoe, and again unload.

The seventeen-year-olds have beached their canoe near Dan's and are unloading. Jerry Wills is approaching. Dan hoists his canoe over his head and starts in. Tim Jones gathers their packs and falls in behind Stephens. David carries the paddles, poles, map, and compass.

This time they get a little farther, but thirty yards in, the trail starts to fade.

"I can't believe it," Stephens says, incredulous. He looks around and sees a nearby cedar with low-hung boughs. In one swift move he slides the aluminum craft up onto eight-foot-high branches. He is happy to be out from under the load. The canoe hangs there, held up by graceful green arms.

Tim looks ahead and sees Dan parking his canoe, realizes it is another dead end, and turns to tell the others not to unload or follow them up the trail. He retraces the thirty yards to shore. Jerry Wills and his companions are still in their canoe.

"Looks like another moose trail," Jones explains.

The others shrug, knowing the real portage must be nearby. Jerry Wills unfolds his map and takes a closer look.

Back in the woods Dan turns to David and asks, "What's the map say?" In part it is a rhetorical question. Dan Stephens has stared at Fisher Map F-19 for the last two days. He can close his eyes and read its title—*Saganaga, Seagull Lakes*—and its accompanying key and assorted lake locations with enough clarity to trace it in sand.

One thing he has always found disappointing is the way the map's landscape relief ends at the Canadian border. North of that line there are no indications of swampland, topography, lake depths, or elevations. Just yellow and blue swatches depicting land, lakes, and rivers. Enough, he has long realized, to easily guide him in a canoe, but insufficient to give him an idea of the country they're about to enter until they cross into it.

"The map shows it's right around here," David finally answers.

"I'm gonna do a cloverleaf," Dan says. "See if I can find it."

The young Scout nods. "Okay," he says. David turns and starts back to the shoreline. They are familiar with their guide's method for finding obscure portage routes, though none of them have ever followed him into the woods.

Still sitting in the canoe, Jerry Wills reviews his map. But when he sees the young Scout walk out and tell them Dan is searching for the trail, he rebukes their young guide, at least to himself. *Bushwhacking,* he thinks, displeased with Dan's decision to strike off and look for their trail through woods as dense as these. He has watched Stephens disappear before, and never worried about it until Janice Matichuk's comments back at the Cache Bay station.

"It's easy to get disoriented in this bush," he remembers hearing the ranger say. "Make sure you stick to the trails."

Well inside the woods, Stephens peers at his watch. He has practically perfected the cloverleaf method for finding wayward portages. He walks straight into the woods for one minute. He glances at his watch several times, shifting through the shadowy trees. Overhead branches block the sky. The heavy network of thick tree roots forms an obstacle course. A half-minute into his hike he squints down at his watch and trips, wrenching an ankle. "Damn."

The bugs are starting to swarm. He needs to find that path.

If you know how to wend through swamp trees, one minute of walking can take you a considerable distance. He does not notice it, but he can no longer hear his friends back at the shoreline. In his short time bushwhacking he has covered well over fifty yards.

Dan Stephens has been careful to register distinctive points in the terrain. A particular cedar tree, broken near its base. A wrangled fin of large granite boulders bordering one side of the swamp. After one minute he picks a clear point of departure, and then makes a sharp ninety-degree turn to his left. Stephens is sure he will cross the trail. He hikes in that direction for another minute, but it fails to appear. He returns to his departure point, hikes in the opposite direction, but after another minute still doesn't find it.

Goddammit. They'll have to paddle further up the shore.

He doesn't look forward to returning through that swamp. He angles to his left to where the fin of boulders borders the trees. The rocks will be easier walking, and though some of them are large enough to require light climbing, that way is preferable to being eaten among the shadowy, root-plagued cedars.

He is almost a football field from his starting point, considerably astray from the angle at which he entered. From here he can see less than ten feet into impenetrable brush. The bugs are starting to annoy him.

He carefully climbs over a near rim of rocks. His wrenched ankle feels tight. He comes to a large boulder, ascends it, and from that vantage point looks to the next low rabble of stone. If he leaps carefully, he thinks, he can just reach that one in the center. He tenses. He springs.

In the microseconds it takes to cross five feet of air, his stomach registers the miscalculation before he does. And then his feet fall short of the center stone and he topples headlong into granite.

3

The Start of the Trail

Pow Wow Trail, BWCAW, Monday, October 22, 2001

Just after noon Jason is almost finished with his four-hour drive north. He passes the Isabella Ranger Station, a low-hung, dark log structure resembling all the other DNR buildings built by Roosevelt's Civilian Conservation Corps. Jason doesn't need to stop. He has his maps and the description of how to get to the start of the Pow Wow Trail. And just days ago he had called an 800 number the DNR uses to provide the public with wilderness information.

The ranger had explained that this late in the season, people were scarce in the Boundary Waters. Besides, most people canoed. Jason Rasmussen was hiking. He didn't need to worry about a camping permit. He would have those woods all to himself.

"Just be careful," the ranger added, warning Jason about the weather, which at this time of year can turn on a dime.

"I'm prepared for it," Jason said.

But as he turns off the highway onto Forest Road 177, he sees the two-inch cover of yesterday's snow spread across the road. In among the trees, deeper patches lie tucked along shaded corners of underbrush. He still has twenty miles of backcountry roads to cross. He makes three turns, driving carefully, meeting no one. Over the next forty-five minutes he cruises through thick woods. In places, on either side of the road, the high pine trunks stand like telephone poles. Sparse, leafless brush bedraggles the forest floor.

The patches of snow worry him. *But I'm ready*, he reminds himself, remembering the contents of his pack. He has plenty of warm wear. His sleeping bag is rated to ten below. Jason knows it won't get that cold. But he is also concerned by the absence of recent tire tracks on the road's sand-and-gravel surface. Not many have driven this way—at least not since yesterday's light dousing.

He makes his last turn. The road narrows and becomes much rougher than the back roads he's already driven over. He wonders if his Saturn can take it. He wends carefully over the ruts, dodging left and right to avoid potholes and soft spots, thankful the cold has been sufficient to freeze the ground. After almost an hour he turns a corner and drives into the empty Isabella Lake parking area.

The trailhead parking lot is a scruffy wide spot to the side of the road. There is a sign for Isabella Lake, but there's nothing marking the start of the Pow Wow. He examines the U.S. Forest Service sign, then looks along the edges of the parking lot. Isabella Lake is to the east. The Pow Wow Trail should cut off west of the lot. He walks over to get a better look and thinks he sees the start of a trail under the trees.

Is that the Pow Wow? he wonders.

In the open lot he squints in the light, feels warmed by the sun, though it's a cool 48 degrees. He appreciates the beautiful day. Yesterday had been overcast. The sky thickened and sleet fell in sharp gusts out of thick gray clouds— a harbinger of the coming cold. But for now the sky is clear and the rising temperature is melting pockets of snow and ice.

He returns to his Saturn, hoists his pack out of the back seat, and steadies it on his car trunk. He holds one strap while he turns around and inserts first his right arm, then his left. He bends forward and feels his shoulders pull against the weight. Not bad. It is noticeable, but he feels certain he could hike much farther than the five or six miles he needs to cover this afternoon. He lifts the bottom of the pack, adjusting it until it's balanced and comfortable. Then he cinches the hip belt, lifting it slightly so it rides on the fleshy muscle above his glutes.

His is the only car in the lot. He's surprised. But it *is* Monday, he recollects. Late October. And he remembers wanting it this way, just him and the quiet woods, the entire trail to himself.

He locks his car, pockets the keys, and walks across the lot to where he thinks the trailhead ought to be. He moves into the brush, searching for a path. For several minutes he explores the western edge of the lot boundary, crisscrossing into the woods. Finally, several yards in, he stumbles across a small path that widens ahead. He peers up the narrow trail, decides it must be the Pow Wow, and turns onto it.

Fifty yards ahead the trail becomes surprisingly spacious. His first half mile is as clear as an old logging road, and it looks like it's going to hold.

During the 1960s Tomahawk Lumber Company logged some of the land around Isabella Lake, including this stretch of the trail. The second-stage forest is thick with alder, black spruce, tamarack, and birch.

Jason's pack feels good in the early afternoon sun. The wind is low and the temperature perfect. He is entirely alone. He sees no one, there are no recent footprints, and it feels wonderful to stretch his legs in the afternoon warmth, to hear an occasional bird chirrup and hawk cry. A couple of ravens pass overhead, one of them making a sharp *caw*. He stops and watches them pass. It is quiet enough to hear the sound their wings make as they beat the air.

A mile up the trail, a narrow footbridge crosses the stream that empties out of Isabella Lake. His map shows a small picnic area to the left, but he cannot see it. The sound of water falling away from the lake reaches his ears. A huge boulder in the middle of the cascade reminds Jason of REI's fake waterfall. While it is architecturally tasteful, it's no match for the real thing. He looks for fish in the part of the stream flowing under the footbridge, but can only see the dark, tamarack-stained water running over black rocks.

He revels at the heavy pull of pack straps against his shoulders, how it makes him feel clear and independent. This is exactly what he wanted.

Yesterday's sleet and the ensuing thaw fill the air with the smell of humus. The trail is spectacularly vibrant, and Jason pauses to fish his disposable camera from one of the zipper pockets of his North Face jacket. He looks up the stream toward Isabella Lake. There is a faint haze near the lake. He snaps a photo of the stream falling away from the big water, threading toward him. Then he keeps hiking, looking for the right place to take a trail shot in the long clear path. Finally he sees it and stops.

The leaf-strewn trail runs out in front of him, narrowing in the distance into a brush wall, or maybe it's a turn. In the left foreground there's a small balsam fir. Further down there are some popples and a couple of tall, moth-eaten birch. Also on the left, a white pine rises out of the trees, and further on sits a wall of balsam fir mixed with thick young alder. On either side the first-tier forest growth

Creek running out of Isabella Lake, from the Pow Wow Trail bridge (courtesy Jason Rasmussen)

FIRST STEPS

forms an impenetrable wall. The brush is so thick, if a school bus were parked ten feet into it you wouldn't even know it was there.

He pauses and snaps the picture. The trail is clear ahead, carpeted by a thick shuffle of leaves stretching toward an opaque dome.

For most of the 2.6-mile start of the Pow Wow, the path's

Section from the start of the Pow Wow Trail
(courtesy Jason Rasmussen)

openness holds. It is so clear, in fact, Jason doesn't refer to Pukite's trail description, his compass, or his more detailed Fisher map. The hazy sky shows no sign of storm. The weather is exactly what he had hoped for. Cool walking in quiet woods, but warm enough to require only his light sweater.

Parts of the trail are wet. Some areas are a little boggy, and he is careful to step on the high points, keeping his feet dry. Otherwise the way is clear, and after just an hour and a half hiking he crosses over a large marshy area. There is water to his right, backed up by an enormous old beaver dam. He crosses on what must be the top of the dam, then enters into a stand of jack pine.

On one of the largest trees is a familiar wooden marker. It isn't much: a dark brown, six-inch diamond of wood with clear yellow arrows pointing in opposite directions.

He is at the Pow Wow circuit juncture. To the left, the arrow points clockwise, wending in a west-northwesterly direction. To the right, the trail is just as clear, but strikes off in a more northerly direction.

He turns right, hiking north-northeast, and immediately the trail narrows to a thin footpath. He walks on a damp, moss-covered path through the trees. It is cool in the shade of the trees. After a quarter mile he is glad to notice an opening ahead. But as he approaches it, he sees it is a long beaver dam, its outer edge built directly over his path.

He skirts its back side. There's plenty of seepage beneath the thick mesh of remarkable engineering, but enough high spots to enable him to keep his feet dry if he moves carefully.

He pauses at the dam's apex, looking out over the still, clear water. An assortment of leaves litter the pond's surface. Its bottom is a mosaic of fall color. The dam itself is so long and thick—its back side laid out in a gentle slope of branches and sticks, some of them over two inches in diameter—he wonders how many beavers there are. He scans the surface of the pond and sees, tucked back into a far corner, a beaver lodge grown over a bank.

He watches for a while. Water seeps from beneath the massive dam, trickling in hundreds of narrow rivulets on its course through the woods. He is surrounded by the music of water. He pulls his camera out of the pack's side pocket and snaps another picture.

Over the next hour Jason traverses three more beaver dams. The whole area is marshy and wet, and though he has tried to keep his feet dry, he can feel his right foot damp along the boggy trail. He hikes carefully, pleased by this minor trail obstacle—something unexpected and interesting.

When he passes another dam, the path widens. He pauses, looks up. An unexpected thickness to the sky has come in from the west. The day is still mild—warm by late October standards—but the bright glint has faded to a flat, metallic hue.

Jason still has no reason to consult his map, compass, or *Hiking Minnesota's* description of the trail. His path is clear. The day feels good. The walking is relatively easy. After more than two hours of hiking he crosses the last beaver dam and continues along the path, which is narrow but still clear.

In fact, the part of the trail that hooks up with the old Pow Wow—the eastern branch abandoned years ago—is clear and straight in front of him. The place where Jason is supposed to turn is covered over with weeds.

But Jason recollects from his earlier map reads that it is just about time for his ninety-degree turn to the northwest, toward Pose Lake, and there is a faint opening to his left. He studies it, but when he compares the gnarled, grass-covered rise to the broad opening in front of him, he is uncertain which path to follow.

In the days when lumber companies foraged trees through this part of the Boundary Waters—before it was the BWCAW—small logging camps were set up at key points in the forest. The open, straight path in front of Jason is the old trail to Calamity Lake camp, over two miles further east. After the camp was dismantled, the trail served as the northern loop of the old Pow Wow, before beavers had their way. Over the years, enough men, horses, logs, and hikers traveled over the spot to make it easily discernible through the trees.

Truth is, the entire area is crisscrossed by old trails. But Jason knows nothing of old logging camps or abandoned hiking paths, and there are no clear markings on any of his maps—not, at least, the ones he carries with him.

Finally, he decides to turn left, continuing along the new Pow Wow until he feels certain he has made the right choice. But he is somewhat puzzled by the straight clear path from which he veered, which was too big to be a game trail. Still, the afternoon is quiet and haunting, and he quickly settles back to enjoy the scenery, the hike, and the rare luxury of abandoning himself to his own random thoughts.

Jason hikes for another hour, lost in the beauty of the afternoon, traversing some messy low spots as he walks. He passes a few more old beaver haunts. Beavers can significantly alter landscapes within a matter of two to three years. He assumes, judging from the poor state of the trail, they've been at work here. He keeps walking in a straight northwesterly line, happy to be in the woods, oblivious to the passage of time.

He reaches another key point in the trail, where it bends left—not quite in a ninety-degree angle, but significant enough to be noticeable, at least on the map. But he is not looking at the map.

Because this turn in the trail is especially difficult to find, someone once built a stone cairn at the spot. Over the years, wild growth covered the cairn, like everything else in the area, and now it appears to be nothing more than a glacial pile of stone. In fact, the turn onto the new, western, proper Pow Wow is little more than a narrow gap in the forest tangle, easily disregarded. A hiker would have to be searching for the turn, knowing when to expect it. Jason is enjoying his afternoon, lost in his thoughts.

Since he's not anticipating the radical shift in direction, he keeps to the obvious path that lies before him, still wide and clear. There was a time this was a main trail, the old portage trail to Insula Lake, and part of an old logging road. A mile ahead it links up with another old logging road, angling east into another old timber camp. That was fifty years ago. The wide path before him is the only trace of the camp or the acres of harvested timber.

For now, it is the clear choice. Unaware that he has missed his turn and is gradually hiking deeper into impenetrable brush, dangerous bogs, and a landscape beavers have had decades to transform, Jason continues walking.

4

Lost

Jerry Wills sits in the middle of his canoe and studies the map. He sees where Dan headed into the trees, but as he hovers in the water he thinks Dan's point of departure is off by about fifty yards. Further down the shore, there's a huge cedar twisted out over the lake's surface. It obscures the shoreline behind it. He and his Scouts paddle down around the tree, and they find what appears to be the start of a portage trail.

Wills remembers the ranger's warning, and he won't bushwhack a portage if it isn't apparent. But this definitely looks like the start of something. He and the Scouts get out of their canoe and examine the path. It appears flat and wide enough to be the portage. They beach their canoe and hike in to have a better look. After forty yards, Bell Lake's blue waters come into view.

"Let's go back and tell 'em," he says, triumph in his voice. The three of them return to their beached canoe and hoist the heavy Duluth packs out of its hold.

From around the side of the overhanging tree the prow of the seventeen-year-olds' canoe spikes into view. Matt and Jake Span have paddled down, searching for Mr. Wills.

From up on the bank, Jerry smiles down at them. "The portage is over here," he says, pointing toward the start of the path.

"We can't find Dan," Matt says. There is concern in the young Scout's face.

"Where did he go?" Wills asks.

"Into the woods up the shoreline, looking for the trail. But he hasn't come back."

"And it's been awhile," Jake adds. He looks down at his watch. "Almost half an hour. Mr. Jones wanted us to find you."

It was not uncommon for Dan to scout the trail. He needed to find it and then be sure there were no fallen logs or places where the path petered out or disappeared. But he'd never been gone more than ten minutes, and this portage was a short one.

From up the shoreline Wills hears Tim Jones and David shout Dan's name. He tells the others to unload the canoe. Matt and Jake get out, haul their aluminum craft up onto the narrow passage opening, and start to unload. After the packs are out of Wills's canoe, he and Justin paddle back to the shadowy bank of cedars.

Tim Jones is happy for the parental reinforcement. "I guess he's still looking," he observes. Tim is concerned, but at this point he expects Dan's momentary return, or at least to hear his answer through the woods. Finally, one of the Scouts finds his whistle, raises it, and blows. Three long piercing signals cut through the afternoon air. They all pause, waiting for a response. But there is only silence and the interminable insect whine. It is as though the canopy of dark boughs has opened, swallowed their guide, and then closed up behind him.

"The portage is down the shoreline, behind that tree," Wills points.

"I heard," Tim answers.

"Why don't you take my canoe, and get the rest of the crew over into Bell. I'll stay here with Justin, and we'll wait for Dan on this end."

Tim is more than happy to leave the ominous swamp. In spite of his repellent he is waving away bugs. It takes them less than a minute to get into the canoe and start off down the shoreline.

Once at the portage, they unload their gear and ferry it across. By now they are an experienced team. They cross the narrow spit of land in fewer than fifteen minutes. On the way over the portage there is no sign of Dan. At the other side, staring out over Bell Lake, they peer down the shoreline in both directions, looking for any movement through the brush, listening. There is nothing.

They wait at the edge of Bell, trying to stay clear of the bugs. In spite of Dan's bizarre disappearance, they are still enjoying the beauty of the day. Some of the Scouts pass time by casting lures into the blue waters. They are certain at any moment Dan will come traipsing over the portage, and they will scoot onto Bell and find somewhere to lunch.

But after almost an hour there is no word from the other side, and still no sign of Dan.

Tim sends Matt back across the portage to find out

what's keeping the others. In fifteen minutes Matt returns and says Dan still hasn't shown up, that they will wait a little longer, that Mr. Wills says they should hold tight.

Tim sighs, annoyed by the temporary inconvenience. He still feels certain Dan is finding his way through the woods, and it will only be a matter of time before he appears on Bell's thickly wooded shoreline, somewhere down along south of them, he guesses. He and his son Shawn get into a canoe and paddle along Bell's southern shoreline. They whistle and call, hoping Dan will hear them. They skirt the shoreline a hundred yards before turning and starting back.

For the first hour Jerry Wills and Justin waited near the edge of the trees, occasionally calling, trying to rest in the midday sun. After a while, they decide to explore the dark grove of cedars, bend into the narrow shadows, yelling Dan's name. But there is nothing. A little later, they push twenty yards into the cedars, well out of view of the shoreline. But the air is thick and heavy, and in seconds they are surrounded by a pestilential storm. That, and the unusual darkness of the swamp, drives them back to the lake.

They continue calling. For more than an hour they stay near the shore, their shouts and whistle blows periodically breaking the afternoon's light breeze. But there is no sign of Dan Stephens. No answer. He has walked into the woods and disappeared.

Matt returns from over the portage, and now the two young Scouts suggest they hike in farther. But Jerry Wills reasons that if their inimitable Georgian guide walked just one minute into those woods and got lost, or worse— attacked by a bear, cougar, or wolves—their own chances of survival are slim.

In the end he decides to venture in far enough to retrieve Dan's canoe. He pushes in a wide semicircle, branching out from the point of Dan's departure, making a deeper and deeper sweep through the trees. He calls back to Matt and Justin near the shoreline, making sure he remains within earshot, careful to keep that connection between them. First his circle arches ten yards. Then he doubles back deeper. Finally, about forty yards into the woods, he sees the pointed stern of Dan's canoe hanging out of cedar boughs like a shining silver star.

Finding Dan's canoe heartens Jerry. Dan's gear tub rests on the ground beneath his canoe. It is a plastic tub in which Dan keeps his food, clothes, down bag, journal—everything but the tent, which is shared with others in the group.

Jerry Wills calls out for Dan, but again there is no response. The bugs are swarming. He looks up at the canoe and knows he is going to need help getting it down. He calls to the tallest Scout to follow his voice in, and together they pull the canoe out of the branches, gather Dan's plastic gear tub, and return to the shoreline.

"He's got to be near Bell," Jerry thinks, out loud. It is a sentiment the others share. They decide to paddle to the portage and cross over.

About the time Jerry and his two Scouts come over the portage, Tim and Shawn are returning from their fourth paddle down the Bell Lake shoreline. There has been no sign of Dan.

There is a touch of worry, maybe even apprehension, in the quiet way Mr. Wills and Mr. Jones bend over the map. They note where Dan went into the woods. It is an area where the two shorelines curve away from each other. Due south of his entry point there is nothing but woods and marsh. But they know Dan Stephens wouldn't hike south. If he did, losing the sun in the understory, he could easily correct his direction as soon as he found some open space among the trees.

But even if Dan took a rounded course through the trees, he should have appeared somewhere along the Bell Lake shoreline.

By now the afternoon is getting on. The two fathers peer at the map, trying to figure out their next move. The unwritten rule in the Quetico is to locate and claim a campsite by 4:00 PM. It is not always observed, but under the circumstances both fathers believe their troop could use a break. They still haven't eaten, and it's late enough to settle down for the day, find someplace close where they can keep an eye out for Dan—when he finally comes crashing through those trees. Then if they have to return and continue searching, there will still be plenty of daylight.

They peer at the map. Bell is a beautiful, long, clear stretch of water. Solid red dots indicate campsites. According to the map, midway down Bell's northwestern shoreline there should be a space among the trees. They are not quite at a vantage point where they can see it, but it should be a relatively short paddle.

The fathers decide to ferry their Scouts and supplies to the mid-lake site, set up camp, have an early dinner—everyone is starving—and if Dan still hasn't appeared, Jerry and a couple of the other Scouts will return and look for him.

They are all still certain of Dan's eventual reappearance. For now it is a momentary glitch in an otherwise remarkable trip. But as the Scouts and fathers cross Bell Lake in the afternoon sun, they wonder what happened to their guide.

BUSHWHACKING

Thought can also intrude when you're walking in the woods. Say you're walking through a tamarack bog, sphagnum moss at your feet, a trail cutting through it. . . .

You're hiking through this forest at a leisurely pace. But ten or fifteen minutes later, you realize that the forest has changed. Now you're in an upland forest of ash, oak, and hickory. . . .

You look back down the trail. You don't see any conifers. You didn't notice the change. You realize you were talking to yourself about something, thinking about something. And you can't remember what it was you were talking or thinking about.

PAUL REZENDES
The Wild Within:
Adventures in Nature and Animal Teachings

5

First Camp

For the next hour, Jason Rasmussen hikes the old trail moving north toward Lake Insula. The sky has turned overcast. He still has plenty of light, but the sun is hidden beneath cloud cover. He walks almost due north, believing he's heading to the northwest, about to encounter the Pose Lake spur and its campsite. Around five o'clock he starts searching for the site. The path narrows to an overgrown game trail, sometimes indiscernible through the trees. After a few paces it reappears, and he keeps to it, searching for the spur.

Finally tired, ready to set up camp, Jason decides he's close enough, and starts searching for the first suitable place to pitch his tent. To the side of the overgrown trail he notices a small opening in the trees, with an old fire ring beside it. A few paces ahead the site runs down into a narrow bog. He sees patches of water along the bog's surface, some of it creek-like, though it appears still in the dusk. According to the *Hiking Minnesota* map the campsite should be overlooking Pose Lake. Clearly, this isn't a lake.

Actually, it is Ahmoo Creek. At this juncture, the creek is a faint seepage through a low spit of land. Further upstream it is wide and clear, a geographic anomaly that might convince you to take a second, closer look at your map. But here it doesn't look to be much more than the back reaches of another dammed-up beaver pond. And Jason is weary. Thankful for the old campsite—which indicates he is still on the trail—he sets down his pack.

His back feels sore, but good. Where the padded straps rode across his shoulders he feels a pleasant, muscular tension. Relieved of the heavy pack he suddenly feels light, with more than enough energy to set up camp. He finds a wide, flat space just big enough for his tent. He crosses it, checking for low spots, root spurs, or rocks. He finds a couple of small, knobby rocks and kicks them aside, smoothing the ground in preparation for his tent. Then he unpacks, spreads the tent across the groomed surface, extends and inserts the interlocking poles.

It feels good to be setting up camp. He marvels at his shelter's simple design. There are no difficult stakes, no directions to pore over. There are only so many ways you can extend and insert the poles. He settles the bright orange tent fly over the top of the tent, fastening its edges to the main poles. Throughout the afternoon the sky has thickened, and now there's a chance of rain. He is glad to have the fly—something that will keep him dry and warm. As he steps away, the tent looks taut and open. He has to tie out its sides with some green and red nylon twine. Now it looks ready for habitation.

Jason forages the nearby woods for firewood. He has brought a small portable saw he uses to size down good chunks of dead wood. It takes less than twenty minutes to stack a reasonable pile of seasoned kindling near the old fire pit. It is starting to get dark.

Jason returns to his pack. He's hungry. He extracts the WhisperLite cook stove and one bottle of white gas. He should have plenty of stove gas for his brief three nights in the woods, but he still wants to be careful in its use. He unpacks everything and sets up his camp pot with water so once the stove flame is lit he can balance it on the delicate tripod. He finds a perfect, flat stone on which to place the stove. Then he pumps the gas bottle, letting a little gas out into the collection ring beneath the burner. He builds up pressure before he lights it. There is a whoosh as the highly combustible gas ignites and burns. He turns the release valve, letting out the pressurized gas until he hears the blue flame hiss and take hold.

While his water heats, he gathers dead grass and leaves from the edge of his campsite. He places them in the bottom of his fire pit. Then he lays small twigs and branches on top, leaving plenty of air to let the fire breathe. It takes only one click of his parents' charcoal lighter. When the flame is thick and rising, he lays on larger sticks.

The fire is warm in the gloaming. It brings a satisfying crackly light to the end of the day. He feeds the yellow flame with larger pieces of wood.

The sky darkens. Since it is overcast, it is difficult to pinpoint the exact location of the setting sun. Besides, Jason is too busy over his stove. He waits until the water starts to bubble, then pours in the freeze-dried sweet-and-sour chicken—one of his favorites.

He waits, watching it steam and bubble, stirring the glutinous mass with his fork. The smell is intoxicating. He stirs and lifts the fork out, careful to bring up some of the mixture on his tines, watching it steam. He blows on it, but cannot help himself. Before it is completely cooled he sticks the hot fork into his mouth.

"Chrise," he says, his tongue stinging from the heat. "Jesus Chrise." But the tang of the sauce and the bit of not completely hydrated chicken tastes better than he expected. His mouth waters.

After dinner and cleanup he adds more logs to his fire. Then he hoists his supplies over a nearby tree branch, well off the ground and out of reach of whatever critters might happen upon them. Probably raccoon, this time of year. But he guesses bears might still be roaming the fall woods. Bears would be attracted to the aroma of sweet-and-sour chicken.

Then he recalls the patches of snow on the ground. He cannot remember, but he thinks he has read somewhere that bears are usually in their dens by late October. Anyway, he is willing to tell himself the recollection is fact—he will sleep better tonight, and he's tired.

He tries to remember a time he has felt so satisfied. He recalls a line from a Robert Frost poem: "These woods are lovely, dark and deep."

He tries to resurrect the rest of the poem, but can only recall fragments: "to stop without a farmhouse near . . . the darkest evening of the year." And then he recalls the last two lines:

> And miles to go before I sleep,
> And miles to go before I sleep.

He looks around. It is almost dark. He feeds the rest of

his pile of logs into the fire and watches as they catch and burn, sending the blaze higher. He stares at his watch, barely able to read its face in the firelight. He reaches up, pressing its Indiglo button, and the watch face comes alive. It is almost 8:00 PM. He cannot remember being this tired, and he knows he is going to sleep well.

He notices a slight breeze high up in the branches. He wonders if it presages rain. Otherwise he is completely without worry, happy to be here, warmed by his fire, just about ready to turn in. Finally, he stands up and walks over to the edge of the brush. He pees on the lower boughs of a young black spruce. The acrid odor of the urine-drenched tree drifts up, wafts away from his tent.

Within fifteen minutes he is tucked into the warm cocoon of his down bag. It is cold at first. Now his body warms its new environs. He marvels at the beauty of deep woods. Outside, the fire has reached its peak and is starting to diminish. The shadows still dance along the nearer trees and against the green tent opening.

So far it has been a wonderful journey. He was not able to find the Pose Lake spur and the campsite overlooking the lake, but it must be very close. He suspects he may have passed the spur, continuing to hike west. He is surprised by how thin and barely discernible parts of the trail have been. And there are no markings.

He has more than enough food. He could live like this for well over a week and not lose a pound. He is warm and dry, and feels secure in the profound quiet, the only sound the slow hiss and crackle of burning wood. He listens, trying to hear something else. The wind soughs through the branches.

He wonders if others who have come this way have felt

this good. It's the woods. He smiles, recalling Thoreau's epigraph: it's "the tonic of the wilderness." Of course they felt good.

He is very tired. His lids are closing, and he is nearly asleep.

Who could have walked through such a day, through these woods, and not felt this good?

Then he falls asleep.

6

The Scream

Bell Lake environs, Quetico Provincial Park, Wednesday evening, August 5, 1998

Dan Stephens's eyes flicker. His head throbs, but a wave of nausea sends him back to unconsciousness. He reawakens, tries to sit up. For several minutes the pain forces him prone.

He is jammed into a low wedge of rocks. When he opens his eyes, he sees a huge boulder towering over him. The sky is clear. He is disoriented, but guesses it is mid-afternoon.

After several minutes he manages to sit upright. A second wave of nausea sweeps over his stomach and chest. He rests on his elbow, waiting for the sickness to subside. His head throbs. There is a dull ringing in his ears. Everything sounds muted and muffled. When he touches his head, he feels a lump the size of a loon's egg.

He must have fallen and struck the rock. He is uncertain

of his whereabouts. He recalls his Tennessee friends, but he is unclear about his location, where they are, where he was headed, or what happened.

From under a thick fog, reason struggles to reassert itself. He calls, but the meager vocalization only intensifies his head-throbbing. And there is no response. Dan struggles out of his low clutch of rocks. He leans against a large boulder, uncertain and disoriented, trying to get hold of himself. Even if he was clear about the purpose of his search, its timing and direction, a return to the shoreline would reveal nothing but tracks. His troop is over a mile away, searching for the campsite on Bell Lake. But he is far from lucid, and his perspective is muddled.

When his head pain subsides he remembers the cloverleaf pattern he uses to locate portage trails. He is thinking clearly enough to recall a simple modification. He can launch out and make a large wheel pattern through the trees, look for his friends. He will walk straight in one direction for a minute. He has his watch. He will find a marker and then walk out from that position until he recovers his friends and their supplies, or stumbles across a familiar trail or lake.

He feels lightheaded, almost drunk. But there is none of the pleasant feeling of inebriation. Instead he feels temporary fits of clarity bounded by long lapses in judgment. He has persistent nausea and a jackhammer head.

He starts pushing through the trees. The trees give way to low brush and boggy marsh. He stumbles through the marsh, recovering his legs, and manages a relatively straight path for almost fifteen seconds. Unfortunately, he moves away from the lake, almost due south, deeper into the brush, in the exact opposite direction from no-name lake, its shoreline, and his Chattanooga friends.

He tries to stay focused, but his peripheral vision picks up a spot of yellow in a patch of sunlight. He is drawn to its vibrant color. It is a wild black-eyed Susan, unusual for these woods. He leans over to consider it. He is struck by its symmetry and design. He pauses, kneels to take a closer look. It might be good to rest a minute. He feels dizzy, his stomach roiling.

Even through his head pain he admires the flower. He has no sense of the passage of time. He stares at the flower, bending in the light. After a while he looks at his watch and it appears to have moved forward half an hour. He gets up, keeps walking.

He returns to the wheel pattern, recalling its clarity and brilliance, remembering his purpose, and strikes off through more swamp. A half-hour later he finds himself in the middle of thick brush. He makes a wide turn in the brush, looking out at a nearby thicket. Along the edge of the thicket, water seeps down a shallow, swampy ravine. Dan turns along the seepage, trying to avoid the deeper pockets of muck. He angles in the general direction he was headed, but still wonders about his position. He moves ahead, toward an area of lowland brush that looks like it might open, possibly onto a lake. But when he reaches the opening he sees an old beaver pond, largely filled in but still covered by a few inches of water. He looks out over its edge and pans the horizon from left to right. Left, there are more swampy, abandoned beaver ponds. To his right, the walking appears slightly easier, with ground that rises high enough to promise firmness. Beyond it he sees what he thinks may be the edge of another lake. It is a long walk, but he starts forward, waving away bugs and lurching across the swamp-bog complex.

After another thirty minutes, maybe more, Dan comes

to the edge of a U-shaped lake. The lake is small and will be easy to skirt, providing he has an idea of which way to turn, and in what direction he should head once he rounds it. He knows he is lost, but still feels confused. He tries to recollect his friends, wondering where they can be.

"Hey," he yells over the water. His voice sounds feeble in the warm afternoon. The weak vocalization makes his head throb. Still, maybe if he yelled louder. "Hey!" he repeats, this time nearly as loud as he can manage until the energy out of his throat moves across his head like a jackhammer. The blow almost brings him to his knees. He reaches up to rub his swollen knot. The large contusion is sore and painful, and he knows he has to sit down. He rests for a minute.

Around the far shore he finds an open stretch of rock reaching down into the lake. At the base of the rock is a huge, white pine, arching up and over the water. He reaches the escarpment and sits in the shade, trying to calm himself, trying to figure his coordinates, trying to reassert some clear idea of his friends and their location. He sits for a while, staring out over the water, before finally realizing he needs a better view. Perhaps if he gets higher?

He considers the tree behind him. In spite of his mental fuzziness and the dull throb of his head, he feels physically capable. In less than fifteen minutes he is fifty feet off the ground, peering out over the massive complex he has spent so much of the day hiking into. He discerns what he thinks is the Man Chain, or at least one of them: it looks like Other Man. He is comforted to find something he remembers, something familiar. He sees that if he strikes off in the direction of Other Man he will have to skirt one small lake before reaching its distant shore. But he knows Other Man is a familiar paddle, a place where he might find his group or some other group canoeing down the chain.

Over an hour later he is still stumbling through thickets, realizing he has not yet encountered the small lake separating himself from Other Man. He thinks he should have found it by now. He wonders if his sense of distance went awry with everything else in this day. Dan finds another boggy beaver pond, with another large white pine rising above it. He scales the pine and peers in all directions until he discovers Other Man behind him, not closer, but farther away! He realizes he must have gotten turned around in the bush and hiked away from the lake. He is stunned. He cannot believe he became that disoriented. For the first time, he feels scared. He descends the tree, realizing that unless he figures out a clear plan, or at the very least a straight direction, he could be walking in massive circles until dark. The thought of walking in darkness unnerves him, and he comes down to sit beside the beaver pond and contemplate his next move.

Along the northwestern side of Bell Lake the Chattanooga Scouts find the campsite and unpack in worried silence. They fix themselves an early dinner, and then Jerry Wills takes two of his ablest Scouts and heads back over the portage to no-name lake. The cave-like gap in trees is exactly as it appeared before. But after swallowing their guide it has a new, ominous quality.

The three get out of the canoe, and Wills starts bushwhacking long semicircles into the perimeter of trees. The apex of the semicircle is the exact location of Dan's departure. The three of them call out for Dan, but there is still no sign or response. Wills comes back, increases his semicircle by another thirty feet. They call and whistle. Wills pushes deeper into the woods, but it is dark and the mosquitoes hound him. And he cannot get the ranger's words out of his head. He knows that if he ventures too far in and gets lost or attacked, it will only compound their predicament. Like Tim Jones, Jerry recalls their collective prayer prior to leaving Chattanooga. In that prayer they pledged to stay together. They asked God to watch over them. They told the parents their children would be safe, that there was nothing to worry about. They gave their word.

Even now, Jerry Wills believes they will hike back over the portage and Dan will be waiting for them, or already back at camp. Wills is working on the close conversation he is going to have with their guide. Dan shouldn't have bushwhacked. He should not have gone into the woods without them. He should never have walked off alone and left them in the middle of wilderness they know nothing about, with only a vague sense of the trail before them and no clear direction about what to do. He knows Dan Stephens didn't plan to get lost, or worse. But Jerry Wills's worry is starting to rise, and he cannot help but imagine the words he and their guide are going to exchange.

They return to their canoe, hoping to find him, but there is still no sign of Dan. Maybe back at camp, they think.

The late afternoon light is slanting into early evening. Jerry Wills and his two companions paddle back to camp and are shocked to discover there has been no sign of Dan. The others at camp are equally shocked. Everyone is getting tired, and Jerry knows Dan's absence is taking its toll on the group's morale.

Finally, the two fathers rummage for their FM radio phone. The Sommers Canoe Base sends one out with every group. The phone is a bulky, crude device, powered by six

D-cell batteries enclosed in a twelve-inch length of pvc pipe. At one end, homemade wiring connects to the transmission device. If the phone gets damp or is jostled—both common occurrences on canoe trips—the connections can corrode or pull apart. And unless you were paying attention when Dan Stephens demonstrated how to use the device, operating it is not an easy thing to figure out.

And there are rules about its use. It is only for emergencies, and since it is battery powered, the calls must be brief. There is no way for the men to know that in Dan Stephens's entire summer of guiding he never once had reason to take the phone out of its bag. It was periodically tested back at base camp, but the phone has never been field tested.

The assemblage is in the bottom of a pack and damp from riding low. When they switch it on, the red button light glows, but there is only a faint white noise coming from its receiver. When they press down to call, they assume their voices are being carried over the air waves. But there is no response.

Even if they knew where to look, there is no way for them to tell that the slim antenna near the top of the device is broken. It could have been the result of normal wear, or of being jostled. Maybe a previous user sat on it and bent it back, separating the connection from its base. Maybe it had a faulty antenna from the moment the device was assembled.

When the radio phone was tested near the canoe base the problem didn't surface. Reception at that proximity did not require the antenna, and the phone worked fine. Now all they hear is faint white noise, not even sputtering static. Otherwise, the phone appears operational.

"Turn it off," Tim Jones finally says. "We'd best save those batteries."

"I think we need to get closer to base camp," Jerry Wills suggests.

They are thirty-five miles north of base camp. Their situation is tenable at best, grim at worst. On the positive side they have the maps, compasses, Dan's shared foreknowledge about where they were headed and how he planned to get them there. And they have plenty of food and gear.

On the negative side, they are alone in wilderness they saw for the first time just three days earlier. And they have six teenagers, two of them young. Above all else, Jerry Wills and Tim Jones know they will do whatever it takes to keep these kids safe. Their Chattanooga community isn't large. They know these boys' families. These boys and this group are among the best Wills has ever accompanied. And it is a good thing, given their current situation. The two leaders don't voice their concern, but each of them is beginning to mull their options.

Those of their troop who consider their guide's whereabouts worry about the slim Georgian and his engaging smile. It is too soon for any of them to contemplate complete tragedy, but already shadows dog their thoughts. What happened to him? What if he never comes out of those woods? What if they never see Dan Stephens again? Jerry Wills has not voiced this suspicion, but he wonders if Dan encountered a bear. Maybe a mother bear with cubs. Jerry knows stepping between a mother and her cubs is a dangerous proposition.

The two fathers, now absolute and unexpected leaders of their group, wander to the side of camp to talk about their options. Neither of them has paid attention to his mounting anxieties or to the group's increasing, almost palpable, fretfulness. Until now Jerry Wills has been occupied with his efforts back at the edge of the cedar swamp. Tim Jones has been busy establishing camp. He and Shawn spent much of the early evening paddling Bell's southern shoreline, hoping their guide would break through the trees and they could pick him up and paddle triumphantly back to camp.

And then they had been busy trying to make the phone operational, hoping for some kind of guidance from base camp. But nothing. Now they are alone, trying to make a viable plan, knowing these kids and their families depend on them. Truth is, it's a little too much responsibility and surprise. Not that the two men are unequal to the task. But they are in unfamiliar country, a long ways from home, and it is all a little unexpected.

When Dan walked into the woods they were certain he'd return. When he didn't return right away, they were sure it would only be minutes, then maybe an hour, then possibly longer—*but he would return.* They could always make camp and wait for him, they had plenty of supplies, and there was the radio phone.

At every point in the day they had another place to turn, another option ahead of them, another cause for hope. But Dan never appeared, and the radio phone wasn't operational, and now there is every reason to expect they are going to spend this night alone. As the day ended, the two men have few places to go for solace.

In the growing dark, near the edge of camp, the pressure boils over. Jerry Wills thinks that in the morning Tim should take Justin White, their strongest paddler, and paddle back over no-name, Fran, and the other portages they've crossed, climb the Silver Falls portage, and return to the Cache Bay Ranger Station for help.

For Tim Jones, the thought of returning over those portages—portages he is not even certain he can find—and then scaling Silver Falls while carrying his canoe, is a little too much to imagine. And he is worried about Jerry Wills. While Jerry has held his own, the strain is showing. His face is drawn and pinched, and his periods of rest are becoming more frequent and longer.

Tim Jones hasn't expressed it, because until now it has not been an issue. But Jones has wondered why Jerry Wills came on such an arduous journey. Clearly, he was not in the best shape for it. Now the thought of separating the crew, leaving the kids (including his own son) with the strained Jerry Wills for two days, is an option he refuses to consider.

For a moment—before the two men realize the stress and anxiety that has crept up on them—a sharp flare of words threatens to ignite into something more troubling. Eventually they grow silent, each stung. They turn away into the waning daylight and gradually come to consider each other's perspectives, knowing that nothing will be served by either of them losing themselves in darkness.

Finally, Jerry Wills sees the sense of Tim Jones's perspective, and Jones understands Wills's concern. It doesn't take much persuasion to convince Wills their troop won't be well served by separating. They have to get closer to base camp. Tomorrow morning they will break camp at dawn and continue along the Man Chain, paddling for help. They don't believe they can help Dan by going in after him, and they worry about getting lost—or something worse—themselves. The best solution is to go for assistance, and they stare at the map, seeing how it is possible. They are doubtful they can paddle twenty-seven miles in a day, but are hopeful that they can get close enough to make the damned phone operational so they can get word back to base camp. In the early morning Tim and Shawn will cross back over the portage and make one last check for Dan, providing he doesn't find them tonight.

The Scouts have started a fire in the camp's pit. There is plenty of wood. As the long evening stretches into darkness, Jerry Wills instructs them to hang lanterns in the trees near the shore. They will stay up later than usual tonight, tending the fire, keeping it well lit. The campfire and lanterns will serve as reasonable beacons in the dark, should Dan Stephens make it to the opposite shore.

Near the close of day, Dan Stephens stumbles along the edge of the old beaver pond. He is tired. He is not thinking clearly. This deep in boggy woods the bugs are swarming. He locates a dead spruce, breaks off enough branches to make a crude but snug lean-to. He pulls up three-foot-high swamp grass and bundles it tightly enough to line his shelter. He knows he needs to cover himself. It is getting cold. A mosaic of tiny lacerations make his bare legs ache. He watches the bugs swarm over his arms and face. He fights them off, rubbing his body, brushing the insane clouds from his scratched and broken skin.

His reasoning is still muddled and unfocused. Of one thing he is sure: he is about as uncomfortable as he can ever remember being. Darkness is coming. He considers the oncoming cold abstractedly, as though it is something outside him. He is close to water, and coherent enough to know it is essential. He kneels in the high grass at the beaver pond to take one last drink, and an insect swarm rises. Something about the way it comes over him, in the dusky light by the pond, falls on him like a pile of rocks. A dull anger rises in his throat and a scream throttles out of him. It is a long, piercing wail—practically inhuman. It is a call to obliterate all pestilence and malaise. It is a plaintive lamentation for solace, and it is answered by an intensified ache in his head.

The insect whirr pauses, startled by the cry. His anger doesn't subside, but he restrains himself enough to prevent another wailing scream. And then the whirr recovers, and the dark cloud threatens him anew.

Almost a mile away, the Scouts are gathered around the campfire. The entire group is quiet in the growing dark, happy to have the fire to tend, to give them purpose and comfort. In the west, the long northern dusk hangs above the trees. The still water reflects the opposite shore and the fading crimson light. The Scouts are quiet for a moment, gathered around the campfire.

And then out of the southern dark they hear a cry. It is far away and faint, but clear. *Blood curdling* are the words that come to Tim Jones, though he doesn't utter them. Before he can look up to see if others have heard, one of the younger boys asks, "Did you hear that?" The boy's face is pinched and incredulous in the firelight. He looks like he has heard a phantom. Jerry Wills raises a hand to silence everyone, and they listen in the dark for several mute seconds.

"God," Jerry Wills mutters, before he can catch himself. "My God."

"What was that?" another Scout finally asks.

There is no way to know. It could be Dan's voice, or maybe something inhuman. Or maybe entirely too human, filled with misery and anguish.

Jerry Wills thinks that if it is Dan, a bear may have finished the work it started earlier. But he doesn't voice his suspicions. Instead, he gets up and turns to the dark eastern shore. "Dan?!" he yells, screaming into the night. His voice echoes back empty against the trees on the opposite shore.

The others pause after Jerry Wills's call. They stop to listen for a response. Then they all join him in the near dark, calling Dan's name, blowing their whistles. Their efforts are frenetic and hopeful, as though one last chance has been offered at the close of a very long day.

Tim Jones finally makes them stop. They pause, listening in the dark. Some of them have blown so hard, their breathing is labored in the flickering light. The only other sound is the flames eating their way through heavy pine boughs.

"I hope that wasn't him," one of the younger Scouts says.

They all feel heavy in the day's last light. They crowd a little closer around the flames. They all wish for the same thing—that it wasn't their guide who cried out. They don't want to contemplate alternatives: either the depth of Stephens's pain, or the being out of which a cry like that arose.

"Maybe a cougar," Jerry Wills finally suggests, though he doesn't believe it. "I've heard a cougar's caterwaul can sound like a man's scream."

"Maybe a wolf," Tim Jones adds. None of the Scouts quarrel with their leaders, but no one believes them.

After a while Dan Stephens has calmed himself enough to turn back down to his hovel. He has heard nothing in the dark. He is hunkered down near the beaver pond, at a low point in the landscape. He still has a headache, and there's a mild ringing in his ears. He can hear the swarm. He can hear the dull seething mass of bugs fighting to feed on him.

On the way to his lean-to he sees a long pine bole, perfect for a walking stick. It is at least something he can use to defend himself, should a raccoon, moose, or bear come foraging in the night. He reaches down, picks it up in the dusky light. He breaks off the branches and snaps the top. He weighs it in his hands. Then drops the narrow part to the ground. The thicker end fits the grip of his hand.

He lays it beside his shelter, within easy grasp. He is careful to note the last rim of light on the western world, a dull blip of illumination with enough in its center to identify west. He lays the stick in a due east-west position. He'll use it in the morning to double check his position. He turns to crawl back into the grass, to lie down in darkness and the oncoming cold and wrap himself in the crude bundles of swamp rushes.

Gradually the evening fills in with the muted whirr of the forest night and Jerry Wills hopes he was mistaken about the bear. Contemplation of the cry makes his skin rise in bumps across the back of his neck and down his arms. He tells himself he was mistaken, that the dark woods are playing tricks, that maybe it *was* a cougar's caterwaul or a wolf's howl. He and Tim try to put the best face on the cry, their predicament, their angry interchange of words that earlier in the evening flashed like kerosene out of the dark, leaving them both a little raw.

The night stretches before them. For the first time, both men long for their own beds, where their wives would nestle close and their mattresses would assuage back and shoulder pain better than this hard northern ground. Even the Scouts worry about the long, dark night of little sleep and troubled dreams, though they finally know they have to turn in.

As the blackness settles, Dan Stephens tries to sleep. But the bugs give new meaning to *pestilence* and *swarm*.

7

Deeper into Woods

Near Ahmoo Creek, north of the Pow Wow Trail, Tuesday morning, October 23, 2001

Sometime in the middle of the night, rain starts ticking Jason's tent fly. He had been dreaming, though he cannot recall the details. He lies in the darkened tent, listening to the rain drops gathering strength. The wind increases. He feels warm and secure in his mummy bag. From somewhere, perhaps carried by the wind, he feels a rising vague concern. Before he can identify the source of his uneasiness, he rolls over, closes his eyes, and drifts back into a pleasant torpor.

He awakens after daybreak, such as it is. Thankfully, the rain has stopped. But it is still plenty wet outside. Lying in his sleeping bag, coming awake in the cold, wet morning, he can smell the rain. The soft light on his tent flap tells him the sky is cloudy.

But it feels good to be in the woods.

He gets up, puts on his hiking pants and a fresh pullover shirt. He pulls the light jacket over the shirt and zips it. He needs to relieve himself. He steps into the cold boots and arches out of the tent without tying them. He walks ten paces and it's like stepping with cold cinder blocks on your feet. He finds an open space in the brush and starts to pee.

The trees and ground are covered with last night's rain. His own warm stream spatters the low branches of a spruce. He finishes, turns back to his tent, and takes down the pack from where he had hoisted it. He opens the plastic garbage wrap, unties the top, rummages for his camp stove, retrieves it, and returns to the level rock beside the fire pit to fix himself oatmeal. His breath clouds in the early morning. He checks his watch and sees it is just after 8:30.

By 9:00 he has heated water, filled his REI cup with instant oatmeal, mixed it over his stove, and admired the steaming ambrosia of cinnamon-apple oats. While the mixture cools he stuffs his bag and dismantles his tent. He shakes the tent fly in the dull morning light. Water droplets scatter over the camp. He does the same with his tent, shaking it before laying it on the ground on top of the fly and folding and rolling both into a compact ball. Then he stuffs it into its storage sack and tucks it into his pack. He is careful to leave room for the stove, gas canister, bowl, spoon, and cup. Otherwise, his pack is ready.

After his long night in the tent he cannot believe how good the oatmeal tastes. He wolfs down the concoction in about two minutes, then makes himself another batch. The day is overcast, but tolerable. "At least it's not raining," he says out loud. It is the first time he has heard anything other than the quiet of the woods and an occasional bird chirp. He is surprised by how foreign his voice sounds.

He hoists the pack onto a nearby log. As he leans to get into it he cannot help but kneel in the wet humus. The damp, rich smell comes up to him. He can feel the cold soak through his pant leg, but knows it will be fine in about five minutes, as soon as he is warmed by the hiking.

Jason picks up the trail where he left it. It runs down to the boggy creek before rising into dense woods just ten feet across the other side. The place where the trail crosses the bog has been reinforced by fallen logs and boulders, and he carefully wends his way across.

This morning, he realizes the path is not as clear or wide as yesterday's. Still, it appears to be wide enough, shooting off in a straight line through the woods—spruce, tamarack, jack pine, and low-growth alder. Up ahead it rounds a big spruce. Wet branches extend over it, but when he pushes through, the trail on the other side is clear again. As it rounds the tree, it starts moving in a northeasterly direction that gradually bends east—but its change in direction is difficult to notice.

If he had been awake at dawn, he might have noted the dull glow of the eastern sky and been troubled by the trail's direction. Now he follows the meandering path in the opposite direction from which he'd come—the wrong direction.

He recalls the trail's outline on the Fisher Map, how it started turning west. He suspects he turned west yesterday afternoon, well after the sky turned hazy, then overcast. He had been so preoccupied with setting up camp, building a fire, making and eating dinner, he hadn't paid attention to the sky, or the direction of its last dull glow. And besides, the sky was dense and overcast, pregnant with rain. He had been comfortable watching the fire burn.

Now he walks due east on the northernmost loop of the old Pow Wow Trail, believing he is walking west, past Pose Lake, starting his counterclockwise circuit of the proper Pow Wow Trail. Walking with a heavy pack in the morning can make you feel more alive than if you'd stopped at Starbucks for a venti. Despite the low weather, gray light, and wet world, Jason feels good.

For the first hour of hiking the trail is relatively clear. But almost imperceptibly it becomes overgrown. On rare occasions he parts branches, and the leftover rain grazes him like the fronds of a painter's brush. But he appreciates the pine bough sparkle.

After an hour the cloistering brush has soaked the front of his thighs. But hiking with the heavy pack keeps him warm, and he enjoys himself. It isn't exactly as he imagined. He came to the Pow Wow for a hike on an airy, wide trail bordered by solitary trees and bathed by a resplendent sun. This path is narrow and overgrown and the sky's color is closer to unearthed bones than turquoise. But in the early morning it is still pleasant.

Then up ahead the path seems to disappear into some black spruce and alder. Jason forges ahead, looking behind him to remember the direction of the path he has already passed over. He pushes through the thick brush and comes out the other side. And finds it. He locates the narrow path—little more than a game trail, but still clear through the woods.

He continues walking. In another fifteen minutes the same mysterious path disappearance occurs. And his remedy is the same. He pushes through, around the wet brush.

His pack catches on the branches, and he struggles forward. He turns the corner of a spruce. The path reappears clearly through the trees, and he keeps walking.

It is much narrower here. Branches line both sides of the meager trail, swatting the outer reaches of his backpack as he passes. He continues hiking, trying to avoid getting lashed, and then the path peters out entirely.

Damn, he thinks.

But twice he has lost the path, only to push through brush and recover it.

He forges ahead. He plows through more brush. The branches snap back behind him. He dodges left to move around a large popple. He steps to the right to avoid boulder rubble. He pushes forward, stepping carefully over mottled roots, but after several minutes he still hasn't recovered the path.

And here he turns around to consider where he has arrived. All around him the branches are thick. He stands in the middle of an unbroken patch of wood, with almost no room for movement, no visible way around or through the brush, and he is startled by the dense wall. He laughs, but it is a pallid humor. He has to take a picture of this. It is so foreign, so random, so unlike anything he has ever seen, so apparently impassable. And yet here he is, in the center of it.

He reaches into his jacket pocket, pulls out his disposable camera, and snaps a shot of the woods. In the foreground his lens is randomly framed by a couple of spare alders, barely taller than himself. More low-growth alders dot the landscape, intermingled with small six-foot firs. Beyond them, to the left and right, mature firs rise into an opaque sky.

The picture is remarkable because clearly there is no path ahead of him, to the left or right. And when he turns

Jason's view in the pathless woods (courtesy Jason Rasmussen)

around there is more of the same behind. He's flummoxed. He turns again to try and figure out which way he should walk. He feels certain the trail is fifty feet behind him. He decides to recover it and check his direction.

Jason bends and pushes through the swale the same way he came in. Then he hikes back, recovering his direction. But fifty feet doesn't recover anything. He is still in the middle of the wood, with no discernible path in any direction.

He shakes his head. For the first time he feels a dull edge of panic, as though someone has placed the back side of a blade against his stomach.

He turns around. Through the thick brush of trees he sees a sparkle. He can barely discern the pleasant reflection of dull sky off water. He pushes toward it and sees the edges of a lake. It is the first big water he has seen since yesterday's crossing of the stream near Isabella Lake.

Last night he assumed he camped near Pose Lake. He remembers it is the only lake in the vicinity. And he remembers it has islands. According to his Fisher map it has one large island and two smaller ones, which he should be able to see from the bank. And if he is right about Pose Lake, he is close to the trail. It would only take a little more bushwhacking to recover it.

He hikes forward to investigate. When he reaches the bank, his view of the rest of the lake is blocked by a wooded peninsula. He moves fifty yards along the shore until he stands at the peninsula's edge and stares over the open water. Nothing. Nothing except water, and the clear border of lakeshore surrounding it.

There is another tug, lower in his stomach.

He finds a clear place to take off his backpack. The woods have crowded him, providing resistance as he fought his way to the lake's edge. Though he hasn't been hiking for much more than an hour (it's around 10:00), he still feels like taking a rest and trying to figure out his location.

When he consults the map, he doesn't find anything resembling the apparent shape of this lake. He starts to worry, but only a little. He remembers the path behind him, how it was relatively clear and close, and he suspects he should be able to recover it easily enough. And of course, once recovered, he will continue.

Jason remembers times in the past when he's been hiking and gotten lost. Those times he could always recover the trail. He always retained a general sense of direction, of the way he should be hiking, and every other time he has been able to recoup his trail, find his way back, his way out.

But those were in southern woods and state parks, where trails are as prevalent as a rat's maze, and where the park has clear, close boundaries—not to mention being surrounded by roads. These woods, he reflects, are entirely different. This forest is on an entirely different scale. The Boundary Waters is over a million square acres, purposely void of any of the usual markings or signs. Still, he thinks he has a good idea of not only where the trail is, but the direction he should be hiking.

He hoists his backpack and starts hiking in the direction from which he came. For about an hour he pushes through the woods. The branches rise up like a series of flexible walls. He pushes through one wall, and behind it, there is another green lattice of fir branches and low-growth alder. And behind that, another. On occasion there is a small opening, and he takes it, continuing to move in the direction his instincts dictate.

This isn't Jason's idea of a pristine hike in the woods. He fights the entire way, getting wetter the more he pushes through damp brush. And the woods are thick. They are thicker than anything he's been through down south.

There is nothing fun about hiking through wet woods in October. The air is crisp. It is barely above freezing. The sky is overcast, and Jason continues to ruminate on how hard it is to bushwhack through dense forest. He has never seen anything like it.

He is worried, but not yet distraught. He knows the direction, believes he will recover the path. And when he does, he finally concedes, he is going back home. He is going to return to his car, head down to the North Shore, have a bite to eat, and go home. He is tired of the struggle. This is very different from what he imagined. If he had found a better trail, more clearly marked, and been able to locate the appropriate campsite over Pose Lake—and if the weather had been better—then things would have been different. But as it is, walking in wet woods in October with a fifty-pound pack on your back is tiring and frustrating and not exactly on most people's list of leisurely fall activities.

Another branch lashes his pack, swings back behind him, and he stumbles forward. And finally, he is rewarded. He crosses the path. It is clear, straight, obvious. Thank God! He feels a momentary rush of relief.

He stops for a minute, looking in both directions. He gets out his compass, holds it flat, and waits for the needle to resolve itself. Jason thinks he is at the top of the Pow Wow Trail loop, somewhere near Pose Lake, where he camped last night. By now he may have hiked well west of the Pose Lake spur. He believes he has recovered the east-west trail. Now, if he really wants to return, he suspects he will have to hike east.

He looks at the needle. This section of the trail moves in a west-southwesterly, east-northeasterly direction. Jason gets out his map and has another look. He knows he is somewhere near the top of the loop. He knows he must be close to Pose Lake. It is not necessary he find the lake, though it would be a good verification of his position. Still, he is almost certain he's at the top of the loop. To return to his car he will have to continue east along the trail.

He puts away his map and compass and starts walking east—exactly opposite the direction he should be hiking. The trail is reasonably clear. It is a lot like the trail he crossed this morning, before he lost it. It moves in a relatively straight line, and for the first twenty minutes, whenever he loses it in the trees and brush, he comes out the other side and recovers it.

He keeps walking, hiking along the trail, pushing through the deep woods. His mind wanders to his car's interior. He sees the Saturn where he left it in the lot. He sees himself taking off the burdensome pack. He finds his keys, remembering where he stowed them. He opens the trunk, drops his pack in, comes around to the front seat, and starts the engine. In five minutes, moving along the gravel roads, the inside of the car heats up like a warm blanket.

He is tired, and by the time he reaches his car, he reasons, he's going to be dog-tired. But it is going to be a sweet reunion. He can feel the way the car heats up and makes him drowsy. He will have to stop and get some coffee, maybe in Finland. With luck, it will only be early afternoon, still plenty of time to get back to Highway 61, have an early dinner along the North Shore, and return home.

Jason pushes through more woods. He has to constantly look down, watching his feet. One misstep and he could be in a world of hurt. This would be no place to break an ankle or twist a foot. He steps carefully, lost in his warm car daydream.

After two hours of fighting through the woods he pauses, knowing he should be closer to where the path opens up. Then he looks up and realizes the path has again disappeared. He has been looking down at his feet so long, not paying attention, struggling to get through the next section of brush, that he has lost the damn path again. He can't believe it!

A percussive cry gives voice to his frustration, loud enough to silence the red squirrels and ruffed grouse for at least a fifty-yard radius. He turns around, trying to recover the trail, trying to decide which way to move.

And then he sees it. There is a clear sparkle of water through the dense branch weave. At first he thinks it could be Pose Lake. But by now, hiking this long, he should be much farther east than Pose Lake. And there is something about this water, the way it shimmers through the branches, that is eerily familiar.

He cannot put his finger on it, but he suspects the airy tumult in his stomach is because this scene—the sparkle through the branches—looks so similar to the water he saw earlier this morning.

He takes a few more steps toward the lake. He looks at the water, peering through the branches. And then it hits him, not in a pleasant way, or with mild surprise. It hits him like someone placing a well-positioned fist in the center of his abdomen.

"Christ!" he thinks. "It's the same lake. I'm in the exact same spot I was in two hours ago!"

Something like a slow burning panic starts to unravel him. Now he is genuinely scared. When he thinks about how far he's hiked, pushing through the damp woods for the last two hours, hiking in some kind of big circle that has brought him back to his exact point of departure, he's dumbfounded. It is like some kind of science fiction movie in which the universe is confined to the narrow reaches of a wild wood, and there is no way out. He is condemned to walk in huge circles through wet woods. He laughs to think about it, how it could be some writer's sense of hell. Only there is no humor in his laugh.

"Get hold of yourself," Jason whispers quietly in the dense woods.

And after several minutes he manages to calm himself, his disappointment. Of course there's a way out. He pushes to the edge of the lake to make sure, and there's the tree-covered peninsula—the same one he observed this morning. There is absolutely no doubt he is near the exact place he stood this morning, contemplating this very same lake.

He looks at his watch. Almost noon. He is not happy, but knows he has to sit down, take off this heavy pack, and reconnoiter. He is not yet ready to ask himself, "What's the worst that can happen?" For the time being he focuses on getting out of these woods.

8

Bugs and Backwaters

*South of the Man Chain of lakes, Quetico Provincial Park,
Thursday, August 6, 1998*

During the interminable night Dan Stephens lies in the
dark and struggles to breathe. The shelter is tight and
warm enough, but he has not reckoned on the bugs. Mosquitoes swarm over his exposed skin. He suspects they
were nestled in the grass when he cut it. Lying in the tight
enclosure, covered by the thick rushes, he is hounded by
the pests.

He alternates breathing through his nose and mouth.
He cannot help but inhale them. There is a dry, metallic
taste in his throat. He has learned to swallow and snort, but
when he realizes the tinge of copper on his tongue is from
his own blood, panic forces him to wiggle out of his tight
lean-to and take refuge in the cold.

Outside it is cool and relatively bug free. He tries to normalize his breathing. He spits and takes another draught of water. But he is not dressed well enough to stay out long. Dan knows he cannot afford the expenditure of energy required to shake and shiver.

He drinks water. He waits. He has a powerful headache and still feels woozy, but this much he knows: to survive he is going to have to climb back into that bug-infested den and lie down in darkness. He's going to have to separate himself from the reality of it. There is no chance of sleeping. A kind of distant rest is the best he can muster. Finally, when the cold is becoming too great, he wedges himself back into his seething cocoon. And the mosquitoes— apparently warmed by him, apparently attracted to his heat—continue to feed on their meaty course.

If it was any other time, any other place, and he had any other recourse, he would rip out of his makeshift shelter and run screaming through the woods. Several times the swarms bring him near hysteria. The effect of so many needles burying themselves in his open skin, the taste of them in his mouth and throat, some of them engorged with his blood—he manages to hold it at the far reaches of consciousness. He knows if he lets them in, if he thinks about it, considers the pestilential siege, his slight hold on sanity may waver. He is coherent enough to remove himself mentally from the debilitating swarm. He tells himself it is only one night, this night—the longest of his life.

He lies in the boggy grass near the beaver pond, wondering where he is. Consciousness is shallow and fitful. When he rises and seeks refuge in the open, he is keenly thankful for the one good thing about the cold: it makes the bugs docile as pet rats.

When he kneels to drink he knows he is still sluggish from the fall. He remembers leaping across a pile of stone and falling. He sees a ragged field of stone as though it is part of some dreamscape. He remembers his friends from Chattanooga. He has a pounding headache, but through it he still worries about them. He waits until the cold drives him back into the warmth of his shelter. He lies quietly and tries to drift again into half-sleep, waiting for the first gray light of dawn.

His body is one big itch. The previous day's abrasions have left his legs sore and aching. Before lying in the grass he debated taking off his tennis shoes, but he appreciated their protection against bugs and didn't want a scavenger to mistake them for a meal. And besides, if he wants to walk out alive, his shoes are almost as important as water. Finally, he decided to leave them on. Now in the first hazy light he wiggles his toes, and they feel hot—as though sunburned. Trench foot, he guesses. He suspects he'll be walking in pain.

He lies still, waiting for the woods to lighten. When he can see well enough to move through brush, he crawls out from under his makeshift shelter. He is tired, but thankful the long, dark, grueling pestilence is behind him. He pisses and mosquitoes rise to the warm stream, but in the early morning cold they are sluggish and easily swatted away. He is relieved to finally be out of their clutches—at least for now. Now he must move to stay warm. Until the sun rises, the bugs will be tolerable.

In the muted light he looks down and finds the hefty walking stick he trimmed the night before. He notes the direction in which it is laid. He uses it to mark what he thinks is a southern trail across the half-lit marsh. Then he leans over and picks up the pine pole. It feels good to grip, something to hold onto. He walks up to the edge of the beaver pond, finds a clear place to siphon water, and fills his collapsible canteen with enough for a good morning draught.

The bugs are starting to warm to him. He drinks quickly, forcing the water down. He looks to the growing light in the woods and rechecks his position by guessing at the direction east. He is still groggy, but coherent enough to know if he wants to get warm he had better start moving. He knows Sommers Canoe Base lies somewhere south. He takes a vague bearing in that direction and strikes off through the trees.

Believing they are out of range for the proper operation of their radio phone, the fathers rise at first light. Tim awakens Shawn so they can return over the portage and check the dark cave of cedars where Stephens disappeared.

Jerry Wills will let the other Scouts sleep a little longer. They are going to need their rest. It was a hard evening and night, and today they will be asked to do the impossible: to find their way through a maze of lakes they have never seen, locate and cross more than a half-dozen unmarked portages—some of them long—and paddle twenty-seven miles to find a ranger station on the international border. Wills switches on a flashlight and stares at the map. He doesn't know how they can do it, but he doesn't see much choice. The life of their guide and friend, and their own lives, might depend on it.

His hand reaches up again to rub his sternum, where his chest feels tight. The strain, he knows. The hard physical labor of paddling and portaging. Still, he wonders about his heart. Maybe he should have it checked when he gets home.

This part of the Quetico is rugged, with prominent outcrops and high, granite ridges. Jerry Wills recalls Dan describing the Man Chain, wondering if the region's unusually high ridges might render their radio phone useless. The terrain, their concern about schedule and direction, and the vague discomfort they all feel when contemplating a return through the nameless lake, convinces Jerry Wills they have made the right decision—to stay together, keep moving ahead, continuing southwest, hoping they will encounter another group, or at least make it far enough so their radio phone is operational. Finally, Jerry Wills looks up to see Tim and Shawn's canoe disappear into the northeastern shadows of Bell Lake. He turns and starts waking his crew.

In the early morning Tim and Shawn retrace the portage to peer over no-name lake. They carry a small cache of supplies: some food and waterproof matches, a note for Dan detailing their return for help. "Stay put," the note concludes. "We'll be back with help."

They lay Stephens's cache on the no-name lake side of the portage. The portage is dim, but the path is clear. They are surprised that yesterday they couldn't find it. They peer over the nameless lake. The water is calm. The only sign of their crossing are footprints in the muddy transition between lake and dry land. None of them are Dan's.

To look back over the lake where their friend and guide disappeared makes them feel anxious. This far into wilderness their imaginations are unbridled—they picture wolves, bears, cougars, or things more sinister. They call out in the early light, but there's no response. Pondering Dan's disappearance makes their skin rise like a plucked chicken's.

They call again. Nothing. They repeat their call, waiting for some response, but there is only the warm mist rising in half light over the deceptively placid water. They wonder what could have happened, shaking their heads, bewildered. The invincible Dan Stephens walked into the woods and disappeared. What in hell could have happened to him?

"Let's get back," Tim finally says. Shawn couldn't agree more.

The day is warming but the bugs have not yet started to swarm. They turn and re-cross the portage, paddling the short distance to camp. By the time they reach it, the others are nearly loaded and ready.

Jerry Wills has been careful to pare their supplies to absolute essentials. In spite of park regulations, discarded equipment and food sits near Dan's tub at the edge of camp. Jerry reminds himself that today they have to make time. The park has a zero-footprint policy—visitors are not to leave any traces of their presence. But this is an emergency. They will inform the rangers at Prairie Portage, and someone will return for it—providing bears haven't found it and feasted. They don't want to leave these supplies, but neither had they wanted to lose their guide and have to travel at a breakneck pace for help. Jerry Wills knows they will need every possible advantage.

They give one last call into the tree line, screaming Dan Stephen's name. Some of the Scouts whistle, but it is early, and their efforts echo back empty. None of them expects an answer. In the distance they hear a loon cry. A lone blue heron rises in startled flight from the opposite shore.

The Scouts come down to the water's edge. Jerry Wills and Tim Jones take one last tour of camp. Some of the Scouts are starting to climb into their canoes, readying themselves for the long journey south.

"Wait a minute," Jerry Wills calls to them.

The spit of rock in front of their campsite juts into the lake. It makes a long shallow reef, descending gradually toward the middle of Bell. Their canoes are beached on a crevice running up into camp. Now the Scouts gather near the lakeshore.

Jerry Wills comes down and walks into the water. "We need to ask for help," he says. The Scouts know their troop leader. He is a devout man, always ready with a prayer. This morning he has them walk down into the water with him. Tim Jones follows them into the cold, placid lake. They huddle there, join hands like a team preparing for a big game. But there is a somber quality to this gathering. They are starting an arduous day's journey, and they're anxious, wishing they were breaking camp under different circumstances. Dan's absence hangs over their heads like a thick fog.

Jerry Wills's prayer is brief, ardent, strained. He asks for God's guidance and help through the long day's journey. He asks that God watch over them and give them strength for what they are about to begin. He asks that He watch over their friend, guide him, and bring him safely home.

The boys are used to their leader's words, but this morning they ring with special urgency. Before, their requests for God's blessings were general, maybe even typical, given their adventure. Today the boys and Tim Jones murmur with Jerry Wills, sincere in their entreaties. They close with a collective "Amen," and break silently for their canoes.

"We have to get nearer," Jerry Wills finally says, thinking about their phone, worried about the long portage and paddle in front of them. "Let's cross into Other Man and give it another try."

Dan Stephens fights through alder, cedar, black ash, and tamarack. As the day heats up the bugs rise to meet him.

He pushes through the muck of lowland swamps, struggling to find a clear rise. For most of the morning he wanders through a marsh, vaguely aware that he needs to move south, needs to keep hiking, following the drainage. He believes if he follows the drainage, it will empty into the Man Chain, and eventually he'll pick up a passing canoe group, maybe his own. Twice he rises to tree-covered outcrops, thankful for the light breeze and marginally better view.

He still feels groggy. He knows he has to keep taking water. Whenever he finds a clear pool or light-running stream, he kneels to drink. The rangers at the Cache Bay Station told him the Quetico waters are high this year, and for that he is thankful.

He develops a rhythm, walking through the brush. He uses his pine pole alternately as an walking stick and parting tool. When he is walking through thick brush, he swings the bottom tip out and under limbs, branches, or grass. Then he parts them by swinging his hand and holding the stick wide to the right or left as he passes. Sometimes he fashions a second stick from wilderness windfall. In thick areas he uses two sticks to part whatever lies in front of him. But he is careful to keep his head up, periodically scanning for the next best landmark toward which to move. He wants to be able to see anything that rises in front of him before it becomes a problem. And he struggles to keep hiking in a southwesterly direction through brush that sometimes appears thick as a living room wall.

On this day he begins noticing bear scat, some of it moist. When hiking in Appalachia, Dan encountered plenty of bears. He prefers to let them know he's coming. Twice in the past he has surprised a mother bear with cubs and was able to back away from the snarling she-bear. He would prefer avoiding any confrontation in these woods, so far from any hope of assistance and in such tight quarters.

Truth is, the day is almost a carbon copy of yesterday, with a few notable exceptions. He is lost, hungry, tired, muddle-headed, and not entirely sure where he is, or which way is south. His feet ache, and he is damn hungry. He cannot ever remember being this hungry. He feels his stomach tighten.

He comes to a tiny circular island in the sea of grass and water, about ten feet in diameter. He has a small binocular lens. He gathers some grass and kindling, and tries to use his lens to focus the sun into a fiery laser point. But after several minutes he hasn't even produced a smoky wisp.

He doesn't consider fire by friction. He's had experience with the technique, and knows that without a good hand socket—something he doesn't have the materials to build— rubbing sticks together is a useless, blistering endeavor.

He was hoping a small fire would raise his spirits. If he fed it long enough others might see it at night, or see the smoke. Now he abandons the idea, gets up, keeps moving.

For the Scouts, the remaining mile down Bell Lake is a relatively easy paddle. From the narrow point of its southwestern end they hurriedly cross a shallow twenty-one-rod portage into another nameless lake. The cool morning air quickens their efforts.

Once in the smaller lake, they need to hug the left shore, turning south. It is a half-mile paddle around a point with hidden reefs. Due south of the point there is an island with jutting trees. Surrounded by a morning mist, the island looks eerie against the southern shore, but it tells them their brief four-rod portage should be just ahead.

This portage is low and marshy. The three bowmen get

out and pull their canoes across the narrow, eighty-foot spit. They are thankful they don't have to unpack and carry. They make good time and come into another nameless spread of water—another small connecting lake.

This one has a small island in the middle. They stay to the right of the island, continuing due south, searching for two jutting points of land that almost connect. They need to thread those points and cross a narrow bay to their next portage. They find the points, pass over water less than a hundred feet wide, and see the south shore rise before them.

From the lake the thirty-nine-rod portage is easy to locate. The land rises up and the path over the escarpment is clear. At this hour they are warming to their familiar routine. They know how to divide their tasks, and their supplies and burdens are fewer. But this portage starts out with a vertical climb over a solid granite wall, as though the wilderness is throwing another obstacle in their path. The wall ends in a narrow granite ridgeback, crosses high over the water, and then plunges down the opposite side into a brief swamp before ending in the next lake.

On top of the crest Tim sets down his canoe and brings up the pack with the radio phone. Since leaving camp they have spent more than an hour paddling and portaging. They are much higher here—and farther south. Their location might make a difference.

He switches on the device. The indicator light blinks on, and the familiar, muted, white noise hums through the receiver. He tries three times, but there is no response.

"It's the distance," Jerry surmises, disappointed. "We've got to get closer."

In spite of the portage—one of the most difficult they've tackled—they work hard and fast, ferrying canoes and packs in silence. There is a small point of land that extends into the lake beyond where they enter. They glide over the water, crossing around the point to look down the long, open water of Other Man.

To reach the next portage, they need to push down the lake's length. The day is warming. A light breeze rises at their backs. The lake's surface ripples, but the waves are not high enough to impede their paddling, and the wind eases their efforts. They have two miles of blue water and islands; on any other day they would revel in its magnificence. They are on the north shore, the correct one for crossing. Tim Jones and his crew in the lead canoe start off along the heavy forest edge, thankful for the freshet that helps move their canoes along.

They take well over an hour to paddle down the two-mile length of Other Man. Thankfully, the portage into This Man Lake is open and easy to find. At forty-nine rods, the trail is longer than their first, but it is low, flat, straight—an easy crossing. This Man Lake is almost three times longer than Other Man. They struggle down the start of its length, hugging the northern shoreline. At 10:30, the sun is well off the horizon and the breeze makes a small chop across the water, but they remain thankful for the wind at their backs.

It is mid-morning, and Jerry Wills is tired and already strained from the paddling. When he considers his group, he thinks the boys' faces show the same signs of fatigue. Before they left the Sommers Canoe Base, the group sat in the Great Hall with all the other groups and watched a video about paddling techniques and safety precautions. One section of the video showed paddlers lashing canoes together to make a flotilla and raising a makeshift sail against the wind. Jerry Wills remembers how the pair of connected canoes leaped easily across the water.

It only takes the engineer a second to make the connection. This Man Lake is their longest paddle in the Chain. The gust is at their backs. He thinks of the rain fly they used to stake out over camp, on the few occasions the skies had darkened. It is lightweight waterproof nylon. It would make a perfect sail.

Jerry tells the group he has an idea. The boys and Tim Jones quickly buy into his plan, thankful for anything to ease the morning's labor. They have miles to paddle, and their backs and shoulders already ache with the effort.

The three canoes come alongside each other. The boys lay their paddles across the gunwales and grip them, making connecting supports. Jerry Wills gets out the rain fly and lashes its corners to the bows of the two outside canoes. He fastens long lengths of nylon rope to the rear corners of the fly. They'll use the ropes to hold onto their fly so it can billow and capture the wind.

Now all they need is a mast to raise the sail so it catches the breeze. The middle riders thrust the narrow ends of two paddles up into the edges of their makeshift sail. A small pocket of nylon fabric catches the wind, and suddenly the entire fly billows with the breeze. The three-canoe flotilla surges forward.

A cry of triumph goes up. From the rear of the middle canoe Tim Jones rudders the flotilla with his oar. In this way the small group steers down the three-mile length of This Man Lake, skirting occasional islands and the near shore. Sometimes they skim over the water so quickly they can hear the rush beneath their canoes. They are thankful for the respite. They all wear broad smiles and cheer the rapid progress.

Some time after noon they come to the end of the lake and are again blessed by a portage that is easy to find.

There are two portages from This Man Lake into No Man Lake. The one to the east is thirty-two rods. The one to the west is sixty rods. While both appear flat and relatively easy to hike, the thirty-two-rod portage will leave them with a hundred more yards to paddle. Still, they prefer paddling to struggling with unwieldy canoes across uneven paths. They take the shorter portage into No Man and quickly reload their canoes.

No Man is a mere half-mile crossing. On the north side of the lake there is a campsite below a prominent ridgeline. They decide to beach their canoes at the campsite and give the radio another try. Then Tim and Justin can scale the ridgeline and hail base camp. The others will have a chance to rest and eat.

Atop the ridgeline Tim switches on the phone. There is a slight spit and crackle as the receiver turns on. Then he hears the usual white noise. He tries to raise base camp three times, but there is no response.

"Closer?" Justin asks.

"That, or this damn phone isn't working."

Discouraged, the two climb down off the ridgeline and join the others. They can see by the look of their troopmates they were hoping for better words.

"We need to get closer," Tim Jones says. It's an answer they all understand.

Across a lowland opening, Dan Stephens feels a light breeze. When he can see them, high pillows of cumulus drift across an azure dome. He crosses the opening to the other side and pushes through more brush. The dense weave is sometimes so thick he raises his arms in front of his face for protection. His forearms start abrading like his legs. At one point he bends down to avoid a branch and gets poked in the eye. The scratch is watery and painful. Blinking, he struggles toward the next rise.

He feels aimless in the swampy bogs south of wherever it was he stepped into the bush and kept walking. He feels desultory and lost. He thinks he is heading southwest. He positions himself by the sun. Whenever he stops to drink he pauses long enough to peer at the sky and check his direction.

He feels relatively certain he's heading in the right direction. But hiking the lowlands is like walking through a shallow hell. The bugs are pestilential, the brush is thick, and the day progresses windless and hot. And now the vision in his one eye is blurred. He still feels a huge, periodic ache on the side of his head.

After a twenty minute rest he re-examines the sky. Dan double-checks his position, glances off through the trees in what he thinks is a southerly direction, and again strikes off through the bogs.

Progressively, Dan Stephens comes to feel as low as the country he traverses. He has a vague notion he needs to angle toward the Man Chain, veer toward the possibility of finding a portage trail and maybe staying put until the next group of Scouts comes along. But he also has doubts.

Before leaving the canoe base with his Chattanooga group, he had asked others about his planned route. But he could not find anyone who had made the wide circle through the BWCAW, then up through the Quetico, then turning back around to come down through the Man Chain. He doesn't know of anyone who has come down out of the Cache Bay Station in quite the same way. It could be awhile before anyone else came along. And then he would be waiting on a bug-infested stretch of trail, for how long he has no idea.

He's thinking well enough to know he's not entirely lucid. An aching cloudiness hangs over him, muddling his thoughts. His vision is still bleary. He is trying to maintain his rhythm, moving carefully through the brush, parting the sharp branches with his stick, moving forward, always moving south. But he is uncertain, and through the long midday his spirits ebb to a wavering crawl.

The Chattanooga group crosses the quarter-mile distance to their next portage, and this, too, is easy to find. They are blessed, but only slightly. The portage from No Man into That Man Lake is a blistering 101 rods. The climb isn't high, and the path is straight, but at over a quarter mile, it is one of the longest portages they've crossed. By the time they reach the other side, they are exhausted. Back at the campsite on No Man Lake, Tim had told the group there was something more than the normal white noise, at least when he first switched the set on. Now they are keen to give it another try.

Tim is doubtful, but willing. They are at lake level, but they've closed some distance. And from this vantage the extreme length of That Man opens empty in front of them. Maybe the clear space will make a difference.

He extracts the phone and flips it on. The light blinks, and the receiver sparks with more static—at least a little more than they heard on the ridgeline over No Man. Surprised, Tim presses the transmit button and speaks into the phone.

"This is Group Number 801C," he begins. He releases the button, waits. The receiver is silent.

"They ain't even listenin'!" one of the Scouts moans.

"Quiet," Tim says. He again depresses the transmit button. "This is Group Number 801C," he repeats. "We're at

No Man Lake portage, about to enter That Man. Does anybody read me?"

From the other end of the line not even a crackle. And then the light blinks off.

Tim Jones can't help himself. He cusses, says, "Looks like it went dead."

The other Scouts take the news hard. The two youngest boys' eyes start to water, and they look away, embarrassed.

"We're on track," Jerry Wills finally says, trying to reassure everyone, trying to be optimistic. "Let's keep moving."

Well after noon Dan Stephens comes to a small stream. On the other side, the forest rises to another rocky outcrop. He kneels to drink. Tannin dyes the slow-moving water the color of dark tea. He has already crossed a half-dozen small streams like this one. He can barely see six inches into its murky depths. It looks shallow enough. He steps into it, expecting to hit bottom.

For the second time in two days his stomach registers the miscalculation before he does. He watches his foot disappear into murk. He waits for it to grip bottom. He is already too far in, with too much weight moving forward, to pause or retract his step. One leg is still on the bank and the other disappears into the stream and in half a hiccup he falls forward into the narrow, deep water. He plunges forward up to his neck before his feet sink into the muddy bog bottom.

"Goddammit," he cusses, thrashing through the deep, mucky water. *What in the hell is it going to be next,* he wonders, struggling to reach the other side.

9

Rasmussen Hikes South

North-northeast of the Pow Wow Trail, Tuesday, October 23, 2001

He drops the pack in a meager clearing, takes out his water bottle, and drinks. He is thirsty. He's been working through these trees, and he hasn't realized just how thirsty he is. He almost drains the bottle, knowing he can filter more when he needs it.

He has to figure out how to recover the trail and get back to his car.

He returns his water bottle to his pack's side pocket and takes out Fisher Map F-4: *One, Two, Three, Four, Bald Eagle, Insula Lakes.* He spreads it out before him and squints over the yellow and blue features, trying to figure out his location in relation to the trail.

Lowland swamps are marked by small swatches of

speckled blue. The lake water is solid blue. When he looks at the map, gazing over the top of the Pow Wow, he thinks it could be Hush Lake. That would mean he hiked farther west than he thought, camping last night between Pose and South Wilder lakes. Had he wandered off the trail and headed northwest? If he were further west could he have hiked northeast?

He stares at the elevation numbers. Math and science have become Jason's strengths. Since junior college, academics have usually come easily to him. Map reading is simple. But trying to discern his own peculiar location from the myriad striations in front of him is difficult. When he gazes over the map, he assumes Pose Lake is someplace near—within an hour hiking, tops. He gazes over the Pow Wow circular trail and realizes he could have strayed south of the trail. He gazes south and sees Hump Lake, almost in the middle of the twenty-six-mile circular Pow Wow.

And then he gazes even farther south, to the vicinity of the Isabella parking lot where his Saturn sits, patiently awaiting his return. He notices the forest road he used to drive here. It runs the entire length of the trail, due south of it, probably less than four miles. It is not exactly straight but it's long enough so that if he hiked due south, eventually he would have to cross it. And Jason knows to miss a road would be impossible. If the bottom half of the Pow Wow is more discernible than this top half, he should cross it long before reaching the road. When he crosses the trail he can hike east, pick up the spur that brought him here, and be back at his car in two or three hours. And if he misses it—entirely possible, given the state of the trail he's seen—he will eventually hit the road. He cannot miss a road.

He fishes his compass out of his pocket, holds it flat,

and lets the needle resolve itself. When he locates due south, he looks up into the impenetrable trees. It feels south. He can see himself hiking through the woods, only this time he will keep the compass out, checking it regularly to insure his constant southerly direction.

He squints again at the map. If he is near Pose Lake, two or three miles should bring him to the bottom of the Pow Wow. He examines the key, measuring off the distance with a finger, moving it south over the yellow terrain. If he misses the trail, he still crosses the forest road by late afternoon. And once he hits the forest road, he hikes back to his car. Either way, he is back at the car well before dusk.

It's a plan, and he feels better after resting and making it. He likes using the compass, knowing his location—at least in regard to magnetic north. He is not looking forward to all that bushwhacking, but now that he has the compass out—*and it will stay out*, he tells himself—he won't double back on himself. He will check it regularly and keep moving due south.

He gets up and hoists on his pack. He straightens the shoulder straps and shifts the weight of the pack until it's comfortable. He folds his Fisher map and decides it should be handy. The inside of his North Face jacket has a pull string he can tighten around his waist. He tucks the map inside his coat and pulls the string taut, zips his jacket shut, takes another compass reading, and then looks up. He peers into the thick brush and strikes off through the trees.

For the next two hours Jason struggles through difficult terrain, climbing up and over small ridges. The lower parts sometimes hold small pockets of water. He steps over them carefully, skirting boulders and rocks, tree roots, pushing through the heavy brush.

The bushwhacking is difficult. But he keeps his promise to himself. He constantly checks his compass, navigating carefully through the woods. He follows the narrow point of the needle due south. He is good about maintaining his ragged direction through difficult terrain.

After two more hours of hiking, he's getting tired. He pushes through another block of impenetrable brush. He is weary and wet, and he knows if he stops longer than five minutes he will start to get a chill.

He pushes through the back end of the block of brush and suddenly it opens. He can't believe it. He stares across an almost seventy-five-yard length of bog. A bog, for Christ's sake. He's stunned.

Jason knows about bogs. If at all possible, you should avoid traversing them. They are deceptive islands of grass hummocks and small forest growth, and they can float over depths of water black as tea. If sphagnum lips part, if he falls through, and if it is deep enough, his death will be fast and agonizing, and the bog will swallow him whole. No one—not his parents, not rescuers, not seasoned hunters with dogs—will ever have a chance of finding even a hair.

He suspects he is being overly dramatic, but he has read about bogs. He knows you're not supposed to cross them. But he has a plan, and he has promised himself he'll stick to it.

He looks to the left. Maybe he can walk around it. But the bog appears to have no western or eastern edge. It looks like one large bog river, and he sees no way of maintaining his direction other than striking straight out across it.

It is such a large bog he wonders if it is clearly depicted on his map. He unzips his jacket, reaches in to pull out his map, but there is nothing. He feels around the inside of his coat, around his sides, above and below the coat's waist drawstring, but the map is gone! God damn it! He lost his goddamn map! He contemplates turning around and looking for it, but realizes that in the last two hours he could have lost it anywhere. Finding the missing Fisher map in the thick brush he has already traversed would be almost impossible—and that's if he were certain he could hike back over the exact trail he used to get here.

He remembers the map, at least most of its larger features. He remembers the trail and the way it wends over the terrain. And he still has the *Hiking Minnesota* map. It is cartoonish in comparison, but at least it gives him some sense of the trail, and the most notable lakes.

He's angry at himself for losing his map, but realizes there's nothing to be done about it. He looks up and knows he has to cross this bog. He peers over the grassy hummocks. In places he can see water seeping through. It's black. He knows it is acidic, having stewed for eons in a vegetal brew. He thinks he discerns a relatively clear trail, higher than the other parts. He starts out across it, moving very carefully, one slow step at a time, testing as he moves.

Before, when he was bushwhacking through dense wood, he thought he was moving slowly. Compared to how slowly he moves across the bog, his hike through the woods was a virtual sprint.

He steps to one mound, testing it carefully before placing his full weight onto it. It holds. Sometimes it starts to sink, like a very slow spring. But eventually, every step is solid and true. It takes him more than half an hour to cross it, stepping very slowly and carefully. Finally, he reaches the other side.

He pauses long enough to enjoy a momentary sense of relief. He knows he has been lucky. He hopes he won't have to cross more bogs. He thinks he is making good progress south and expects to pass over the southern side of the Pow Wow at any time. Providing it is wide and obvious, he reminds himself—unlike the northern part of the trail—he'll be able to take it, hike due east, and get back to his car in plenty of time.

It's after 2:00. The skies haven't altered since he first looked up. They have been gray and thick all morning, but thankfully not weeping. If it started raining, he knows he would have to stop and set up camp, get out of the rain. It looks like it's just going to be one of those overcast days.

Jason hacks his way south, attending to the bold S of his compass, letting it guide him through boulders and thatch, continuing to push through the wet wood. He cannot remember a harder day hiking—and with fifty pounds on his back. He is going to deserve that dinner. He relishes the thought of the warm car and his drive down a wide, open road, providing he can reach it before dark.

After almost two more hours he still hasn't crossed the trail, but panic is a long way off. He keeps expecting the Pow Wow to appear over the next rise, an open and obvious trail through the trees. But he also knows that he is holding to his plan, moving south, and that even if he misses the trail he will eventually, probably before dusk, cross the forest road that brought him here.

And then he pushes down a thicket slope to an edge of black spruce. And once through it, there's another bog. He can't believe it! Another goddamn bog!

He does exactly what he did this morning, knowing if there is any other recourse he should take it. He looks left. The grassy hummocks recede around a bend as though a river of moss is flowing down the contour of land. When he looks to his right, the same. It would be impossible to hike around this bog. And he remembers he is keeping to his course. He has to maintain his direction south.

Deeply fatigued, he knows he is probably not reasoning as well as he should, but he suspects the trail is just the other side, waiting for him. He examines the boggy surface. He finds again what he thinks is a viable path. Thankfully, this bog is half the width of the preceding one. He steps, tests, and then moves carefully across it. In twenty minutes he reaches the other side.

Again, he breathes relief, contemplating the rise in front of him, knowing there is no other way but up. More tired than he can ever recall, he looks down at his compass and sees he is still heading due south, just as he suspected. He pushes through the heavy brush, climbs the small rise, and comes out on top.

He's very tired now. He knows he should stop, but he wants to recover the trail. He feels disappointed he has not found it. The hike ahead appears clearer. Up here there is a solid granite dome covered over with caribou moss and lichen. There's some grass. And then it opens up wide and clear for at least thirty yards.

As he moves forward, the clouds part. For the first time all day a discernible blue gap opens in the otherwise gray and white cover. It's misty, but definitely blue. And then the sun breaks out, shining on Jason's small clear island in the middle of the brush. He looks up, bathing in it. If he were religious, he would interpret it as a sign. Even though he's not, he will still interpret it as a sign. He moves forward a few steps, and down the other side he sees a long lake.

He doesn't remember a lake on the map. He didn't think he would be coming in contact with a lake, but this one is definitely different from the one he has already seen twice today, the one far behind him.

This place, bathed in the sun over the long, narrow stretch of water, is beautiful. It is the first truly open patch of ground he has encountered all day. He revels in being unencumbered by thicket and brush.

It is almost 4:00, and he knows he is far too tired to continue hiking. It occurs to him that this is the first place he has been all day that appears to be a reasonable campsite. And why not? Why not camp here for the rest of the day? Get out of these wet clothes. Pitch his tent. He is too tired to gather wood for a fire, and besides, after last night's rain, the firewood is still wet. But he can cook some food, and he is near all the water he can drink.

Thinking of food and water he realizes he is starving, and thirsty. His mouth feels like it's lined with cotton. He pulls his water bottle out of his pack, bathing in the sunlight, and finishes his water. He takes off his pack. He has decided to stay. He is too tired to keep moving. He can continue south tomorrow, after he's well rested and fed. Jason suspects the trail is just the other side of this lake. He'll have a look at the *Hiking Minnesota* map and find this lake, now that he has a good landmark.

Within an hour his camp is set up, he has filtered more water, drunk his fill, and his WhisperLite is cooking another fine meal—stroganoff and noodles. The smell is savory, ambrosial. He is dry, warm, and ready to eat. For the first time that day, he feels relatively good. But he is exhausted. Now that he's secure, with the tent beside him and his meal starting to simmer, he can take stock of himself.

Waiting for his dinner to be done, he pulls the disposable camera out of his pack and snaps a photo of his tent on the rise. The tent's mosquito-net door is zipped shut. Not that he needs it. The afternoon light appears brilliant after his long amble through the gray woods. He has taken all his wet clothes—two pairs of socks, shirt, pants—and laid them across the tent's peak. The extra weight of the sodden clothes sags the tent sides, but it's plenty strong enough to hold.

He turns around and takes a picture of the water through a small stand of spruce. The far lakeshore is buffered by a twenty-foot-wide marshy border. The area beyond the marsh is thick with spruce and fir.

Jason's tent on rise over water (courtesy Jason Rasmussen)

He moves down through the spruce stand, closer to where the slope of his moss-covered hilltop slides down into the lake. Then he takes a picture of the lake disappearing into the distant trees.

The water is still and almost perfectly clear, and he can see the shallow, leaf-strewn bottom. An old beaver lodge sits near the middle of the narrow lake. He turns and takes a picture in the opposite direction, where the lake bends to

The body of water east of Jason's tent (courtesy Jason Rasmussen)

the right around two narrow hillocks of spruce. Beyond the narrow opening, the water appears to empty into a large marsh.

He hikes up the small rise to his tent and his dinner. He cannot remember feeling this kind of tiredness. He knows that as soon as the stroganoff is finished, as soon as he has eaten his fill, he is going to crawl into his mummy bag and slip into well-deserved oblivion.

10

First Word

*Ely, Minnesota, and Quetico Provincial Park, Thursday,
August 6, 1998*

Twenty miles outside Ely, Minnesota, up Moose Lake Road,
the Sommers Canoe Base main lodge and building complex lies nestled in deep woods. In summer the only visible
trace of the base from Moose Lake is the radio tower rising
above the trees. The signal ends in the main lodge, a heavy
log structure built in 1942 by Finnish craftsmen.

An attendant is nodding over paperwork. It's 2:29 in the
afternoon, one full hour after a late lunch. In many coun-
tries it's time for a nap. But at Sommers the afternoon is
drawing out slow and hot. The FM radio receiver crackles,
sending a signal across the office. Seldom does the receiver
make even a pop. And then the attendant hears a scratchy
voice.

"801C," the voice comes over the console, faint, but

plenty clear enough to hear. The attendant writes it on a piece of paper. "No Man Lake portage," he notes. "About to enter That Man." He knows the phone is only for emergencies—an infrequent occurrence. He crosses to the console and presses the transmit button.

"This is Sommers Base Camp. Come in, Group 801C."

Then he releases the button, waiting for a response. The group repeats its number, adding its location.

"We copy, 801C," the attendant repeats. "What's up? Over."

But the group doesn't answer. And then the line goes dead.

The attendant takes the cryptic message to Doug Hirdler, the camp's general manager. Hirdler has been working at the base long enough to have witnessed most kinds of emergencies. Usually it is a bad sprain or a knife cut. But nobody uses the phone unless there's something to report. Hirdler starts to worry.

"Just keep tracking it," he instructs. "See if they send anything else." He gets up to chew over the news with Joe Mattson, the camp's program director. When they look to see who is leading Group 801C, they're reassured. Dan Stephens, one of their best. Whatever comes up, Dan will know what to do. Still, the phone is for emergencies, and knowing Dan is guiding that group doesn't entirely calm them.

While That Man Lake is almost as long as This Man Lake, islands cross its middle, making a sail impossible. The Chattanooga group enters the water and starts the long hard pull down its length. They have almost reached the halfway point. It doesn't take long for their aches to return. They bend their backs and arms into it, straining against the paddles.

The wind remains behind them, assisting their efforts. Tim Jones murmurs a prayer of thanks and feels as though God is watching over them, giving them assistance at a time when their spirits are flagging.

They make slow progress. They pass by the big islands, keeping to the northern shore. It is a hard three miles. At least the lake is long, narrow, and straight. If they stay along the north shore, they should paddle straight to the portage.

At their last portage they rummaged through their supplies to find the right map: F-11: *Snowbank, Knife, Kekekabic Lakes.* They've seen the portage that awaits them. At 136 rods, it will be the day's longest. The two fathers don't look forward to the haul, particularly as the afternoon stretches out before them. They are all tired, and they can see the younger boys struggling with the effort. Jerry Wills is particularly fatigued, but there is no alternative. He appreciates these Scouts. In the last twenty-four hours they have done everything they've been asked to do, and more. Now they bend into the hard labor, fully aware of the long portage ahead of them.

There is a narrow connecting river between the two lakes, but in places the water drops over some small falls and the white water foams. Their portage ambles along the southern side of the river, concealed in the trees. They can hear the water rushing when they make the crossing. They struggle with canoes, packs, and paddles. Thankfully, it is relatively straight and clear, with few rises or drops. The gradual descent to their next lake—Sheridan—is a long hike, but manageable.

The group pauses and rests at the end of the portage. Some of them grab fistfuls of gorp, washing it down with water. After fifteen minutes they launch their canoes into Sheridan. They cross it in silence, making slow progress across the water. It reaches a short mile south, bending around a spit of land and turning almost due south to their next portage into Carp Lake.

After another hour they locate the fifteen-rod portage, and thankfully it is an easy crossing. The Scouts are tired. They've made remarkable time coming down from Bell, but they are weary from the long haul. Still, they know they must keep pushing.

They enter Carp Lake and after fifteen minutes paddle around a small island just outside the portage bay. Jerry Wills raises one tired hand to rub his sternum. As if in answer he sees a silver flash from down the long lake surface in front of him. It is another canoe party. He calls out to the others, and they squint into the blue afternoon, watching the same silver flash across the water. Then they dig in their paddles to close the distance before them.

Dan Stephens crawls out of the deep channel and knows he has to get himself dry. He climbs a small ridge to get out of the swamp. A light breeze gives him temporary respite from the insect swarm. The sun warms him. He takes off his clothes and hangs them in nearby bushes where the afternoon breeze will dry them.

He sits down, naked, starting to realize he had better stay put until his head clears. He's starting to feel better. It is as though the wilderness stream bathed his entire body in dark tea, and the total immersion is having a clarifying effect. Gradual lucidity begins to wash over him, dissipating his muddled thinking. He sits for a while, resting.

After several minutes there is a sudden onrush of clarity, as though someone has switched a light on in his brain. Its illumination is startling. He remembers his Tennessee group, the start of their trip, their journey north, the canoe race. He recalls their search for the unnamed portage, and his cloverleaf in the cedar swamp.

It all tumbles forward and with sickening clarity he realizes he should have remained in the rocks where he fell, stayed until his head cleared. Instead, he started walking, bushwhacking deeper into the woods, his path aimless and ill-defined, hiking into the wilderness with only a half-wit's sense of direction and a vague plan.

He remembers the Fisher map. He gave his compass and map to young David. He tries to recall the wide yellow swath north of Bell Lake—at least ten miles of wilderness before reaching another noticeable body of water, a course that would take him much farther into the woods. If he had hiked north, he would have moved deeper into the Quetico, making his chances of being found, of surviving, nearly impossible. But he feels certain he is headed south.

He knows they must be looking for him. He curses the stupor that made him leave those rocks. He feels a brief surge of shame for having put himself in this predicament. He imagines the call to his parents, their understandable worry. But he is okay. He is all right now. For the first time since falling he feels clear headed, and he knows he can find his own way out of the Quetico bogs.

He takes stock of himself. He is wearing shorts, a polyester shirt, a deflated polyurethane life vest, and light hiking shoes. He has a collapsible canteen, a knife, lip balm, some string, pocket binoculars, sunscreen, and a small roll of duct tape. His legs are badly abraded. His scratched eye is bleary. His shoes, soaked and filthy, cover over one of the worst cases of trench foot he has ever seen. Hiking is just as he expected—painful.

He takes off his shoes and tries to dry his feet in the afternoon sun. He allows himself one brief moment of self-pity.

"I need a plan," he says out loud. "And I will sit here until I figure one out."

The sun is still two hours from setting. Two-thirds up the hillside the rock is open and warm. But he can already feel the onset of coolness with the fading day. Last night it must have dropped below sixty, and the mosquitoes were so bad he slept fitfully, if at all.

Dan likes his position on the hillside. He is high and open enough to keep the bugs at bay—at least until dusk. He faces near west, where he'll soak in the day's last rays. And in the morning he can crest the ridge and walk to the other side to warm himself in the rising sun.

He takes another reading. He finds a long stick, locates the westerly sun, and lays the stick in a clear east-west direction. He knows he has to move south. He looks in that direction. The hill slopes down to a long, thick valley where it bellies out for a half mile before rising to another ridge. In the morning, he will hike to the next ridge. He doesn't look forward to crossing that bush, but he has to move south. He recollects the map. He remembers the yellow and blue swatches north of the Canadian border. The lakes form a straggling northeast-to-southwest band. Below Bell Lake the yellow is almost solid to Ottertrack. Ottertrack Lake is a familiar, well traveled canoe route.

He has to make it to Ottertrack. Once at Ottertrack, he will wait, forage whatever food he can, and intercept another canoe group. Dan Stephens doesn't like the notion, but he knows he can make it to the shores of the long border lake, where he will eventually encounter another group.

"What other choice is there?" he mutters.

He is thinking clearly now. He will stop making mistakes. He begins to lay out the next day's travel. He will force himself to take a water break every ninety minutes. He will keep himself well hydrated. At every water break he will double-check his direction. He will forage whatever berries he can find. And there are bugs. He has read about survival, how most bugs have high protein and fat content. If need be, he will forage bugs.

He needs shelter for the evening. Rain and the mosquitoes could seriously diminish his reserves, and he knows he has to sleep, to replenish energy for tomorrow's trek. He looks over the hillside, fingering his knife.

Midway down the hill he finds a widow-maker birch. He recalls the reason for the tree's nickname: When high winds or storms break off a tree's top dead branches, the trunk fills up with seep water. The tree rots from the inside out, the bark remaining to the end. Anyone who tries to fell a widow maker topples a pile of logs heavy as cement bricks. But he thinks about the bark, one of nature's most waterproof substances. The natives used it for canoes, water baskets, drinking vessels, *even their shelters.*

He puts on his boxer shorts, shoes, and shirt, and limps toward the dead birch. He pushes in his knife, and after piercing the bark it sinks easily into rotting wood. But Dan doesn't want the wood. He busies himself cutting and peeling three long circles of bark from the dead tree.

11

A Plan to Recover the Trail

In the morning Jason awakens to a light rain pattering on his tent fly. He opens his eyes to the gray light, comfortable and warm in his mummy bag. Then he rolls over, closes his eyes and listens. The drops make small pelting sounds directly overhead. He feels as though he is completely alone in the universe. The immediacy of having a paper-thin layer of nylon between himself and wild woods makes him feel alive.

He feels a satisfying ache that leads him to quickly recall yesterday's trek. As he comes more fully awake he remembers his long peregrination through the woods. He can feel the dull muscle ache from yesterday's heavy hauling through wet brush. It is the kind of stiffness that reminds him of the value of hard exercise. But he doesn't want to feel that level of discomfort again—wet, cold, and bone-tired.

Warm and dry in his mummy bag, he is not thinking about being lost and is certainly not awaiting rescue. He has plenty of water, food, and shelter. If he is careful with his supplies, he could last two weeks, though it would never come to that. With a fire, and the bright tent on the treeless escarpment, a plane could easily find him. It would be over in a day.

But he is not yet ready to concede being entirely lost, and after all, it is only Wednesday. He is still disappointed with himself over carelessly losing his Fisher map, but he knows he has plenty of time to find his own way out. This morning—rested, warm, and dry—he feels more optimistic than he did yesterday, after a long day wandering through wilderness. The rain outside keeps him tent-bound, but he is happy in his comfortable surroundings. And he will use the time to figure out his whereabouts and make a plan.

He squirms out of the bag, opens the tent flap, and stretches in the light, cold rain. He steps a few paces across the bed of caribou moss. Walking on the moss-covered wet rock is like stepping onto an icy sponge. He looks down over the long, narrow lake in front of him. It is surrounded by the usual thick tree line, the occasional low-hung cedar bent out over its surface. Under the muted sky the lake is slate gray. It appears to stretch more than a quarter mile south. There is mist at the far end of the lake and it looks beautiful in the early morning rain.

But it's cold outside, and he climbs back in out of the rain and slips into his mummy bag. He pulls the opening up to his neck and waits until his body warms the bag. Then he reaches out, rummages through his pack for a granola bar, and happily munches, washing down the breakfast snack with lake water.

He pulls out the *Hiking Minnesota* map and studies it. There isn't a lot of detail. He examines the lakes on the simple depiction. He is looking for something resembling the lake in front of his tent. He stares at the map for a couple of minutes.

His first night he thinks he camped near Pose Lake. According to the map he should have been close to it. Even though he made more turns than an interstate cloverleaf, he suspects he ended up somewhere in the middle of the circular trail. That is, somewhere inside the twenty-six-mile-long oval that marks the trail's boundaries.

He considers the lake in front of him, long and without islands. As he stares at the map he sees an obvious choice, a thin gray strip inside the Pow Wow circumference. Fallen Arch Lake stretches near the eastern end of the oval, its southern end reaching down almost to the bottom of the trail. If he is correct—if the lake in front of him is Fallen Arch—Jason realizes he may be closer than he thinks to getting out of here. If he walks along the western side of the lake and strikes off beyond its southern shores, at some point he will cross the Pow Wow. He examines the map, looks at the key, and uses a brief length of finger to determine the distance from the bottom of the lake to the trail. It looks close, less than a mile from the southern tip.

He opens the tent flap and looks out over Fallen Arch Lake. Some of its shoreline doesn't exactly align with what he sees on the map. But the map's depiction is so simple and without detail, there is no way to be certain. They are both long and narrow, they are both north-south. When he examines the simple map, the only gray swatch that even remotely compares to it is Fallen Arch. It has to be Fallen Arch.

The rain is still pattering his tent. From inside his pack he extracts the pamphlet he purchased at REI, Suzanne Swedo's *Wilderness Survival: Staying Alive Until Help Arrives.* He's not going anywhere in this rain. He hungers for something to read, and apart from the map and a copy of some of the pages from the Pukite text, this is it.

He begins at the beginning. The pamphlet is small, and he is a good student. Within an hour he has skimmed the entire booklet.

It's a clear, well-reasoned approach to surviving in the wild. The author is emphatic about the three most important requirements of staying alive: shelter, water, and food. She explains their relative importance, given climate and terrain. In the North Woods, Jason realizes, water is abundant. No problem there. But in October in these woods, shelter rises in importance. The human body, he reads, can survive a long time without food, as long as it is well hydrated and reasonably warm. Reading about starvation makes him hungry, and he rummages his pack for another granola bar.

As Jason reads through the text, he notes he has all three covered. He could live like this for over a week. Longer, truth be told. He reads about some of the forest's edibles — which don't really sound that edible. Cattails, conifers, and grasses. The inner bark of some trees. Earthworms and grubs. He is amazed by the forest flora and fauna that can sustain life. The text says very little about flavor, and he doesn't recall seeing pine bark, cattail roots, or raw larvae on any restaurant menus, but if you need to stay alive there are at least a few wild comestibles offering nourishment.

When he is finished it is still raining. He reads through the text a second time. Water, shelter, food—in that order. He is well positioned for a long stay in the wilderness, though he knows it will never come to that.

He peruses the text a third time, absently opening it to chapter six: "Shelter From Cold and Heat." He reads the first paragraph.

Should you become involved in a wilderness emergency, you are statistically much more likely to succumb to hypothermia, otherwise known as exposure, than to any other problem. If you can stay warm enough to make it through the first night, you're probably going to make it to safety or at least survive long enough to be rescued.

He reads about "the recipe for hypothermia: cold, wetness, and wind." He considers freezing from a clinical perspective. In the last five years he has learned plenty about the body's operation. But this discussion of hypothermia from a wilderness-survival perspective is new. When they covered it in medical school, it was brief and cursory. Today, in his tent, the notion has an immediacy difficult to ignore. *People in the northern climes*, he thinks, *are always close to the possibility.*

He dog-ears the page on hypothermia and lays the book down. He leans back to consider the world's northern climates. He loses himself in contemplation, wondering about it. And then he notices the pattering has stopped. There is only the sound of water forming large drops near his tent's ridgeline, rolling down its sides.

Jason returns to his pack and gets into the warm clothes he'll need to hike through the woods. While he dresses, he decides it will be much easier hiking through dense brush without the encumbrance of his backpack. He recalls yesterday's struggle through tree branches and fallen boughs.

His jacket has more than enough pockets, and he has brought along a fanny pack with two water bottle slots. Now he rummages his pack for some of the items he'll need for his short hike south to find the trail: a couple of small packages of crackers, a can of tuna, two Tootsie Rolls, a package of cocoa, his compass, a Swiss Army knife. He considers the items randomly, trying to figure out the minimum required to hike through the woods for probably less than two miles. All he needs are sufficient supplies to get him south of the lake point and less than a mile into the trees. He should be able to discover the trail's whereabouts and identify the easiest path to get there. He can focus on finding the southern loop, and on marking the best trail for returning to it when he recovers his supplies.

He places two water bottles in the slots on either side of his waist pack and picks it up, weighing it. Not bad, he thinks. *Much easier getting through these woods without that damn pack*, he thinks.

By noon the skies have been quiet for almost an hour. The world is wet and overcast, cold, but not freezing. Jason laces his boots, puts on his olive drab jacket with the internal hood, fastens his pockets, and zips up the coat. He decides against taking a pair of gloves and a hat. It is above freezing, and he is trying to be careful about packing light. He doesn't want his jacket bulging and catching on the brush, and he doesn't want unnecessary weight hampering his progress. Finally, he feels ready. He fastens the fanny pack around his waist and steps out of his tent, bending back to zip up the fly and close the opening.

He carries his disposable camera out of the tent. He starts down the hillock toward the western edge of the lake. After ten paces he turns and takes another picture of his tent. The rise looks dull, gray, and wet, with a small backdrop of spruce. He knows it would be hard to find by dead reckoning, but he has an entire lake to assist him. When he returns, all he needs to do is find the lake. Find the lake, he reasons, and he can easily recover his tent.

He turns and in the midday gray descends the granite rise. After being cooped up in the tent through the morning he feels good to be walking. Within five minutes he is in trees so dense—cedar and low-hung black spruce—that he cannot even see his tent or the granite rise behind him. But he is careful to keep the lake on his left.

Walking this close to water, he finds that parts of the shoreline are heavily bouldered. Fallen branches form an obstacle course. Whenever necessary, Jason climbs over, ducks under, or walks around large toppled trees. His progress is slow, but he is happy to be hiking again, particularly without his pack. Hiking through thick wood with his pack isn't going to be easy. Periodically he reminds himself to look for the best route. But for the most part he moves down the shoreline toward the end of the lake on automatic pilot, attending to the next ten yards, the part in front of him he can see. He is careful to keep the surface water in sight. As he walks, he ruminates. Wander a tenth of a mile in any direction, and unless you are consciously attending to your thoughts, they can stray far from your immediate trail.

After half an hour Jason comes to the southern lake tip. He peers into the woods. The land's surface makes a gradual rise through the trees. That's good. He wants to stay on higher elevations, no matter how slight. He does not want to encounter another bog. These woods are thick and shadowy, but as they rise away from the lake they appear to open. It looks easier walking just up ahead, and Jason moves toward the space, plotting his next twenty yards.

Well into the trees he turns and can no longer see the lakeshore. He pauses long enough to fish his compass out of his waist pack. He takes a reading and notes the direction due south. He looks ahead and finds a landmark—a huge fallen white pine—that is almost exactly due south. Its path lies a few degrees to the west, but not much. Jason makes for the tree, bending, weaving through the brush.

He was correct about this part of the woods; they are easier to traverse. Here it appears to be old-growth forest with the high tree canopies blocking enough sunlight to minimize the understory growth. He appreciates the change in elevation and more spacious woods. He keeps walking south.

There appears to be a meandering height of land that jogs south-southeast, then south-southwest. If he stays on it, the walking is much more comfortable. Periodically he pulls the compass out of his pocket and takes a reading. The higher jag of land moves in a minimal slant southwards, and it is easy walking in the midday. The forest growth, with towering red firs and occasional white pines, is haunting and beautiful, like walking through a cathedral.

But in places understory growth is still plentiful enough that his pant legs remain damp. Hiking beside the lake, pushing through the dense weave near water's edge, Jason can't help getting wet. But he is dressed for it and comfortable, and the exercise warms him.

He keeps moving vaguely south, admiring the forest. After an hour he is well south of the lake, pushing through another high patch of trees. He hasn't seen anything resembling a trail. Not even a deer trail. Jason wonders if these woods—these woods he is now hiking through—have ever seen the print of man. He tries to imagine what it must have been like to live here, to survive like the indigenous Ojibwe. And while it summons pictures out of books and the cinema—*Dances With Wolves* occurs to him—he knows that their life of hunting and gathering is well beyond his powers of invention.

Nothing in his life—his childhood, his years in med school—was anything like what indigenous people had experienced here before whites arrived. And it wasn't that long ago. One hundred years before, on this very spot, he would have worried about wolves, bears, cougars, and staying alive by whatever he could hunt or hack out of the woods. One hundred years, he reflects, would have been 1901.

He revises his estimate to two hundred years. Two hundred years would have put the date at 1801, a time of traders and voyageurs. At that time, he thinks, trying to recall his early American frontier history, it would have been the Hudson Bay Company and the Northwest Company. He vaguely remembers reading about it as a kid—how the two fur companies fought over this fecund landscape. Fought over beaver to make hats in England, battled over all the fur-bearing animals to make stylish coats and fur-lined gloves. He smiles to remember how the absurd fashions of the time compelled the exploration of a far-off wilderness, and then the death of so many animals thousands of miles away. He has seen enough MTV and cinema—not to mention sitcoms—to know that changing tastes can dictate some bizarre perspectives, if not lives.

He looks up through the trees and realizes he has been walking for the last fifteen minutes without much of a sense of his own direction. He pulls out the compass, examines the needles, and sees his current course is more east than west. And he still hasn't discovered the trail. He has tried to hike where the walking is easiest, staying on higher ground, though in places there wasn't much difference. He has skirted fallen trees and rocky outcrops, but he hasn't even come across a game path, let alone a hiking trail.

He pauses in a cathedral of red and white pine. The walking here is beautiful and relatively open. He could keep moving in a southerly direction—at least for the next fifty yards. Beyond that distance it is difficult to see anything. He reasons that if he hasn't yet discovered the path, maybe he hasn't moved far enough south. He would have guessed his hiking this long would take him at least a mile, but it is hard to determine in the woods. And truth is, he hadn't paid that much attention to the exact time of his departure. He looks down at his wristwatch. It's 1:30. The sky is gray, but there is still plenty of light. He has at least another four or five hours of daylight, and he's still hoping he will discover the trail.

Until now Jason has felt confident about his plan. He'd found the lake on the map and could see the trail just beyond it. Hiking down to the trail was the obvious choice, but he wonders where it is. He may have crossed it, but if so, it is virtually invisible. Now he wonders. He recollects the map, but cannot remember any of the other lakes in the area even partially resembling the lake in front of his tent. It has to be Fallen Arch, which would place him very near the bottom section of trail.

He wonders if he has truly moved in a southerly direction. He takes out the compass and balances it to take another reading. If he continues, he will be moving south-southeast. He wonders if he should try veering west. He looks in that direction, and the forest makes a gentle descent for the next fifty yards. He can't see anything except tree trunks. But the hiking appears to be as easy as it is here.

Maybe if he moves in a westerly direction he will encounter the trail. Maybe he just hasn't gone far enough. And so he decides. He moves in a south-southwest direction. He picks his way carefully through the woods. He wanders as he walks, skirting fallen trees and wet brush. Occasionally he takes a compass reading, but not often. Barring yesterday's anomaly, Jason believes he has a pretty good sense of direction, of dead reckoning, even in woods as dense as these.

He hikes for another half hour, but does not find the path. He decides to try something radical, and hikes due east. Perhaps part of the trail moves in a north-south direction. He tries to remember and thinks the southern end of the trail had plenty of wobble. He guesses it would likely traverse high ground, rather than wet low patches. He stays on the high ground, moving for another fifteen minutes before finally stopping.

When he finally realizes he is not going to find the trail, it is another difficult moment. He cannot believe it. He remembers the map, the way Fallen Arch was so close to the trail. Can the DNR have been that obtuse about marking the Pow Wow Trail? He recalls reading something about signs being prohibited in the BWCAW, something about pure wilderness. *But Christ*, he thinks, *what if the trail's not marked at all?* He thought it would have been traveled enough to at the very least be a visible path. Much of the trail he started on was clear, and wide enough for an ATV. Where is the blasted trail now?

He looks at his watch: 2:30. He guesses he has been walking for at least two hours. Although he has been walking back and forth, he figures if he hikes due north he can make camp in less than an hour. His journey south, east, and west has been so halting and hacked up, he knows if he is determined he can make it back to the lake and then his camp in *less* than an hour. And he is starting to get hungry. He reaches down and pulls one of his water bottles out of his waist pack. A long draught quenches his thirst. He feels for one of the Tootsie Rolls, unwraps it, pops it into his mouth, savors it. He chews slowly, takes another drink, swishing the water to fill his mouth with the dark, chocolaty flavor.

That was good, he thinks. He reaches in for the other roll, eats it with the same relish, knowing he can replenish his supply when he returns to camp.

The water and the Tootsie Rolls temporarily sate his appetite, at least enough to hold him until he gets back to his tent. He hasn't decided what he's going to prepare for supper, but he still has enough hunger to spend a few moments contemplating the possibilities. Another stroganoff? This time maybe his turkey teriyaki? *Whoa,* he thinks. *I've got to get back.*

He fishes out his compass, takes another reading, and strikes off through the trees.

After hiking north for more than an hour Jason looks at his watch, looks at the woods in front of him, at the climb of bush and trees spreading away from him. It all appears new, as though it is totally virgin territory.

He fishes out the compass, takes another reading. Yes, he is hiking north. He scours the landscape for a familiar tree, outcropping of rocks, tracks through the leaves. There is nothing.

He keeps walking, and after what he presumes is at least

another half-hour he feels something stronger than worry. A first clear wave of panic flows over him. He had been worried when he stopped and took another bearing. Now, not only is he not finding his camp, but the lake itself seems to have disappeared. How could he have lost a lake?

There is still plenty of light, he reasons, trying to calm himself. *There is still time.* He doesn't want to contemplate alternatives. He puts aside other possibilities and keeps walking.

After another hour he can no longer deny he is lost. He can no longer keep walking and expect to encounter the lake, or his gear. But it has to be around here! He hasn't wandered that far. By Jason's recollection it has been a brief two hours, maybe two and a half. And for more than half that time he was heading north, *closer* to his camp. At least he was supposed to be returning.

But where is the lake? Where is Fallen Arch and the beautiful escarpment with the orange tent perched atop it? Where is he? He doesn't want to think about consequences, but as the light continues bleeding from the afternoon sky—already an opaque gray—another wave of panic washes over him. This one threatens to engulf him.

He keeps walking. He pushes through brush and trees for another half-hour. Another wave of panic threatens him, rises inside and crashes along some inner shore, leaving him desolate and mute. And then he sees the opening ahead in the trees.

It has to be the lake! He scrambles toward the opening, elated. He cannot believe he's been that stupid—stupid enough to miss an entire lake. But now he has recovered it. Now he can use the last hour and a half of dull gray light to move up Fallen Arch's shoreline and recover his camp.

And then he pushes through the trees and sees—another

bog. Another damn bog? He peers to the west, turns and stares into the gray eastern light. He squints across the bog's surface.

If there is a landscape of the soul its lowest point must be a bog. Jason struggles to get a grip on himself. He can feel some part of him getting sucked into shadowy desolation. For now, the mottled and tangled surface of the bog—knowing he must cross it—is the single tangible expectation keeping his panic at bay. For now, crossing the bog occupies an imagination that might otherwise drown in the full realization of his predicament.

He turns into the brush, finds a dead tamarack bough, and trims it down to a sturdy five-foot pole. He starts picking his way across the tangled bog's surface. And he makes excellent progress. He is almost to the other side when his last leaping step breaks the bog's surface, starts sucking him down, and he lunges for the far edge. He topples onto firm ground, but his feet and legs are cold and soaked to the upper calf. He watches the black water runnel off his legs and boots. The feeling of cold is far off, and he sits and stares into the tangled surface of the bog, unbelieving, the panic now full in his throat, disarming, forcing him mute and still.

Jason doesn't know how long he has been sitting. Profound panic has given way to catatonia. He cannot move, cannot think. He is trying to figure out how he got here. He is trying to understand it, his legs soaked with water and his boots full of it. The bog has reached up and taken his spirit and he hunches on the edge of it, wanting the sick feeling to be over, wanting to awaken from this nightmare.

Where was the lake? What happened to that lake? The question rises and words form, but there is nothing behind them. He feels outside himself, or in some other landscape. It's starting to occur to him. Gradually, like a far-off wave coming in to curl and crash, his awful predicament is starting to rise over him.

He is wet, cold, tired, and there is not much more than an hour of light left, possibly less. It is the waning light that strikes him, slaps him at least partially awake. If he has to stay in these woods for the entire night, with the temperature dropping fast, the smell of storm in the air, he might not see tomorrow's dawn.

The thought of dying makes him rise. He has no idea where to turn, where to find shelter. He looks across the bog but knows a return south is out of the question. He has to push north. He climbs through the boggy shoreline into the trees. He is looking for something, he doesn't know what. He is searching through dusk for some place to hide—some place to pack himself away for the evening where he can roll up in a fetal ball, conserve his heat, and survive.

He stumbles through the woods like a somnambulist. He is devastated. He is trying to remove himself, trying to bring himself awake, but he's beyond conscious thought. He is tired, and he tries to focus on his mission—to find someplace to hide, someplace to sleep, someplace safe, out of the weather, out of the cold.

But he *is* cold. He can feel it as he walks. His legs are still wet and stiff and his feet are numb. His brain isn't functioning. It is as though the freezing water has reached around his cerebral cortex and deadened it with an icy grip.

Up ahead he comes to a boulder as large as a house. He walks around the base and sees a very small depression. He gets down on his hands and knees, looks at it abstractedly. He might be able to dig it out. He pulls some small boulders out of the space, but then looks at it and realizes it would be more work than he has time to burrow. And besides, the rocks are cold. The entire landscape is freezing.

He walks away from the boulder. He wanders another five minutes through the woods, absent and searching. He doesn't know what to think. He doesn't know what to look for. He is dimly aware this may be his last walk anywhere. He tries to put it out of his mind, to keep moving through the woods.

Up ahead he sees a huge, fallen pine. It's in a forest of giant trees. The woods are dark and forbidding. The tree is fallen on its side, at a slant where it snapped off a few feet up its trunk.

He walks up to the toppled tree. It has been lying here awhile. He considers building a lean-to. He looks around the woods for material, but there are only thin boughs and dead wood. These would afford no protection from the wind. And he didn't pack matches. He has no means to build a fire. *I didn't pack matches.* He repeats it to himself, but he is a long ways from registering its full impact. He is numb.

The air is turning colder, and he thinks he smells snow.

He looks at the fallen tree, at the dusky woods around him. It feels hopeless. *Maybe somewhere else*, he thinks. *Maybe if I keep moving?* He turns and walks another fifty yards. When he comes to the end of it, he is in the same woods he has been in for most of the day. There is still a half-hour of light, but it is rapidly getting dark.

He stands and tries to think. He suspects he has seen something he could use to make a shelter, somewhere in the latest ground he's covered. It is one of his first truly coherent thoughts since panic first set in. He tries to recall the landscape. The boulder. The tree.

He could keep moving forward, searching through the woods until they darken. But he knows there's not much time. He needs to use whatever he's seen in the last twenty minutes. There is no time to keep searching. He turns and starts retracing his steps. Fifty yards later he is back at the tree.

The boulder would take too long to burrow out. It would be well after dark before he could fashion a cave big enough. And then what about the cave's mouth? Cold seeks the lowest elevation. The cold would sweep into the gap and freeze him into a fetal fist. He stands beside the fallen tree, reconsidering his idea of building a lean-to. He tries to recall something from his book on wilderness survival. He can't remember anything. He can't figure out how he could make a lean-to with enough cover to retain his body heat. Its sides would be a sieve, and the wind would sough through it all evening. He'd be dead by morning, or near dead. He reaches up and absently breaks away part of the end of the huge fallen tree. It is rotted. Its center is heavy with decay.

He tries to focus. Something he has seen over the last thirty minutes could save him. He knows the forest has something to offer—other than devastation and the end of his life.

He reaches up and dislodges another piece of wood. It falls from the center of the trunk. Chunks of decayed wood tumble down after it. The surface of the trunk is still strong. Because of its angle, water seeped into the trunk and apparently rotted its inside. Absently he pulls another chunk out of the trunk.

And then it occurs to him.

Suddenly he starts digging in the middle of the tree. At first, he's careful, too uncertain to believe he might have found something, some kind of shelter. But in seconds his care dissipates under the real possibility of shelter. His hands are flying. Suddenly he feels energized. The feel of swamp water on his legs evaporates. His hands move with frenetic energy.

It is cartoonish, as though he is a dog burrowing into a hillside at breakneck speed. Hope and energy flood his veins. Lethargy is replaced with a hard rush of adrenaline. In five minutes he has dug out a cave large enough to hold his entire upper body.

He keeps digging. Hands flail, arms pull and throw. As the daylight continues seeping out of the western sky he fashions a deeper hole. There is at least two inches of firm wood surrounding the rotted center. Within fifteen minutes he has used his knife and hands to dig a hole out of the wood wide and long enough to hold almost his entire body. He keeps working, keeps digging.

Just before dark he turns into the woods and forages pine boughs, slashing them off with his blade. He is working quickly now. He has purpose. He has a plan and he is certain it's going to save his life. He gathers three loads of boughs and carries them to the trunk.

He can now wiggle down inside the trunk with his head well concealed inside, his legs bent but not folded. He lines the nest with spruce boughs.

It is almost dark, just barely light enough to make his final preparations. He finishes lining the trunk with boughs. There is just enough room to squeeze into his makeshift house. He brings the last bunch in behind him, closing the overhead gap.

It is cold in the tree, dark and enclosed, but he can feel his body heat starting to warm the inside. He has laid enough boughs across the entrance to make a thick mat.

He cannot see anything in front of him. There is no light, just the sound of a spare, cold wind. The inside of the tree smells like rich, moldy pine.

He is starting to feel tired now. For another day he has hiked through difficult woods much longer than expected and with entirely different results than those he anticipated—at least when he started. Now he doesn't want to think about it. Now the half-hour adrenaline rush is dissipating as quickly as it rose. A dull ebb of tiredness washes over him. He is well beyond panic, unable to think of much but closing his eyes. And after a few more minutes, totally exhausted, Jason falls asleep.

In the middle of the night Jason awakens to howling wind and fierce pain. His calf feels as though it is being lanced. He has little room to move and can only sit and come awake to the pain. He shifts his leg, hoping to assuage the pain.

An enormous windstorm has come out of the sky. He hears a tree topple and fall. It sounds far away, but it must be a large tree. The wind howls and the tops of the trees knock and snap. He has never heard this kind of wind. Even through his pine-bough covering he can hear the blow whipping the tops of the trees.

The pain is back, and when he moves again, slightly, the pain moves, too. There must be a small hole in the side of his shelter with an icy blast spearing through it and cutting into his calf. He shifts again and tries to maneuver a section of tree bough between his leg and the hole. He is only partially successful, but it's enough to give him some respite.

The wind picks up. Jason wonders if the notorious Fourth of July storm from the previous year, the one that blew down a million trees, was kin to this one. Another tree falls, this one closer than the last. More wind, and he hears another tree fall, like a tottering giant in the woods. He cannot believe it, but this one shakes the ground. He can actually feel the ground shudder when it falls. Then another, and another. Giants are falling in the woods. It must be some kind of centennial storm, and he is smack in the middle of it. He is too incredulous to wonder. He realizes that if one of those huge trees topples over on him he'll be crushed. His tree trunk will crumble like an egg.

He closes his eyes and prays, but all he can hear is howling. He asks for deliverance. He doesn't want to be crushed by the forest, though he feels that the woods are doing their best to finish him. But he's a scientist. He is a med student, and he doesn't give much credence to the idea of forest malevolence. He knows there is nothing to be done but lie quietly and try to recover his strength—and hope like hell the storm passes without crushing his narrow home.

Somewhere from inside him a question cannot help but rise unbidden to his lips. *What next,* he wonders. *What in God's name is it going to be next?*

12

Assistance

Prairie Portage Station, Quetico Provincial Park, Thursday, August 6, 1998

As the Chattanooga group nears the other canoe party, they can see it's from Sommers, their base. They paddle like hell across the blue expanse of Carp Lake, hailing as they deepen their strokes. By the time they skid up alongside, it's a little after 5:00.

"Wha's up?" one of the other group asks. He is weathered and lean and sits comfortably astern with a paddle across his legs.

"We've lost our guide," says Tim Jones. He is winded from paddling, and bends over to catch his breath.

The leader scans the group. His body bends forward and stiffens, unsure he has heard it right. "Lost your guide?" he wonders.

"Back up on the lake before Bell," Jones says. "He walked into the woods looking for our portage and never came out."

The guide is incredulous. He looks for a smirk. He scans the group, searching for a familiar face. He knows that nameless lake—the connection between Fran and Bell. Like most of that country, it is rugged and remote and surrounded by brush. But in his brief season of guiding he doesn't think he has ever heard of a guide disappearing. He looks at their faces but can only discern sharp worry and weariness.

"Who was it?"

"Dan Stephens."

Christ, he thinks. *Stephens? He's one of the best, with paddle know-how and more savvy about the woods than almost anyone in camp.* "Did you call it in?"

"Our radio's out."

The leader leans forward and rummages through his own pack, pulls out the crude radio phone, and fires it up.

Back at the base there is static on the wire, but this time the attendant is ready. He listens to the voice on the other end, recognizing the guide from a different group. He reports the group number and their location: Carp Lake. The guide is with the 801c group. It comes across the air waves clear enough to hear. The attendant waits for the pause and then responds.

"We read you loud and clear. What's up?"

Hirdler and Joe Mattson have also heard the call. They come out of their offices and cross the room as the other guide explains Stephens's disappearance. There is universal disbelief. Over the raspy radio phone, all they know for sure is Stephens has been separated from his group. They need more details. They instruct the Chattanooga group to continue to the Prairie Portage Ranger Station, at least another two hours' paddle. At Prairie Portage, Mattson and David Japiksi, the camp chaplain, will meet them. It's 5:19.

Prairie Portage is a Canadian ranger station. It has two good rangers and radio connections to every emergency location across the Quetico. Whatever they need, they should be able to call in from there.

Doug Hirdler is worried, but he knows Dan Stephens. "If anyone can walk out of those woods in one piece," he tells others in the office, "it's Dan." Joe Mattson, the one who hired Stephens, who saw his résumé and had a chance to work with him through guide training, agrees.

"*If* he can walk," Mattson qualifies. In the back of Mattson's mind he remembers a statistic about people who get lost in the woods. Most lost people are found within seventy-two hours. Mattson is not sure, but he thinks he recalls that those lost in wilderness over seventy-two hours are—more often than not—gone forever. For Stephens, he realizes, it has already been more than a day.

Carrie Frechette and Cathy Antle, Quetico Park rangers, are busy sunup to sundown. The Prairie Portage Ranger Station is one of the primary checkpoints for anyone crossing the Canadian border. Even though the station is a half-hour boat ride up Moose Lake north of Ely, Minnesota, and in the middle of wilderness, on August days it can be more like an urban transit depot than an outpost in the Canadian woods. The log structure is small. The Canadian flag waves high on the station pole. And Carrie and Cathy busy themselves changing money, stamping and checking papers, dispensing licenses.

Two hours earlier, at about 5:00, they received a call from Doug Hirdler at Sommers. He told them one of his groups was in some kind of trouble and Joe Mattson and David Japiksi were coming up to meet them. Now Carrie and Cathy hear the low whine of an outboard motor—they assume the boat from Sommers. Cathy looks up long enough to see a distant party of canoes crossing Bayley Bay. It must be the Sommers group.

"Here they come," Cathy observes.

"Maybe we'll find out what's up," Carrie suggests.

Normally the Prairie Portage Station is staffed by a married couple. The previous year, the couple decided they'd had enough—of the outpost, and their marriage. If the couple's divorce had a silver lining, the two current rangers were its beneficiaries. Carrie Frechette, Cathy Antle, and the Quetico Park system all took chances, and so far it had paid off in spades.

The two women were almost through their first season, and they were happy with their choice. It was remote. At times it was as quiet as dusk light on a spellbound lake. At times it was anything but. They were open for business at dawn, and closed just after the sun dropped below the lake's far western shore, making canoe travel difficult. But they loved the wilderness and reveled in the deep-woods feel of the place.

It had been a busy season, and except for a few temporarily lost people and some minor accidents, their days were mostly spent regulating travel. The station is sparsely furnished. They have a satellite phone that operates sporadically, currently on the blink. They have a two-way radio—the Teleconnect—that is somehow patched into the phone system. That is the device Hirdler used to contact them.

As the two remote parties approach—one from the north, one from the south—Cathy and Carrie are glad to know that at least they have means to contact the operations specialist at Quetico Park HQ in Atikokan. They suspect they'll be on that line before the evening is out. There is still plenty of light, but it is fading and casting sideways shadows across the trees.

"Better make sure there's a clean spot for all of them to stay," Carrie suggests.

"Good idea." Cathy walks out the door to check the nearby yard. As she scans it, looking at the approaching canoe party and the boat from the south, she knows it is large enough to manage them.

By 7:30 everyone is assembled, and the entire bizarre episode has been explained. Cathy and Carrie ask as many questions as Mattson and the chaplain. What surprises the rangers is that Dan disappeared clear up on no-name lake. That was one hell of a long way to paddle in a day. And the Cache Bay Station was half the distance closer.

By their own admission, the Chattanooga group had panicked. They left Dan and came south partly from fear, but mostly in a run for help. Some of them should have stayed put, but the two fathers in the group couldn't decide who should stay and who should go. Besides, they had promised the parents of the kids that they would stay together and keep everyone safe. They thought Dan would be better served by their alerting the proper authorities. And there was the Silver Falls portage. There was no way all of them could have climbed back over that arduous rise of rock and mud, particularly with canoes and equipment. Unbelievable as it sounded, it was faster coming south.

To the others it sounds reasonable enough, unless you considered they have stranded their guide in the middle of the bush with no means of transport, no maps, and a food cache that can't last. Cathy Antle sometimes reflected on the wide variety of outdoors experience she encountered among the Boy Scouts. Sometimes, like Dan Stephens, they were as savvy as deep woods trappers. Sometimes, like this Chattanooga group, they had no sense of the measure of true wilderness.

But this group had solid reasons for what they had done. They insisted they had come south because they figured the Prairie Portage Station and the Sommers Canoe Base were the best places to turn. And they had paddled like dogs to get here.

Everyone nods in appreciation of their speed and effort. No doubt about it, that was one hell of a paddle. It has to be some kind of novice record, and they can see the group is exhausted, nerves worn thin as bare wires.

Cathy and Carrie have heard enough to radio HQ. After they help the group get settled, the two fathers return to the station. Mattson, Wills, and Jones huddle over the station radio while Cathy makes the call. Static comes over the line, but also a voice—and this time it is clear enough to hear. Dave Maynard, Quetico Park's operations specialist, sounds cheerful and ready to assist.

"What's up?" he asks. "How are things at the Prairie Portage?"

"Beautiful, buggy, and busy, as always. Especially tonight," Cathy says. "We have a group down from Bell Lake say they lost their guide."

It takes five minutes for Carrie to relate the pertinent

details of Stephens's bizarre disappearance. What Maynard can't figure out is what the Chattanooga group is doing at Prairie Portage. They should have returned to Cache Bay. He knows valuable time has been lost. *Every passing hour* expands and complicates a search area.

The Mattson Method is the methodology used for determining the Probability of Area (POA) for every possible search area or route choice a lost person might take, providing he is mobile. Search coordinators compile all known facts about where the person disappeared, who he or she is, and any other corroborating information. The data is used to lay out a search area. All subsequent air and land efforts follow the quadrants laid out in the process.

If Maynard recollects his details correctly, each hour a person is lost expands the POA by five kilometers. More often than not, lost people wander, ignoring the axiom about staying put. This one is a guide, so Maynard hopes he had enough sense to sit still. But it is very odd. No one disappears. People sometimes go missing and are never found, but they're somewhere—alive or dead.

Something is seriously wrong, and he knows the sooner he can contact the Ontario Provincial Police (OPP) and get the Emergency Rescue Team (ERT) involved, the better. This guy has already been gone over a day. If Maynard's math is correct, that has expanded the search area by over one hundred square kilometers.

He tells everyone in the room to stay by the radio. He is going to contact the Ontario Provincial Police. He knows they will assign a constable to the case, and the constable will have questions. He will have to know the details before he moves it up the line to the shift sergeant. The shift sergeant will have to contact the duty officer. Once the duty

officer is briefed on the pertinent details, he or she will decide if ERT's participation is warranted. Maynard wants to
make sure it all happens in record time, because every
passing minute matters.

SURVIVAL, SEARCH, & RESCUE

Survivors don't expect or even hope to be rescued. They are coldly rational about using the world, obtaining what they need, doing what they have to do.

LAURENCE GONZALES
Deep Survival: Who Lives, Who Dies, and Why

"Forget it," he said. "You'll do someone else a favor sometime. It's all part of the Big Circle."

I liked the concept. Because of the nature of bush travel, you often can't repay those who help you. But you can help somebody else, somewhere down the trail.

Sooner or later, it all comes around again. That's the Big Circle.

SAM COOK
Up North

13

Linda Rasmussen Worries

Northeast of the Pow Wow Trail, Thursday, October 25, 2001

In the morning Jason awakens to a silent world. He is tucked down inside his dark shelter. His leg still burns and his feet are numb. He blinks and discerns pinpoints of daylight through his woven-branch hatch. It's quiet outside, almost eerie. He can hear a faint whisper, but he doesn't think it is wind.

He did a good job covering the trunk opening. Now he pushes on the overhead weave and it dislodges, toppling forward. A light dusting of cold, white powder drops down onto the edges of his tree-trunk hole. It's snowing! Jason struggles up to the mouth of his opening and the world is blanketed in thick white. The trees and brush and the large stump from which his own sheltering trunk has fallen are smothered with several inches of dry white fluff. The thermometer has taken a wicked turn south. This snow isn't melting.

At least the howling wind has subsided. He recollects the midnight storm, how he could have been crushed by the felling of one of these old giants. His leg still hurts. His feet grew numb in the deepening cold, and now he cannot feel his toes. He didn't bring his hat or gloves because he didn't plan on spending the night in a tree. In a tree! When he considers the cold white world he is beyond shock. What else could happen to him?

But now he has to get up and walk around, stamp his feet, return them to some semblance of normalcy. Normalcy? There is nothing even remotely close to normal about any of this.

When he was young, the first snow was an occasion for happy wonder. Now the weight of the cold presses on his life, as though this is one more rock on the pile, another nail in his coffin, another place where the wide sanity of the world is slipping.

He recognizes almost nothing about the muffled landscape in front of him, and he knows there is no returning. To try to turn back through this field of white, through woods where no trace of yesterday's journey remains—where he would be unable to tell if he was walking over a bog, a flat forest opening, or his grave—is unthinkable. The deepening of his predicament is devastating. He tries to focus on his surroundings, to distract himself.

When the huge pine toppled over—probably in one of those wind storms, Jason suspects—part of the tree's side splintered away from the trunk and remained connected to the ten-foot-high stump. The rest of the tree fell away. But the slab of splintered siding formed a long, wide, bark overhang. It extends from the stump to the top of the fallen tree. It is like a giant, rough-hewn tent awning, and in this snow it provides some cover over the ground in front of him.

Jason struggles out onto the bare patch of ground. He stamps his feet. His breath clouds the air. His hands are very cold. His feet are numb, and he continues walking in a narrow circle near the tree opening, stamping his frozen boots. Gradually, the movement warms him. At least enough to allow him to walk off ten paces and relieve himself.

But to get there he has to walk through snow. Normally it might be fun wading through the season's first good accumulation. Now all he can think of is the way the white powder sticks to his boots and lower pant legs, melting and forming a thin layer of deadly ice.

From the vantage of ten feet of distance he turns and looks at the woods in which his narrow hovel stands. Under the snow, the woods form a thick wall of white. There are a few large pines still standing, similar to the one that now lies on the ground in front of him. But most of them have toppled, either in last night's storm or in the notorious July 1999 storm. Around them the open forest floor is thick with new pine growth. Much of it is Christmas tree–sized, some of it taller, some smaller. Taller poplar trunks rise out of the green pine understory. There is a thick red pine near the backside of his hollowed-out tree. Otherwise the world is a smothering blanket of white.

Jason tries to take stock of himself and his wintry abode. He has to consider the unthinkable: hiking out and trying to find his tent. He needs his food. He needs matches. He knows his only chance of getting truly warm is to find that tent.

He gathers his water bottle and places it in his waist pack. But the truth is, he has no idea which way to turn. His tent, he knows, could lie north or south. He is looking for a good, open rise above the lake, just on the other side of a bog. He is hoping he can recall the location by sight, but he wonders at the world's transfiguration. Trees are covered. Saplings heavy with snow are bowed over near the ground. He figures that yesterday he must have passed east or west of the lake and then traveled north beyond it. He takes a compass reading south and starts hiking.

He's soon wet from his effort. Pushing through the snowy terrain only makes him colder. And the world is so different. Nothing looks familiar. Finally, he is forced to retrace his tracks and return to his hollowed-out tree.

He survived last night. The tree should provide shelter for another day. At least he has shelter, he thinks, remembering his book's clear delineation of the basic requirements of survival.

Today is Thursday. He won't be coming home. He hopes his mom remembers his admonition just three days earlier. If they don't hear from him by Thursday night, *call the Lake County sheriff's office.*

He realizes the best he can do now is try and stay warm, to conserve both his energy and his heat. For now, he has plenty of water. And he can always melt snow. He pulls up his water bottle and takes a long drink. He's hungry. He doesn't want to think about it, but the empty gnawing in his stomach is difficult to ignore. He still has a can of tuna, some crackers, and the rest of the water.

He cannot stay out in this weather for long. It is still snowing, and he cannot afford to get wet. That would be inviting hypothermia. Hypothermic people don't think clearly. They make stupid decisions, Jason knows. They die.

After the feeling has returned to his feet and toes, he turns back into his hollowed-out home.

Later, in the afternoon, he rummages through his pack and extracts one pair of crackers. He eats them carefully, one at a time. He sips water in between the satisfying bites, knowing they will be his only food today. He decides to save the tuna. He doesn't know how long he'll be out here. Probably tomorrow, he thinks. They will probably send people out tomorrow. Certainly they will find him then.

He waits until late afternoon before turning back out into the nearby bushes. He has noted the spots where his

Jason's tree at dusk (courtesy Jason Rasmussen)

shelter is weakest, where holes and cracks in its sides and top let through water or wind or the cold air. He takes pains to make his shelter more snug, covering over the top with a latticework of cut pine boughs. He stacks splintered wood near the sides. He plugs the holes as well as possible, from both inside and out.

Throughout the day the cold presses down, holding the entire region in an icy grip. His hands ache from working outside over the tree. When darkness finally comes, he is ready to return to the narrow confines of his wooden cave. *Tomorrow*, he thinks, pulling the mesh of pine boughs over the trunk opening. He feels certain they'll come for him tomorrow.

Over two hundred and fifty miles south, in West Bloomington, Minnesota, Linda Rasmussen is anxious to get home. The kindergarten teacher is helping chaperone a roller-skating party with her school's kids and their families. She enjoys the work, likes teaching children. It suits her disposition, her patience, and natural empathy. But right now all she can think of is the end of the party—in just moments— and a trip home to hear about her son's adventure.

If Jason gets home early, Lee will hear the entire saga: what it was like, where he camped, what he saw, words about the weather, and Jason won't want to repeat it. She knows Lee. If she asks for the trip details, Lee will say, "Sounds like he had a good time."

So she hurries to her car. She covers the distance from party to home, anxious to see her son, to hear about his trip. The first thing Linda Rasmussen notices is the absence of Jason's Saturn. She hasn't missed his stories—but she is not entirely happy about it. All day she had been on a field trip with her kids at the Minnesota Zoo. Although the weather was a blizzarding, sideways slant, she was unconcerned about Jason, because she knew he was already out of the woods and on his way home. Then after school she returned home, and Jason still hadn't arrived, or left a message. Now, after 8:00 PM, he is still not home. She pulls into the garage, knowing there will be a message from him—that he is running late, probably because of the storm.

She is a little concerned, but tries to consider the positive side. Now she will hear all the wonderful details of his remarkable northern trek. Lee is downstairs watching television.

"Any word from Jason?" she asks, coming into their kitchen.

"Nothing," Lee yells back. "When did he say he was coming home?"

Linda is surprised. The absence of a message worries her. She tries to recall the details of her conversation with Jason prior to his departure, the one here in their kitchen. She places her coat over a chair.

Outside, it is clear, but blustery. The snow has long since ended, and by tomorrow—weather reports indicate—a warming trend will most likely melt the small accumulation. Neither Lee nor Linda worries about the weather, since it has been a relatively warm fall and the last few days have been mild. Jason was careful to pack for the possibility of colder northern woods. And right now they don't know that the storm up north was much worse than the weather in the Cities. For all they know, Jason has been enjoying the same unseasonable warmth.

"He said sometime later today," she finally answers.

"Was he going to get home this late?" Lee wonders.

Linda tries to think. Details like this one, told to her four days ago when she wasn't completely focusing, are sometimes difficult to recall. At the time she remembers there was little reason to worry. Jason was organized, is organized. He is careful and he was more than a little prepared—with two maps and a good trail description, a clear idea about where he was heading and where he planned to camp each day.

She remembers looking over his map. And that causes her to recall the detail about the only optional part of his plan—a possible side hike up the Superstition Trail Spur. She remembers Jason talking about the spur. If he had enough time, he was going to hike it.

And now that she is recalling details, another one shakes loose. She is certain she remembers Jason telling her that he would call them Thursday afternoon.

She walks downstairs. Lee is sitting on the left side of their corner couch, waiting for the 9:00 PM news, killing time.

"No messages?" she asks, wanting to be sure.

"Nothing," Lee says. She can tell from his voice he's concerned, a little edgy, worried about their son.

"I'm going to call," she finally says.

She doesn't know what the sheriff can do, but she knows that by now she should have heard from her son. The storm complicates his absence, but she remembers Jason's admonition.

"If I'm not home by Thursday night, call the sheriff."

The Lake Country Sheriff's office is six blocks off Highway 61, in Two Harbors, twenty miles up the North Shore from Duluth. With just 3,600 inhabitants, Two Harbors isn't a big town. The highway cuts through the middle of it. Grouped along the highway are restaurants, gift shops, a couple of liquor stores, gas stations, bait shops, and the usual assortment of establishments catering to the tourist trade. On the far northeastern end of town sits a Dairy Queen. Turn right at the DQ, drive six blocks to Third Avenue, turn right again, and the sheriff's office and jail sit in a squat, yellow brick facility next to the county courthouse.

Two Harbors, home of Agate Bay—billed as the busiest harbor north of Duluth—is also the county seat for the second-largest county in Minnesota, at least in terms of land mass. With over 2,000 square miles, the county covers over half the state's northeastern Arrowhead Region. It runs from Two Harbors, over fifty miles up the North Shore of Lake Superior to the Cook County line, just northeast of Little Marais. From this southern border it plunges north in a broad, straight swath to the Canadian border.

Over three-fourths of the county is comprised of four state parks, the Superior National Forest, and the Boundary Waters Canoe Area Wilderness. The populated quarter is mostly made up of small towns like Knife River, Two Harbors, Beaver Bay, Silver Bay, and Little Marais, all hugging the frigid waters of Superior's North Shore. There are 11,058 citizens in the entire county. Except for Finland, Isabella, and Fall Lake—tiny inland communities—the vast majority of people live on the North Shore. Everyone is surrounded by trees.

At 8:38, Linda Rasmussen's call comes through to the on-duty dispatcher. Linda explains about Jason's hike, that he was due back hours ago. She tells the dispatcher where he was going, how long he planned on being away, and his final directive.

Missing persons are law enforcement's stock in trade. The dispatcher takes down the information. Then she explains about the weather, particularly further north. There is some snow, but it's not too bad—at least by Northern Minnesota standards. She should be able to get a vehicle up in that area before too long. She will check on Jason's car and get back to the Rasmussens, probably within the hour.

Seventy miles of highway and backcountry roads separate Two Harbors from the Pow Wow Trailhead parking lot. Fortunately, Lake County is large enough to employ eleven full-time deputies. The deputies divide the county into three geographic regions, or stations. There are four deputies in the Two Harbors station, four in the Silver Bay station, and three in the Section 30 station, located near Ely at the door to the BWCAW.

The three Section 30 station deputies cover the northern wilderness areas of the county. Truth is, Two Harbors and the southern part of the county are far enough south so *turf knowledge,* or having plenty of first-hand experience of the northern woods, can be significant. On this night, Joe Linneman is Section 30's on-duty deputy. The dispatcher reaches him on the radio and relays Jason's story and the make, color, and model of his car.

Joe Linneman has been working as a northern Lake County deputy for over twenty years. In fact, the three Section 30 deputies have a collective sixty-three years of law enforcement experience. Linneman knows the Pow Wow Trail. Since the 1999 blowdown they have had more than a few calls from people getting lost in the area.

From Linneman's station outside of Ely he takes Highway 1 a little over thirty miles to the Tomahawk Road, then turns left. From here it is another twenty miles, primarily on dark, unmarked forest roads. But Linneman knows the way.

Linneman's four-wheel-drive Chevy truck is more than equal to the task of crossing the snow-covered roads. It is a white truck with "Lake County Sheriff" emblazoned on its side, and the usual overhead lights and siren gear. On the way in he notices the snow here is deeper, and the road is a wide blanket of white. Moreover, no tire tracks are breaking the pristine plane; there has been no traffic on this road for the last twenty-four hours. It is the only exit out of the Pow Wow.

In most missing-person investigations—or at this point, late-person, Joe reminds himself—the vehicle is gone by the time he reaches the last known parking point. Usually the missing people are just late. They end up reappearing within a few hours, having pulled to the side of a road for a quick nap, or checked into a hotel. *That's how most of these incidents end—little more than wild goose chases*, Joe thinks.

Finally, a little after 10:00 PM, his headlights shine over the trailhead parking lot. The lot is well marked, in large part because of Isabella Lake. This is one of the less frequently used entrances to the BWCAW, but it is at least popular enough to warrant a poster board and a lockbox where canoeists, in season, can drop their BWCAW registration forms.

At this late hour the deputy's headlights turn around the first entrance corner. And there sits a compact car, tucked up against a wall of winter brush, indistinct under six inches of white powder.

Deputy Linneman gets out of his truck. He brushes snow off the car's hood and shines his flashlight on its metallic finish. Green. When he brushes the rear bumper, he sees it is a Saturn. He flashes on the car's interior. Other than a few food wrappers and the usual assortment of car junk, the inside looks empty and cold. He takes down the car's license number—478 NJA—just to be sure it is Jason's.

As he suspected, this is the only car in the lot. He shines his light onto the wall of brush in front of him. It illuminates thick white branches bowed over in the snow. The night is cold and quiet. Linneman walks out far enough to flash the beam of his light over the remaining lot. There are no cars or tracks. That is fortunate, Linneman thinks. At least no one else is out on that trail.

He returns to his truck. He switches on his flashing lights. The snow-muffled trees shimmer red and yellow in the spin of lights. He squawks the siren—one good loud burst. If Jason is within earshot, he should hear the siren. He switches it off and listens.

The wall of brush in front of him is thick with white fluff. He tries the lights and siren a second time and waits again for a response. But there is only the thick snow and the enveloping darkness beyond the edge of his lights.

From this northern reach, radio reception is spotty. Fortunately, the Isabella Lake lot is one of the good spots. He tries to contact dispatch, and her voice comes back scratchy, but intelligible. He tells her about the car and gives her the plate number so she can run the license and make sure it is Jason's. Dispatch comes back affirmative, and Joe Linneman knows they will have to reconnoiter in the morning. He tells dispatch he will get back to the office and give Nick Milkovich a call. Milkovich is the on-duty deputy whose shift starts tomorrow morning.

Joe Linneman suspects the kid is hunkered down on the trail. Linneman knows hiking on a poorly marked wilderness trail in a snowstorm can be difficult at best, treacherous at worst. If it was him, Linneman knows, he would set up camp and wait for the storm to blow over. In the morning, he supposes, Milkovich will go up in one of the Forest Service planes. With all this fresh snow, Jason will be easy to spot.

"We found Jason's car," dispatch finally relates, when she is able to speak with the Rasmussens. "And I suspect I know what's happened."

For the next ten minutes the woman in dispatch relates a theory. They have dealt with this kind of thing in the past. The Section 30 deputies are well acquainted with the woods, especially in winter. If you are on a trail when it starts snowing, it is damn easy to lose your way. More probably, the deputy surmised, Jason recognized the difficulty of traversing through a winter storm and decided to hole up somewhere safe. Deputy Linneman is certain Jason is near the end of the trail, ready to hike out in the morning, when the storm passes.

What dispatch doesn't tell the Rasmussens is that snow deeper than a couple of inches can obscure everything, particularly a BWCAW trail. Boundary Waters trails aren't supposed to be marked—it is part of the Wilderness Act's requirements. And trails up here are seldom traveled, because most enter the BWCAW by canoe. Hiking out through a foot of snow isn't going to be easy. Linneman is worried, but upbeat.

"They'll be ready to search for him at daybreak," dispatch tells the Rasmussens. "We have people up here that know the area. I suspect he is close, hunkered down in his tent," she repeats. "And fine. I'm sure we'll find him in the morning."

The Rasmussens share a few more details about their son. He is intelligent and prepared. And he has a pretty good idea of what to do in the woods. They also tell her he has maps, a compass, and he was planning on hiking the trail in a counterclockwise direction.

"Good to know," dispatch says, thanking them for the additional information. For now, she thinks, the most viable theory is the one Deputy Linneman proposed. She also knows it is the most comforting. She hopes it is the right one.

14

The Science of Search & Rescue

Quetico Provincial Park, Thursday evening, August 6, 1998

Just after dinner, Constables James McGill and PC Jones are nosing their cruiser out of Atikokan, heading out to Highway 11 to start the evening's first patrol. The constables are part of the OPP's mandate to provide the public with general law enforcement across Ontario's non-municipal territory. Like a state patrol in the U.S., the OPP is responsible for patrolling provincial highways.

Back at cadet school, general law enforcement had an abstract quality. In the country outside Atikokan—a mining town that dropped from 10,000 to 4,000 inhabitants, after the market for ore ran out—the phrase usually meant dealing with domestic disturbances, driving while intoxicated, speeding, parole violations, and the occasional missing person.

Now the hard-working Atikokan townsfolk make their

living cutting lumber. The town rests atop the million-acre Quetico Provincial Park, a vast forest of thick bush, lakes, and rivers. While no one in Atikokan can touch a sapling in the park, to the east, north, and west, the Ontario woods stretch for miles.

Ontario itself is over a million square kilometers, much of it rivers, lakes, and woods. With its comparatively small population spread across such a huge geography, the province's police force owns an unusual assortment of tools to cover the territory. Snowmobiles, four-wheelers, Beaver planes, and helicopters augment the typical patrol cruisers, and a vast telecommunications network keeps it all connected.

The constables are turning onto Highway 11 when a call comes in from the OPP communications center in Kenora.

"411 Kenora," the dispatcher announces.

McGill picks up the receiver and confirms his number and location. "Kenora 411, Highway 11 east of Atikokan. Go ahead."

"Sounds like we got a lost person in the Quetico," says the dispatcher. "We need you to go back and check it out. Contact the Ministry of Natural Resources over in Atikokan. He's got the details, over."

McGill thumbs the receiver. "10–4," he says. "I will return to Atikokan and contact the MNR. My ETA is twenty minutes."

There is a pause on the other end of the line before the definitive response is heard. "Kenora clear," the dispatcher concludes. Jim McGill hangs up the receiver and turns the cruiser around.

That evening the acting staff sergeant, Phil Donald, works over the forms with McGill. Donald and McGill know ques-

SURVIVAL, SEARCH, & RESCUE

tions have to be asked, some of them hard. Laid out on McGill's evening desk are two pieces of paper—the Search Urgency Chart and the OPP's Lost Person Questionnaire. Beside them, his hands finger a white legal pad and a number two pencil. McGill is trying to concentrate.

Tools like the Search Urgency Chart and Lost Person Questionnaire make his job easier, but McGill knows enough about human nature to realize these tools are only the surface of the process. For starters, the Mattson Method for defining a search area relies heavily on whatever information you can gather about the lost person. Woods knowledge, character, and personality are top on the list but never easy to plumb. Interviewees are always quick to tout a lost person's strengths. The initial responses to "what kind of kid is he?" are as pedestrian as a dollar bill. For example, tonight he has already heard "great kid," "smart," "kind of quiet," and "capable." He has also heard plenty of testaments to his Eagle Scout status. All of it McGill patiently transcribes.

Jim McGill wants to know about Dan Stephens. He is interested in the kid's dark side as much as the color, sweetness, and light he's been fed during his initial interviews. And he wants to know about the group's dynamics at the time Stephens disappeared. He spends the first hour on the phone with Tim Jones and Jerry Wills. He masters the details quickly enough, bizarre as they sound. But he has to ask. Was there any tension in the group? Has Stephens come down on anyone for, say, an inability to keep up, or not doing their fair share? Was he a taskmaster in the bush? Did he have any problems with the kids? Any issues with the fathers?

Jerry Wills is surprised by the questions, but he answers them all the same. "No."

In every way, it's as though Stephens was the perfect guide. Knowledgeable, trustworthy, considerate, and except for walking into the woods and not coming out, he has been practically ideal. *A regular Mark Trail*, McGill thinks. *Was anyone even tired of the guy's cooking?* But to all of these questions the answer is the same. Nothing was amiss. He just walked into the woods and disappeared.

McGill spends the next hour questioning Doug Hirdler at the Sommers Canoe Base. Did Dan have any history of depression? Did he seem gloomy? Did he have a girlfriend? If he was from Georgia, what was he doing in northern Minnesota? Any inconsistency or nuance in the kid's character would draw McGill's eye for salient detail. Only in this case there aren't any problems with girlfriends or disputes with bosses. Dan Stephens doesn't seem to suffer from some post-teenage angst or wanderlust. He doesn't seem to be the kind of young man who would take off on a lark just to prove something—to himself, or anyone else. To James McGill, Dan Stephens sounds like everyone describes him—a pretty good kid with plenty of backwoods savvy. In fact, if someone had to go missing in that area of the Quetico woods—with deep ravines, craggy bluffs, walled bush, swamps, and more bugs than an Amazonian rain forest—Dan Stephens sounds like one of the better choices he had seen. Not only is he an Eagle Scout, he's also familiar with the Quetico.

Before McGill rings off with Hirdler, Hirdler asks to be the one to call Dan's parents down in Georgia. It is against protocol and McGill hesitates. But given Hirdler's excellent cooperation, James McGill decides to make an exception.

"If they have any questions," he reminds Hirdler, "tell them to call the OPP."

After hearing all the details, McGill wonders about the

kid's absence. When he walked into the woods to find that portage, what happened?

He can tell that Jerry Wills and Tim Jones were new to the Quetico woods. But they had been able to guide themselves through over twenty miles of lakes and rivers—making it to the Prairie Portage Station in pretty good time—and he is impressed by their rapid pace. There were plenty of questions he could have pursued. Why hadn't they spent more time searching for Stephens in that cedar swamp? Why hadn't they set up camp there and waited? Why hadn't they at least kept someone, maybe a couple of them, on the scene while the others went for assistance? The protocol for emergency situations like this one called for the group to split up.

But Wills and Jones were adamant about the need to keep their group together. They were responsible for these kids, and above all else they had taken that job seriously. They had left Dan Stephens a cache of supplies and instructions to say put. But food in that part of the woods doesn't last long. Most likely it would satisfy the appetite of a passing bear, or a couple raccoons.

Jim McGill is familiar with one of the woods unfathomables. When you step off the grid in a place as thick and wild as that part of the Quetico, the wilderness can do strange things to your head. Reason sometimes takes a back seat to instinct, and he can hear it in the fathers' voices—the drive they had to survive, to bring all their kids out safe.

McGill and Phil Donald work their way through the Lost Person Questionnaire, completing the *Place Last Seen, Subject's Trip Plans,* and *Subject's Outdoor Experience* sections. Stephens scored high on that one. Most of that subsection's check boxes—from "familiar with the area" to "will stay put"—are marked in the affirmative. McGill hastily completes the *Contacts Upon Reaching Civilization,* and *Actions Taken So Far* sections. After speaking with Doug Hirdler at Sommers Canoe Base, he has completed the Search Urgency Chart. The Chart comes up with a score of 11—*Emergency Response.*

Scores on Search Urgency Charts range from 7 to 21. The lower the number, the more urgent the search. Scores of 7 to 11 merit an *Emergency Response.* Scores of 12 to 16 require a *Measured Response.* And 17 to 21, *Evaluate & Investigate.* The only reason Stephens's score isn't lower? Outdoor knowledge and alleged character—so far as McGill can ascertain. If you disappeared in this part of the world, it was good to be Dan Stephens—providing he could walk and he had no other serious impairments. What didn't make sense was his absence. An Eagle Scout knows to stay put. It deepens the mystery of his disappearance, and makes McGill wonder what complicating factor has occurred.

After a couple hours and the compilation of the necessary data, McGill hands over the forms to Staff Sergeant Phil Donald. McGill recommends an immediate ERT response. Donald reviews it, then forwards the information to Duty Officer Hugh Dennis with the same recommendation. Hugh Dennis and Inspector Dave Wall give McGill and Donald's work a cursory review. Dennis and Wall are familiar with ERT triggers. It only takes a glance at the paperwork to see that an immediate effort is warranted.

Back on his escarpment, the light has all but drained out of the western sky. Dan Stephens descends to a near creek and forces himself to drink water. He climbs to the hillside and rechecks his stick marker pointing east and west. He breaks off another and aligns it perpendicular with his east-west marker, pointing due south. Then he forages on the hillside for broadleaf. He takes off his boxers, ties the legs closed with pieces of twine, and stuffs them with leaves. He lines the birch bark rolls with the broadleaf and with black spruce boughs. This time he vigorously shakes everything lining his bed, careful to make sure it's bug free. There isn't much grass up on this hillside, and after last night he knows better than to use it. The spruce and broadleaf is a whole lot less comfortable, but at least it's not a mosquito housing complex.

He lies down on the scratchy, makeshift bed, carefully pulling the huge coils of bark around him. He aligns their seams so they overlap. If it rains, he should stay dry enough. The leaf-stuffed shorts are near his head. It is dusk, and the bugs are starting to swarm. As darkness comes he lies on the ground, staring through a narrow slit into the night sky.

There are so many stars. He is always amazed by the thick Milky Way and profusion of starlight. He stares into it, trying not to think of all the people he suspects may be searching for him, of his parents and their worry.

And then he has a sudden, disturbing thought. Why are there no search planes? Not that they'd be able to see him. In order to find him in this brush they would have to be right on top of him, and it is doubtful they would even see him then. Where are the aircraft? It is a question as prickly as a cockle burr. On the one hand it implies his disappearance hasn't yet been reported. That is good. He can get himself out, and he doesn't want to worry people, particularly his folks.

On the other hand, *why* isn't his absence yet known? Where are his Chattanooga friends? Their plight worries him. He is still their guide, even if he isn't with them. Still, it would be nice to be located by air and picked up. He is hungry. He is damn hungry. He has never been hungrier. He stares into the glittering night sky. So many stars. So many questions. The night is blazing with them.

It takes Dan half a second to know there is nothing he can do about his friends, his parents' worry, or the others who may very soon be looking for him. First, he has to take care of himself. He has a plan, and it's a good one. He will walk out under his own power. But he is only partially comforted by the thought. Finally, he pulls his shorts over his head and tries to quiet his mind. It's a worrisome night.

At 9:15 PM, Doug Hirdler is sitting near the phone, a place he hasn't moved from for most of the evening. He is wondering how he can convince Constable McGill to let them assist in the Stephens search and rescue. His crews know that country. They have portaged Bell Lake plenty of times and are very familiar with the Man Chain. He's feeling frustrated when the phone rings for the last time that evening.

It is Jim Stephens, Dan's father. Jim is back home in Monroe, Georgia. Every room in the house is filled with boxes. He and his wife, Mary Ann, Dan's mom, are in the middle of a move from Monroe to Fayetteville. When Hirdler first called—8:40 PM, Jim jotted on a note pad as soon as he got off the phone—they had been hip-deep in the innumerable details of packing up a household that had been years in the making. They were stunned.

But Jim Stephens served twenty-four years in the Army, with time in Vietnam. He knows about government response, knows it can sometimes be dubious, ill-considered, and incomplete. He has also seen the opposite. This time Hirdler hears it in his voice. Any previous consideration of packing, moving, attending to the vagaries of household transport, have fallen like so much chaff. Jim Stephens is more than over his moment of stunned silence. Now he is focused one-hundred-percent on the mission at hand: finding and rescuing his son.

For the second time that evening sharp questions fly over the line.

"Who's in charge?"

"Was his group still out there?"

"Why didn't anyone hang back?"

"If you've known about this since 5:30, why in hell did it take so long to call the police?"

Jim Stephens continues grilling Doug Hirdler on their search and rescue efforts, wondering why so little is being done, wondering about his son and how they plan to find him. He wants to make sure everything that can be done is being done.

Hirdler answers with as much candor and support as he can muster, but it has already been a long day, and the affable officer is grim at the prospect that it is just starting. To Jim Stephens's final question, he wishes he had a better answer. It is one Stephens asks after getting a full sense of where everyone's at in the search for his son—Hirdler, the Sommers Canoe Base, the rangers, and the OPP.

"Is anyone even looking for him?" Stephens wants to know.

Hirdler pauses and swallows. "Not just yet," he manages. "It's night, tough to fly in, and they wouldn't be able to see anyone if they did. But they're on it," he offers—shallow solace, he knows, given the facts.

A frustrated expletive fires back on the line.

After a long pause he offers Jim Stephens the only hope he has. "Morning," Hirdler manages, low and faint.

A thousand miles away in Monroe, Georgia, Dan's

mother hovers over her husband's shoulder. Mary Ann is waiting for some good news. She is waiting to hear her son has been found. Instead she can barely pick up Hirdler's voice over her husband's ear, and his faint effort to console.

"Morning," she hears Hirdler repeat. "We should know a lot more then."

Jim Stephens is not satisfied with Hirdler's answer, and tells him so unambiguously.

It is a sentiment Doug Hirdler understands. He nods behind the phone and tells them as soon as he hears anything they will be the first to know. But when he hangs up he wonders if Dan Stephens is okay. He hopes for the best—knows the young guide, expects him to survive. But the truth is, he doesn't know.

Doug Hirdler has spent his life working in the Boundary Waters and Quetico woods. He knows in wilderness unexpected things happen. He is hoping the young guide got lost, but it doesn't add up. He suspects there was something else, and he hopes like hell the kid's okay.

He has tried to assure Dan's mom and dad, but he shares their concern. For now, all they can do is sit, wait, and pray.

15

Lake County Search & Rescue

Northeast of the Pow Wow Trail, Friday, October 26, 2001

Before first light, Lake County Deputy Nick Milkovich cruises through the small town of Ely, heading toward the U.S. Forest Service's hangar on Shagawa Lake.

Late last night he received a call from Joe Linneman. After the usual banter over the 11:00 PM harassment upsetting the comfort of Nick's home, he listened to his friend and fellow officer. He took down the information about Jason Rasmussen, noting the car in the trailhead parking lot. Nick told Joe he'd be in the skies by first light, providing he could commandeer a pilot and a plane. Given the day's snowfall, its flawless white background, and tomorrow's weather forecast—clear, cold, and calm—Nick suspected Jason Rasmussen would be sipping one of those fancy coffee drinks at Ely's Northern Grounds Café by noon.

Milkovich has been working as a Section 30 Lake County

deputy for over twenty-five years. He knows the pilots. He knows their routine. He could requisition a plane properly, going through Forest Service HQ in Grand Marais, completing the proper forms and getting the requisite sign-offs and head nods. But the bureaucratic fine points would set his air search back a day. With lost persons, Nick knows, time is critical—particularly in weather like this. So he chooses the more expeditious method, the one with which he's most familiar. He pulls up to the hangar at dawn and knocks on their door.

In the early morning light Jason Rasmussen crawls out of his narrow home, stretches, and starts to stomp, trying to return circulation to his feet and toes. It is cold, but clear. The air is crisp and he can hear a long way off—though on this morning there is only silence. The snow has muted everything with a heavy blanket and creatures far and wide are resting beneath it.

He guesses there is a foot of snow on the ground. At this point, Jason has no idea of the extent of the storm, the exact snow depth, or the distance it reaches. In another quirky twist, Jason's hollowed-out tree sits in the heart of a mile-wide band of these remote woods where the fall was heaviest. His orange tent, which sits less than a half-mile away on the bare rise above the water, was also situated in the storm's path. Its sides sag under the heavy accumulation. More importantly, you couldn't have done a better job of covering every inch of his orange tent fly if you were spraying it on with a paint gun. Jason would have to be right on top of the igloo-like lump before recognizing it as an anomaly in the landscape—possibly his tent, more likely a boulder. From the air, it's invisible.

Just five miles southwest, Jason's car sits in the trailhead parking lot in less than twelve inches of snow. Further south, there is less.

Jason stays out long enough to stomp his feet and restore some circulation and feeling to his numb toes. He knows the temperature has dropped. Ultimately, the biting cold drives him back into his narrow shelter, where he can better preserve heat and wait for his rescue.

He feels certain that today he'll be found. He knows by now his parents will have called the sheriff's office. He knows they will be out looking for him. Maybe they'll send planes. Today he feels confident that—in spite of the snowfall—they will spot him from the air, or call to him from the surrounding forest. He crawls back into his tree, pulls the limbs over his head, and tries to doze.

The U.S. Forest Service hangar sits on the edge of Shagawa Lake, near the Ely city dock and swimming beach. From here the Forest Service operates its northern air fleet—three vintage red-and-white DeHavilland Beaver planes. The planes have been in operation since the 1950s. Milkovich knows if you give any of the three pilots half a chance, they'll wax poetic about their planes, how cheap they are to operate, and how perfect they are for keeping tabs on a canoe wilderness area.

In summer they are rigged as float planes, in winter, outfitted with skis. The three pilots—Wayne Ericson, Dean Lee, and Pat Loe—divide their time between fire spotting, wildlife telemetry tracking, search and rescue, and medevacs.

Because air resources are scarce, the Forest Service has an informal loan agreement with the region's county governments. County sheriffs are the point of first contact for search and rescue. Depending upon the nature of the case, the sheriffs have a wide net of government and volunteer resources on which to call. Today Deputy Milkovich is the point man in the search for Jason Rasmussen.

The Lake County deputies are given plenty of leeway for managing their own investigations. On the sheriff's website the deputy's page notes simply, "All of the deputies do their own investigations as well as performing various civil duties as assigned by the sheriff." In fact, the only reason Milkovich would ever contact Sheriff Steve Peterson regarding an investigation is if he needed more resources. But because Milkovich knows the area and the immediate resources, he has taken matters firmly in hand.

On this morning, Pat Loe answers Nick's early morning knock. Within the first hour of sunlight Pat has the engine revved and is ready to take off over Shagawa's still, unfrozen waters. The area's lakes are on the verge of freezing, but the pilots are still two to four weeks from replacing the Beaver's floats with skis.

The northern Minnesota branch of the Forest Service is one of few in the country with its own planes. The three DeHavillands are loud taking off, loud in the air, and conspicuous. This isn't an advantage for wildlife spotting, but it is helpful in search and rescue.

Nick Milkovich has flown on enough search and rescue missions to suspect this one will be over in a matter of hours, if not minutes. The Pow Wow Trail is a quick fifteen-minute fly-in from the Shagawa hangar. While they cover it, they revel in the conditions. A cloudless sky. The air crisp and settled. Their vertical flying column ranges from a low of four to five hundred feet to a high of four to five thousand feet, depending upon the nature of their search. Today, regardless of their elevation, they will be able to see anything that moves. If Jason is out there, and if he's whole, they'll find him.

They are hoping he lights a fire. If he does, they will follow the pillar of smoke like a homing beacon. Barring a fire, they are hoping he is on the move, or has the common sense to carve a big s-o-s in the snow, providing he can find a big enough opening.

Nick Milkovich has been in these woods long enough to have hiked over most of its acreage, and plenty of the area surrounding it. And he knows something about the area's history and its plethora of abandoned trails.

Twenty-five years ago, Milkovich was broken into his present position by an old deputy named Martin Carlson. Carlson remembered the days when the small logging community of Forest Center sat smack-dab in the middle of the current Pow Wow Trailhead parking lot. The Forest Service has done an excellent job erasing all traces of the old town. But there was a time, Milkovich remembers, when the small community had businesses, a small logging train station, and logging roads that spun out from Forest Center like spokes on a wheel, connecting a series of makeshift logging camps set up all over the woods around the village.

Milkovich knows some of the oldsters who worked in Forest Center, before the Forest Service re-claimed the land. They've told him stories, and during the first year he was working, Martin Carlson showed him around.

Now Deputy Milkovich and Pat Loe turn over the area and examine the parking lot from a few hundred feet. They locate Jason's car, Joe Linneman's tire tracks, and the footprints from his late-night perambulation around the vehicle. They use the spot to plot a course that starts taking them in a straight line up the two-mile trail to where the Pow Wow circular path begins.

First they do a complete circuit of the twenty-six-mile oval track. Because of the weather and perfect snowfall most of the track is a clear white line through the woods. Much of the Pow Wow Trail and many of the old logging roads are relatively clear from the air.

From this height, with binoculars, they can easily discern wolf tracks. In the past they've even seen lynx in the snow, pouncing on snowshoe hares, forest voles, or field mice. They've seen plenty of deer, but not many in this area. But the Pow Wow, they know, is moose country. The bogs and swamps of the region make it ideal for the solitary, horse-sized creatures. They marvel at the numbers they fly over. But there is no sign of a solitary hiker, his tracks, or his orange tent.

Milkovich knows the natural boundaries around the Pow Wow Trail. They are marked by long water or high ridges, or both. Beyond the western side of the trail rises a high ridge and rough country. That area is also littered with the detritus from the 1999 blowdown. The deputy has struggled through those areas on foot, and it is virtually impassable. Few people would trouble themselves crawling over and under so many fallen trees.

Arrow Lake lies three or four miles to the east of the trail. That entire area is covered over by beaver ponds, bogs, and swamps. Milkovich would be surprised if Jason was anywhere east of the trail. Just to double-check, not more than an hour after they have been up over the trail, they fly out beyond the east side of the Pow Wow, their eyes scanning bogs, swamps, beaver ponds, and occasional islands of pine.

Around 9:30 AM, Jason is roused out of his tree by a low, far-off drone. It sounds like a plane. He has been dozing, off and on. Now he is suddenly awake. He is pretty certain it's the sound of a plane. He pushes off the top branches of his hovel and quickly wiggles out.

The sound grows louder. The plane—it is definitely a plane, now he's certain of it—is coming closer. It veers in from the west-southwest. He hears its approach. The drone rises in volume over the trees. He doesn't know what to do. He tries to move to the most open spot, but the cover around his tree is thick. He moves ten paces from the fallen log, and then he sees it—a small red-and-white plane with floats. It comes up fast, and Jason jumps up and down, waving in the middle of his narrow opening.

The plane passes over without a sign. Jason reaches down to the orange lanyard around his neck and pulls out his whistle. He starts blowing. He blows frantically, waving—though the plane is moving away, starting to disappear. In a matter of seconds it pushes east and disappears over the treetops. He listens as the drone whines down like a dying insect.

He whistles again. The piercing signal shrieks over the woods. He blows off and on for at least another minute. Then he stops, his heart pumping and breathing heavy. The view of the plane gave him a sudden rush of hope. Jason knows the plane cannot hear him, but the plane, he assumes, must be accompanied by ground searches. To hear his whistle they would have to be close, probably within a mile. But they must be out, already combing the trail and the woods around it. And by his own estimation he is near Pose Lake. The small lake is close—so if searchers come up the trail and make noise he will hear it.

After a minute he repeats his efforts with the whistle

and then stops and listens. Nothing. Still, the sight of the plane stirs his optimism, and he hopes it will be back for another foray.

The pilot and deputy swing east over the long north-south boundary of Arrow Lake but see nothing. There are one or two stray moose east of the lake, struggling over the snowy terrain. But otherwise, nothing.

Jason could have strayed north, but in just two to three miles his path would be blocked by the massive Lake Insula and its connecting waterways. Still, they wing northward up to Insula and along its ragged southern shoreline. Nothing.

Every twenty to twenty-five minutes, Milkovich or Loe is in touch with Lake County dispatch or the Forest Service hangar. Throughout the morning they give periodic updates of their progress—or lack thereof. Twice they return to the hangar to re-fuel. But the Pow Wow is only fifteen minutes from Shagawa, and it takes less than forty-five minutes before they are back up over the area, resuming their grid search. Other than the wildlife, the woods appear empty.

After their initial circumnavigation of the trail and their review of the natural boundaries east, north, and west, Pat Loe lays out a grid—minding Milkovich's designated borders. For this initial grid, Milkovich and Loe agree. The smart money is on the area inside the large oval trail. Both of them believe it would be the most obvious place to run astray.

They spend the first half of the day covering the ground from a high elevation, looking for smoke or some other sign. Over the course of the day they lose track of the number of moose they see.

By early afternoon they are flying lower—under one

thousand feet, crisscrossing the trail's center and pushing out beyond the trail on all sides. They hope the closer look will yield a better examination of the ground. But by this time both men believe they should have found him. They should have seen his tent, or—if he moved at all—seen his tracks, or caught him struggling through the snow.

Three more times throughout the day Jason hears the plane's steady, low drone. Once it swings south, but almost out of ear shot. Another time it passes south, but just barely, coming in closer. Both times Jason waves and dances on his small clearing of snow. He picks up his orange whistle and blows.

Once, the plane passes further north, but too far to be seen. In the hopes of extending his reach, he picks up a long spruce bough from the side of the hollowed-out tree—one he used earlier for insulation. Now he waves the tree branch high overhead, waving it back and forth like a deep green flag.

After the plane starts to recede Jason blows his whistle and yells. *Maybe the on-ground searchers are close*, he thinks. And the effort to signal them comforts him. More importantly, hearing the plane search all day has been re-assuring. If he is not found today, then tomorrow.

Part of him worries about how long air searches will continue. But for now, he places that anxiety aside. He knows they are going to find him. He is certain it will be soon. Though they haven't given him any indications, he secretly wonders if the plane may have spotted him and is even now signaling his coordinates to the ground searchers. He tries to keep himself from too much idle dreaming, but it is quiet in the snowy woods, and he has time.

For most of the day he stays in his hollowed-out tree,

struggling to retain his heat. This day is cold and clear, and he needs to conserve his energy. He spends his brief outside moments tightening and insulating his tree. He cuts nearby boughs and lays them against the side of his log. He lines the inside with as much greenery as he can fit into the narrow enclosure. He looks for cracks and holes and plugs them.

Later, in the afternoon, he remembers his last small package of crackers. Without anything to eat all day he has grown progressively more hungry. He has only a little water left in the one bottle. His other bottle has been lost under the snow, but in any case, it was already empty. He decides he has to eat something. He figures the crackers might assuage his pangs better than the tuna. Jason knows he has to keep some in reserve. If he is not found in the next hour, he will be here another day. He only has the pair of crackers and the canned fish.

Finally, he unwraps the crackers and nibbles them down meditatively, drinking the rest of his water. Tomorrow, he knows—if he is still here—he will have to eat snow for water, or fill his water bottle and somehow try to melt it. By bringing it into his home, he thinks. But he has little choice.

Before dusk he takes one last look at his tree and his efforts to tighten and insulate it. He cuts more boughs, but in the oncoming cold it is only minutes before he starts to shiver. The shaking drives him back inside.

With less than an hour of search light left Milkovich radios down his worry. Since their freshest clue is the location of Jason's car—a clue four days old—Milkovich knows Jason could be anywhere. A healthy hiker can cover a lot of ground. And from what they have heard, Jason is young, reasonably fit, and there are more than enough trails in those woods to choose from—and to go astray.

He tells dispatch to call search and rescue. What they cannot do from the air, they may be able to accomplish on foot. They are going to get searchers into those woods. Milkovich knows that on a search like this one it would be best to get as many feet as possible. They are all volunteer, and at any one time he can only expect a partial response to his call. But tomorrow is Saturday, he thinks. The weekend could be in his favor.

"Better call 'em all out," Milkovich finally advises Lake County Dispatch. "Maybe the ground pounders can turn up something."

Pat Loe and the tired spotter angle their wings westward and in the day's last light return to Shagawa base. Lake County dispatch signs off and starts the page.

When the directive comes in over Jim Williams's pager, he is winding down his Friday labors. By 3:00 PM his latest remodeling effort is coming to a close—at least for the weekend. When his radio pager beeps, he recognizes the voice of the Lake County sheriff's dispatcher.

"Calling Two Harbors Search and Rescue," she says. Her voice crackles over the small device. "Please report to the garage for a woods search." She repeats the directive and then signs off.

Since its inception over three decades ago, Lake County's volunteer search and rescue has grown progressively more sophisticated. In the late 1950s and 1960s it was little more than a group of concerned citizens. Today the fifty-plus volunteers are divided into three squads: Two Harbors, Silver Bay, and Finland. Each squad has trained individuals who can stand in as incident commanders, the leaders responsible for guiding and directing searches. And now the volunteer groups have plenty of the right equipment: all-terrain vehicles (ATVs), personal watercraft, and boats; gear for water searches, wood searches, climbing rescue; radio equipment; even their own command vehicles. The Finland squad's vehicle is a used ambulance and trailer, gutted and refurbished with communications gear, a table, and a sleeping berth. Two Harbors has an emergency van specifically manufactured for search and rescue. The equipment is a far cry from what the volunteers scraped together just two decades earlier.

Among the group of altruistic citizens there has been talk of more training. Most of them have attended CPR and related courses. And most of them, either by practice or on the job of an actual search, have acquired reasonable familiarity with handheld radios, diving equipment, climbing ropes, carabiners, helmets, woods search packs, and assorted other equipment.

But Jim Williams, the head of the Two Harbors unit and the first commander to answer the sheriff's page, knows there is little substitute for practical experience, particularly in the woods. He and his sons Darren and Ryan (also volunteers on the team) run a construction company on the edge of town. Jim and his boys mostly remodel, though he also owns the Minnesota distributorship for pre-manufactured log homes from a Canadian outfitter.

As he winds through town, he wonders who is lost in the woods this time. It doesn't take long to reach the Two Harbors Search and Rescue garage, where the group's equipment and emergency van are kept. Williams is on the phone getting more information when his son Darren walks through the door. Jim smiles and nods. His sons love the woods as much as he does. When calls like this come in, it is difficult to keep them out of the fray.

The dispatcher doesn't give him much additional information. Jason Rasmussen is lost on the Pow Wow Trail. Jim doesn't recognize the name, so he suspects an out-of-towner. Almost all their search and rescue involves people unfamiliar with the woods, usually from the Cities. Every year hikers come up, claiming they are knowledgeable and prepared. And then they go missing. Fortunately, Jim Williams knows these woods as well as people from the Cities know their streets.

The dispatcher tells him to take the van and head to the trailhead parking lot, where Undersheriff Steve Van Kekerix will meet them. Sheriff Steve Peterson is out of town and won't be back for at least another week. Van Kekerix has all the information about Jason, the search, and what has already been done.

Jim Williams signs off, and he and Darren get into the van, starting the seventy-mile drive north. They are joined by Jim's other son, Ryan, and six others from the Two Harbors squad, all in their own vehicles. Jim knows the Silver Bay and Finland squads will also be answering the page. By the time they hit the north end of town, it is 5:00 PM.

Williams knows that area around the Pow Wow and the old Forest Center site well. The summer of his seventeenth year, in 1963, he cooked and made coffee for the crews of Tomahawk Lumber, which operated the town of Forest Center. He drove plenty of lumber trucks on the back roads out of the small lumbering community. He remembers the town, its chapel, small café, grocery store, lumber mill, and pulp operations. It was the site of an old Civilian Conservation Corps camp before the town started. For twenty-five years, Forest Center was the logging train's last stop. There was a school, too, with classes through the sixth grade. Beyond that, kids had to be farmed out to relatives down in Two Harbors or boarded in local homes. The distance from Two Harbors to Forest Center was too far, and the roads too rough, for daily trips.

Forest Center supported at least seventy families. At the time, the log harvesting practice was to set up remote camps from a base, work the area for a year or more, and then move on, setting up another camp somewhere else. The men headed out on the trails to remote logging camps at places like Calamity Lake, or Crystal Bay—now well inside the Boundary Waters borders. The theory was that, in the years it took loggers to circumnavigate a logging center, the trees replacing the ones they'd cut down would be ready for harvesting. The reality, of course, was slightly different. In the end, Tomahawk Lumber ran out of trees and time.

Williams graduated from Two Harbors High School and made his first professional purchase: a chain saw. He knew the area and was ready to log. If Tomahawk hadn't been on the verge of bankruptcy, the company would have hired him. But they folded in 1965. He found plenty of other logging work, and for the next couple of summers his young chain saw hummed.

Then the Wilderness Act was passed, and Forest Center and everything around it closed up and moved away. But if you wanted to build a complex maze in the woods, with sucker trails and misplaced routes, you would be hard pressed to improve on the region.

Williams has crisscrossed the bogs, swamps, and woods his entire life. He has mastered compass and map. He has perfected a way of moving through woods, whether along trails or in rougher terrain, in strides that are almost precisely three feet long. There are 1,760 yards in a mile. With a compass and his map-reading skills, it's likely that Jim Williams could pinpoint an area in the middle of dense woods with as much accuracy as a handheld GPS.

When asked about getting lost in the woods Williams is matter-of-fact and self-effacing. "I've never been lost, but I've been confused many times," he explains. "I was a timber cruiser." In those days, the only maps were aerial photos. "You had to be accurate with what you were doing. I trained myself to take three-foot steps. And I was fairly accurate with where I'd be. But you have to pay attention to the wind, sun, terrain, the trees and streams. If you're observing those things—other things—there is really no reason for someone to get lost."

Williams knows many hikers enter the woods unprepared, whether physically or psychologically. When people are lost, he's used to hearing families say that they're experienced hikers. "That may be," he says, "but they're not experienced woodsmen."

Most of the people they search for are like Jason—urban people. The city, Williams says, is a place where "I'm just as far out of *my* element as hikers are when they get up here."

Jim, Darren, and Ryan Williams, along with the other Two Harbors searchers, reach the trailhead parking lot well after dusk. There are a handful of others assembled from Finland and Silver Bay. They have already done some preliminary searches along the nearby trails. They have signaled with heavy sirens and flashing lights, but there is no response. The call has gone out for dinner, for fifteen volunteer searchers must be fed. Some are still in the nearby woods. Others are milling around, waiting for their first crack at pizza.

When the searchers have assembled, Steve Van Kekerix is joined by Rebecca Francis, the U.S. Forestry Service law enforcement officer. They tell the group what they know. Steve and Rebecca explain where Jason went in, how long he has been gone, when he was supposed to return, and where he was going. Van Kekerix has already spoken with the parents. In fact, Steve is heading over to Ely from here. The parents have come up from the Cities and are staying in an Ely hotel, ready to help out with more information, or by entering the woods themselves, if need be. Everyone knows that's a bad idea. The best thing the parents can do is let the pros handle the search and rescue.

Steve Van Kekerix is already mulling the delicate diplomacy he'll use in his conversation with the Rasmussens. He has plenty to share about what has already been done, and the number of search-and-rescue folks who have answered their page. He is hoping the kid's parents can tell him more about the maps he is carrying, his equipment, and his backwoods savvy.

It sounds like Jason Rasmussen is experienced, fit, and more than equal to surviving in the woods. He appears to have the right equipment and plenty of food. And he's a med student. If he has broken a leg or is wounded, he should be able to keep himself alive. But they are all troubled by the failure of the day's flyover efforts. Steve tells them the Forest Service plane has covered every inch of that trail and much of the area inside and out of it—but they didn't see a thing. Not a tent. Not a hiker. Not even tracks. Deputy Milkovich will be heading up tomorrow to spend another day in the air, but they need some ground pounders in those woods—to see if they can find something, anything.

It's a puzzle. All of them—seasoned woods people and

those familiar with the area—know anything could have happened to Jason. He might have fallen into a bog, slipped and dropped into a ravine, broken a leg, sunk to the bottom of a lake. They hope their imagined calamities are just that—imagined.

Jim and Darren will spend the night in the van, just in case Jason comes out. But it is cold tonight, Williams knows. In this first good snowfall of the season most critters will be hunkering down. Jason would, too, he suspects.

Van Kekerix, Rebecca Francis, and the other searchers leave. Everyone promises to return at first light. Over cold pizza Jim and Darren Williams plan Saturday morning's search. Jim peers out at the places he knows they will search first. These first, obvious places are referred to as hasty searches. Seasoned rescuers know hasty searches have the highest likelihood of getting results. In the morning, they will be ready.

16

The OPP Emergency Rescue Team

Quetico Provincial Park, Friday, August 7, 1998

At 3:00 AM on August 7, Jeff Moline, a constable with the Dryden Detachment of the Ontario Provincial Police, is awakened out of a deep sleep. The goddamn phone is ringing and it sounds like an alarm going off in his head. His hand reaches to stop it. He brings the receiver to his ear at about the same time he musters his single-word response.

"Yeah."

"Jeff Moline?" the voice asks.

Moline barely manages an affirmative.

"Out of bed, Moline," someone on the other end of the line directs him. "We've got a Scout lost in the Quetico."

Moline recognizes the dispatcher's voice, but can't come up with a moniker. He is still groggy, not entirely certain he's awake.

"Get your crew and report down to Atikokan lickety-split," the voice commands. "We'll see you there in four hours," he says.

It is the Dryden on-duty communications specialist. Moline still cannot remember his name—but he manages a dull "okay," then hangs up.

The OPP has two Emergency Rescue Teams, each comprised of sixteen men. Moline and Kevin Hunter, out of the OPP's Thunder Bay Detachment, are the two search coordinators for Moline's team. Jeff doesn't know if this search will require a second team—unlikely—but he knows there will be at least sixteen searchers heading into the woods.

Jeff's team would be assembled from the other detachments: Atikokan, Fort Francis, Kenora, Dryden, Red Lake. In all, there are over a dozen detachments from which the members could converge. Given their location across the massive Ontario province, they will arrive in Atikokan at different times.

Atikokan is the central point for this operation because it is perched like a tiny bug atop the million-plus-acre Quetico Provincial Park. It takes a little over a minute to drive through the town. Apart from the hospital, a few bars, a half-dozen stores, and some lumber mills, the ranger HQ and the OPP station are just about all there is to the place.

Moline knows everyone on the ERT will follow the same process: review the case, learn about Moline and Hunter's plan (after they create one), and head into the wilderness to help set up a base camp and start searching. Moline, like everyone else in the ERT, knows that every minute matters.

By the time Moline wipes the sleep out of his eyes, he is already on the phone to Scott Moore, the other ERT member from the Dryden Detachment. "Look for me within half an hour," he tells Moore.

In the middle of the Quetico night, Dan Stephens stirs. This night his coiled bark and pine bough bed is rough and scratchy, but relatively mosquito free. He doesn't actually sleep. He enters a kind of half-consciousness in which his tired body rests. But it is not sleep. He feels a large ant or spider move across his legs. He feels a point on his abraded skin where something bites him. He flinches under the microscopic jaws. He wriggles to be free of it. He closes his mind, trying to reach toward darkness, to find rest, but it is a long time coming.

He feels more of these critters crawling on him. He wonders if he has lain down on some kind of ant hill. He made sure his bedding was bug free before coiling it around him. But he guesses they are attracted to his legs.

He has been careful about drinking, and now he is going to pay for his compulsive hydration. He has to peel out of the bark coils and throw off the boughs. He tries to do it carefully, because he knows in just minutes he will have to crawl back inside.

He pees and looks at the stars. They are brilliant in the cool August night. He focuses on the North Star, high in the sky but still pointing north. He finds another stick and lays it down, pointing toward the bright sphere. In the morning, he reasons, he will use it to double-check his coordinates. He will have three pointers. One marking east-west, tracking the setting sun. One laid perpendicular, pointing south. And this one pointing north. They should all line up. If they don't, he knows he will have to reconnoiter. But he feels better, now that he has a plan. He is confident his markers will align.

He is about as comfortable as you could expect, recovering from a concussion, lying on the ground in tree bark with black spruce boughs for bedding, surviving a cold northern night in a light shirt and shorts, not having eaten anything in more than a day. His stomach gnaws at the thought of food. He tries to recall everything he knows about wild food. He believes he remembers reading about the inner bark—cambium layer?—of northern white pine. It can be harvested and chewed. He also recalls arrowroot and knows he has crossed through plenty. He resolves to try both in the morning. Then he crawls back into his birch-bark coils and gathers the pine boughs and broadleaf around him.

Later in the night he feels the ants crawling. One crawls near his arm. He reaches down, picks it up. But instead of smashing it with his hand or brushing it away he feels the large black shape wriggling, recognizes the outline of a large carpenter ant. And then he pops it into his mouth. He bites and swallows and in darkness feels a satisfying twinge of vengeance at having turned the tables on at least one of the gnawing beasts.

Dryden to Atikokan is almost two hundred miles. With enough coffee and the right wheels you can run it in a little over three hours—providing you are willing to bend the rules. At this time of night, on this emergency, Moline's only worry is a big mammal—moose, deer, or the rare woodland caribou—straying out of the woods.

They take Trans Canada 17 almost eighteen miles to Provincial Highway 502. There they settle into a comfortable ride for almost one hundred miles. This highway is broader than 17—safer, given their speed, and they make excellent time.

Moline's trip is made only marginally easier by the company of Scott Moore, the other ERT member from Dryden. The two men hurtle through the dark Ontario night. Not long after starting on the long haul down 502, Moore nods off.

Moline turns from 502 onto East Provincial Highway 11. He guns the last eighty-five miles in just under an hour. At that time of the morning he sees only the occasional oncoming car, but thankfully no big animals sticking their wary heads out of the thick bush.

They arrive in Atikokan before first light, right on schedule. Before leaving, Moline was briefed on some of the details, and now he knows he wants to be in the woods with base camp set up no later than noon. They will have to hustle to make it.

In the hours before dawn Dan Stephens tries to return to sleep. As he begins to drift off he does not think about God. If he paused to consider, his heart might fill with recrimination. Instead, he feels determination. He knows God has provided him with everything he needs to survive. God has done his part in this bargain. Dan has the resources of the woods, water to drink, and the know-how to put it all together. In the bush, Dan reasons, everything watches out for itself. Unless you get in step with the wilderness program, the bush will devour you whole.

He wants to assuage his parents' worry. He wants to stop the search and rescue he suspects is being waged on his behalf. He doesn't like to think about the time and money being spent, or of his parents' anxiety. He can imagine them in knots, fraught with fear. He wishes he could reach out and let them know he is fine, that he can walk out under his own power. He wishes they would call off the search, but knows it is an idle thought. They will search until he gets out under his own power and lets them know he is okay. Hungry, but okay. A little torn up over the legs, but otherwise fine.

Now Dan Stephens knows he needs to rest. He is determined to execute the plan he feels certain will take him to safety—and not make mistakes.

Sometime before dawn he dreams. Fisher Map F-19 is laid out over a huge table. He cannot see the edges of the table, but knows the portion of the map in front of him is the country he now traverses. He stares at the map, searching for the point that will show him "You are here," but there is nothing. He again notices the lakes spread across the map in a northeast to southwest direction. There are no topographic numbers, no indications of elevation, but he realizes, staring at the map in his dream, that the ridges he is now crossing must conform to the striations of water. They move in the same direction.

On the dream map he notices a series of ridges and valleys before encountering Ottertrack Lake. Before the dream evaporates he makes note of the realization, and in the morning, he remembers.

At dawn he throws off the coils, rises, and crests the ridge, dropping over the other side. He watches the sunrise, shivering in the early morning cold. It was a reasonable night: no rain, with temperatures in the sixties. It was hard sleeping—he was too keyed up, ready to get underway. He shivers now, starting to feel the sun warm him.

He takes note of the sun and lays another stick in an easterly direction. He marks the location, comparing it to the three sticks he laid last night. He wants to be absolutely certain of his southerly direction. The pointers line up, and he crosses back over the ridge. He looks out over the low slope of land. In the distance he can see two small ponds, connected by small creeks, laid out in a southwesterly direction.

Halfway down the slope is a large white pine. Dan starts down the hillside toward the tree. He is ravenous. He opens his knife blade and digs into the fragrant wood. He peels off the outer layer, revealing the resinous white cambium. It smells strongly of pine. The smell reminds him of solvent, or air freshener. But he is hungry. He peels off a long strip. It is like a damp length of flattened bailing twine. He puts an end of it in his mouth and starts to chew, but it is like chewing on a piece of Pine-Sol–soaked leather. He tries for almost a minute trying to gag the bark down, then spits it out. There is a little water left in his canteen. He drinks a mouthful, swishes, and spits, trying to get rid of the bitterness.

He turns and continues down the hillside, moving into the lowland, alert for berries or anything else he can eat. He is careful to keep the landmarks in front of him, the ones that guarantee his southerly direction.

In the lowland he finds occasional thimbleberries. Most of the ripe ones have been eaten by the birds or bears. Some have fallen on the ground. He gathers a few near-ripe ones and devours them. They are sour. He sees a few on the ground, eats those, and is thankful for their sweetness. He is especially thankful that the taste of the berries overrides the bitterness of white pine bark.

In the morning Constable McGill and Staff Sergeant Donald brief the assembled team at the Atikokan station. They explain everything they know about the case: where and when Stephens disappeared, Stephens's experience, what the group was doing in the Quetico, the fact that his friends left him, the location of his friends now. They cover it all in detail, answering ERT members' questions.

Moline has chartered two Beaver planes to take them into the bush. They will set up base camp at no-name lake, at the precise location Stephens walked into the woods. He has also requisitioned the OPP's helicopter, which will take a while to arrive from Sudbury. This time Scott Moore pulls the lucky job of spotter. It pays to have one of the search co-ordinators come from your detachment. After Moore helps set up base camp and determines a likely landing spot for the OPP's twin-engine Aerostar copter, he will be searching from the air, not bushwhacking through that part of the Quetico. There will be plenty of searchers on the ground. Moore has done it often enough, and he smiles to know this time he will have the bird's-eye view of the place.

At the Atikokan OPP station, sometime after 7:00 AM, the shifts change. Sergeant Heather Lacey replaces a tired Phil Donald. Jim McGill has already shared everything he knows with the searchers and Sergeant Lacey. McGill has gone out for donuts and coffee. In all the planning and preparations, McGill and Donald haven't had a chance to get back to Stephens's parents.

"I'm on it," Lacey says. She doesn't look forward to calls like these, but at least she can inform the Stephenses about the OPP's efforts. The small Atikokan station is humming with ERT staff. Supplies are being gathered and packed. Dogs have been sent for, and the first Beaver has arrived. The first contingent of four ERT members is ready to load and take off. Everything that can be done, is being done.

A little after 8:00 AM, Sergeant Heather Lacey calls Jim and Mary Ann Stephens. It has been a bad night for the couple. Jim Stephens stared in the dark, trying to imagine his son's whereabouts, to place himself in the Quetico woods, about which he knows nothing. He is familiar with wilderness, but from what Dan told him earlier that summer, northern wilderness seemed wilder than the southern woods; everything but the water has a sharp edge. And there is too much water. He has looked at the maps. He cannot believe the latticework of lakes and streams. There is as much water as land. He hasn't said it to Dan's mother, but with so much wild water, drowning is a possibility. He knows his son, knows he is an excellent swimmer and water man, careful about life vests. Still, with that much water, anything is possible.

A bleary Jim Stephens answers the phone after the first ring. Heather Lacey introduces herself and the Ontario Provincial Police. She is barely into her discussion about what is being done before Stephens has words of his own.

"We're catching the next flight up," he says. He knows he cannot spend another night in the dark, without shuteye or any sense of what is being done for his son—without doing something himself.

Sergeant Lacey assures him that they are doing everything that can be done. She tells them she will contact them every hour and give them updates until they find Dan. At this point it would be premature for them to come to Canada. They would be helping Dan more by staying home, attending to their move, giving the OPP any other details they think might be relevant.

Stephens is doubtful anyone could turn over as many stones as himself—the boy's father. But he spends the next half hour repeating everything they have already told Doug Hirdler. They are impatient and anxious, but to Jim Stephens, who has an ear for bureaucratic mumbo jumbo, Heather Lacey sounds granite-solid. They are relieved to have the staff sergeant on the other end of the line, and for now are convinced to remain home by the phone.

Throughout the warming August morning, the two yellow Beavers ferry men and supplies into no-name lake. Moline and Moore are among the first to arrive. They fly low over trees and water, examining the entire shoreline of Fran Lake, no-name, and Bell. The place is nothing but trees and brush. They can barely discern where the waters of no-name lake begin and the brush ends. They are looking for some kind of granite promontory, or high ridge outcrop— the best place to be seen, providing Stephens is still around and thinking clearly enough to make himself seen.

The pilot makes two passes over the lake, but there is nothing open about it. From the air they believe they can see where the portage should be and the area where Stephens disappeared. The plane makes one more wide circle and lands on the lake from the northeast. The pilot taxis the float plane down to the far southwestern corner.

Moline and Moore see the wide cobblestone path at the far end—the one Stephens was first certain was the portage. And then almost fifty yards to the southeast, the wide, dark spot and the opening into the cedar swamp behind it. It is the only place that looks like a cave, the way the Chattanooga fathers described it. Behind open space, cedar boughs close overhead in a dense wall. Inside, under the boughs, everything is dark. The first thing they are going to do, Moline knows, is hike into that dark space and explore every cranny of it.

The float plane taxis up to the open edge of water, and the men throw off the rope and tie it firmly ashore. Then they take no more than five minutes to unload supplies for base camp. Tents, coolers, food, bags, radio equipment—

everything is tightly packed and easily handled. When it all sits in a huge pile on the shore, the float plane is untethered and cast off. In moments it wings back out over the lake.

As part of the initial search coordinator setup, Moline and Hunter have laid out a search grid. The grid is divided into kilometer-wide squares that stretch out and away from the point where Stephens walked into the woods and disappeared. By now Dan has been gone two nights, approximately thirty-six hours. That means the search area is going to be wide. When they unfold the map and examine it, the expanse of wilderness is daunting.

Moline, Moore, and Hunter realize that if Stephens hiked north, he is in a world of hurt. That direction disappears into over fifteen miles of heavy bush until the next big body of water—and that's if he hikes *due* north. People in woods without anything to guide them—like a compass—tend to walk in circles. If they are left handed, they tend to veer left. It makes them walk in a huge, left-leaning circle. Right-handed people veer right. Eventually most people pushing through brush end up at or near the place they started.

Due north from Bell Lake is one of Canada's thickest, most impenetrable forests: nothing but big trees, thick brush, blackflies, and mosquitoes. The likelihood of coming in contact with any wilderness travelers would be one in a million. *More like a billion*, Moline thinks, given the fact there are no good canoe routes and certainly no hiking trails. A hike north is a walk into oblivion.

In terms of woods and distance, the hike south doesn't look much better. But at least in that direction he has a better chance of running into someone—providing he can hike all the way to the Canadian border. The search team has spent enough time in the Quetico woods to know the likelihood of making it all the way to the border—to the long narrow strip of Ottertrack Lake that straddles the international boundary—is at best remote, more likely impossible. Even if Stephens knows what he's doing, the hike would be through bush so thick and bug infested most would be turning in circles and unhinged within twenty-four hours.

Stephens went into the woods without a compass or map. That means dead reckoning via the sun, most likely, providing Stephens is savvy enough to compensate for the rule of dominant handedness. He has the season working to his advantage, but even in August it gets cold at night. And the heat of the day, particularly at dusk, will bring out the swarms. He might find some berries, but more likely he'll go hungry—damn hungry. Moline knows the woods have plenty to offer, if you know what to look for. But it takes training and time to recognize the possibilities. The kid might know something about it, given his background and Eagle Scout rank. But people more experienced than Dan Stephens have walked into the woods and disappeared. All in all, they're not feeling good about this search.

The team is well rehearsed in setting up camp. By noon the entire place is a hive of activity. They have already been over every inch of the cedar swamp and the surrounding area, but they find nothing. Not a track, not a sign that the young man has passed. They're disappointed, but not surprised. Searches of people gone as long as Stephens rarely have a rapid conclusion.

Some of the men are already in the woods starting their search along obvious routes. They have ferried in dogs, and the dogs are trying to pick up Dan's scent. If he is in the neighborhood, Moline knows, the dogs will smell him.

The OPP-ERT members preparing to search the Quetico bush; Constable Moline, sitting at left, is search coordinator (courtesy Constable Scott Moore, OPP-ERT)

The helicopter is almost in from Sudbury, but they realize there is no good place for it to land. The area around no-name lake is so thick with brush—trees running straight up to the edge of the water with no flat granite outcrops—they will need to create some kind of makeshift helipad.

Sergeant Norm Mitchell and Moore know the copter doesn't need much. But it should be plenty open, so the rotors have no chance of hooking on a tree branch. The most open place close to camp is the cobblestone end of the lake, but the boulders are too large and tumbled, in the same state the glaciers left them. Its surface is too uneven.

A kind of log-dock landing pad could work. It doesn't have to be much, just spread in an even plane across those boulders.

Mitchell and Moore envision the way the logs could be cut, stripped, and laid out in a simple latticework across the open rocks. Two long log sides with four logs strapped across it. They enlist the help of four recently arrived ERT members and make their way along the shoreline to the cobblestone end, sizing up trees as they maneuver along the tight bank.

While the men build the makeshift helipad, the copter touches down at the Prairie Portage Station and picks up Jerry Wills. He is amazed at the copter's speed. In minutes they pass over the twenty-seven miles of terrain that had cost hours of back-breaking pain and labor the previous day. They fly low over the southeastern end of no-name lake, where a yellow Beaver lies tethered near the shore. Jerry points out the location where Dan Stephens disappeared, now occupied by the ERT. The pilot radios the ERT ground crew and then ferries Jerry Wills back to Prairie Portage.

By early afternoon all sixteen ERT members have arrived, dropped off their gear, and started searching. Jeff Moline and Norm Mitchell are setting up gear, waiting for the Aerostar twin-engine to reappear. They've been in radio contact with the chopper and expect to see it any time now. Moline and Mitchell consider the handiwork of their makeshift helipad. They have both seen the copter land on worse.

And within the next half-hour the copter has put down, picked up Scott Moore, and taken off over the lake, making a wide circle of the entire shore—the most obvious place

A Beaver float plane takes off near the log platform built for the helicopter near ERT camp (courtesy Constable Scott Moore, OPP-ERT)

anyone could be seen. Moore and the pilot have the grid laid out in front of them. They make several wider circles of Bell Lake, but even when you're on top of it you cannot see much more than the conical tops of pines. In another half hour they exhaust the local possibilities. They radio to Kevin Hunter that they are turning south.

For the rest of the day the dogs and men search through the Quetico woods. Scott Moore and the copter pilot make several runs south, covering different grid quadrants all the way down to Ottertrack Lake. But it is as though the trees have swallowed Dan Stephens whole. Even the dogs find no trace of him.

17

No Tracks, No Signs, Nothing

The Pow Wow Trail region, BWCAW, Saturday-Sunday, October 27–28, 2001

Saturday morning at first light there are over a dozen searchers assembled. Jim Williams is serving as incident commander. Rebecca Francis is there to co-command and to make sure proper wilderness authority is available in case BWCAW regulations need explaining. ATVs and overhead planes are entirely allowable, she assures them, in cases of search and rescue.

Brad Johnson, a DNR conservation officer out of Silver Bay, has also answered the call. He was patrolling the area when he heard the radio chatter. In less than an hour he is in the trailhead parking lot, ready to hike into the woods.

Together, Williams and Francis send pairs of searchers along the obvious routes, some in ATVs, others on foot.

Most of them head up the trail. The initial goal is to circumnavigate the entire Pow Wow. They need to walk every foot of it, since the trail is the most likely place Jason could be found. But the early going is difficult. The weight of the heavy, wet snow has clogged the trail and bowed many of the young trees bordering it. The trees and brush have to be shaken and flung upright to make way for hikers and 4-wheelers.

Each pair has a woods pack containing waterproof matches, medical supplies, food, water, and space blankets—durable foil sheets designed by NASA that retain almost 100 percent of the body's heat and fold up into two-inch squares. If Jason is out there and in trouble, they have plenty of the right resources to assist. And they carry radios that can bring down a swarm of rescuers on the spot—if need be.

Last night the weather moderated, and now it is hazy and beginning to warm. The heavy, wet snow starts to melt, growing heavier with each hour and making walking more difficult.

The Rasmussens stop by in late morning. They meet with Steve Van Kekerix, Jim Williams, Rebecca Francis, Brad Johnson, and some of the other search and rescue folks. Van Kekerix makes the introductions, and they all share their initial progress. The officials encourage the parents and reiterate their full expectations of finding Jason alive. But while they review what they've already done, Williams hopes no one calls in from the field to report a body has been found.

Off to the side, a handful of searchers have returned empty handed from their first forays up nearby trails. Quietly, they are beginning to suspect the worst. More than a day of extensive flyovers have yielded nothing—and in nearly perfect conditions. Why didn't they at least find Jason's orange tent, or some other sign in the wide blanket of white?

They know that in ninety percent of search and rescue cases, the hasty searches done nearest the last whereabouts are successful. The odds are not in Jason's favor. Six days gone without any clue but a cold, dark, metal heap—still empty in the trailhead parking lot. The searchers hang on the periphery, waiting to convey their empty-handedness and get their next assignment, which they suspect will be more remote.

Until now, Jason was just another lost person. Now the searchers see Linda and Lee's anguish. It makes their efforts somehow more tribal—as though seeing the family reminds them of their own, makes them recollect their natural, communal connection. It could be anyone out there. Some day it might be one of *their* sons or daughters, brothers or sisters.

Perhaps it is these silent doubts the Rasmussens sense. Their presence impedes the free-wheeling discussion of the search efforts, or any talk of recovery of the body, if it should come to that. Lee and Linda again describe their son's experience, intelligence, and drive. They convey his preparation, and the types of maps he carried with him—details Williams and Francis already know from their discussions with Van Kekerix. In the end, the Rasmussens know their son is better served by their own retreat to somewhere off site, and they decide to drive south to Two Harbors and find a place to spend the night.

All day the searchers ply the nearby trails. Two pairs reach the juncture of the circular trail, and head in different directions—hoping, by late afternoon, to meet somewhere on the west side of the trail. But it is a long hike, and not easy in this snow. Before their routes are half done they are forced to turn back, exhausted and discouraged.

By late afternoon the most remote half of the trail hasn't been touched. Hiking is not easy—either plowing through the accumulation, or recognizing the trail through the trees—especially in blowdown areas. Jim Williams and Rebecca Francis have been at the command center the entire day, tracking the searchers' progress, getting periodic radio reports from the field.

Overhead, Pat Loe and Nick Milkovich have been crisscrossing the sky since first light, but there is nothing to report. No tracks, no signs. Nothing.

Jason Rasmussen shuffles around his hollowed-out home. If he had an aerial view (and if his orange tent fly weren't smothered in snow), he would see he was less than half a mile from his camp, and less than six miles from the swarm of people now assembled in the trailhead parking lot, spreading into the woods like trailing ants.

But he would also see the difficult nature of the terrain. As the crow flies, it is a short distance to safety. But for all the bogs, swamps, beaver ponds, and thick forest brush he would have to cross—providing he could maintain a straight line and knew which direction to turn—it would be impossible to hike it in a single day. And he would get wet. Jason remembers his *Wilderness Survival* book back in the tent. He was reading the section on hypothermia when he finally noticed the rain had stopped. He had folded the corner of that page and set the book down. The natural sequence: exposure, hypothermia, disorientation, and death. *But that was a lifetime ago*, he thinks.

Three times he has heard the drone of an overhead plane. He has been careful to scramble to the nearest brush opening. But the opening is small, and the flights are not directly overhead. He waves. At one point he climbs on top of the six-foot stump beside his hollowed-out home. When the Beaver comes into view—this time nearer than any of its previous flyovers—he waves his arms and shouts. He is a full eight feet closer to the plane, and at least from a sideways vantage eminently more visible.

But if you saw Jason from the air you would see a man in olive drab, the color of trees and brush, standing atop a stump wide enough to conceal his every gesture. He would have been far better off standing on snow. Nick Milkovich and Pat Loe see nothing.

In the plane's wake he whistles and whistles. But there is only the gradual ebbing of the plane's engines. Any hopefulness he was feeling at the start of the day bleeds out with the passing plane. By the time his narrow opening returns to silence, he begins to realize it may be another day before he is rescued. His disappointment threatens to plummet into something much deeper.

If he is not found this day, he knows he will have to spend another night in his tree. He recalls the adage: idle hands are the devil's workshop. He busies himself making more repairs, sealing more holes, covering over more cracks. The effort makes him lightheaded, and later in the day he begins to feel weak. He knows he is starving. He hasn't had enough water or food—for at least the last three days.

Finally, by late afternoon, he opens his small tin of tuna. Canned tuna has never smelled so good. The salty sea smell wafts into his forest opening like ambrosia. When he digs it out of the can, it flakes off on his fingers. At first he tastes it carefully. He sucks down every particle before returning to the tin for more. Its saltiness makes his stomach weak. Then he takes one large bite. He tries to chew it meditatively, but cannot help himself. Within five minutes he is licking the can, careful not to cut his tongue on the tin's sharp edge.

Now he is thirsty. He cannot believe how much his throat burns for one long drink of water. It is in part the effect of the salty tuna, in part the cumulative effect of one cup of melt water per day. Now he eats snow to slake his thirst. He packs his remaining water bottle with snow. He begins shaking. He suspects it has as much to do with the salt intake and his need for water as the cold. And eating snow hasn't seemed to help his thirst. Well after dark, he lies inside his tree and continues to tremble and sweat, feverish in its wooden heart.

On Saturday night, BJ Kohlstedt and her husband John return from a week in New Orleans. Kohlstedt is one of Finland's key search and rescue personnel. Unlike Jim Williams, she is not a native northern Minnesotan, but she is one in spirit.

When she was a senior at Lakeville High School, down in the Cities, her science teacher took a group of students on a one-week course to the Environmental Learning Center (ELC), just outside of Isabella. For an intensive week Kohlstedt traipsed through subzero temperatures and deep snow, observing white-tailed deer. Her fellow students complained, longing for the warmth of their own beds, the restful sanctuary of their homes. BJ Kohlstedt's eyes opened to the northern starlight. In the transcendent beauty of winter wilderness she found a calling.

After graduating from the University of Minnesota-Duluth she managed to find work teaching at the same ELC she visited when in high school. Over the years she added an EMT certification to her credentials. And she has been working on the search and rescue squad out of Finland, not far from home, for the last several years.

BJ is one of the few volunteers who has had extensive training in search management systems. Every year, the second weekend in October, the Emergency Response Institute offers a class—Managing Search Operations—at Vermillion Community College in Ely. This year BJ taught the course. It was another opportunity to augment her expertise on the topic. And it is a great place to meet others in the field. On her last trip she met Carla Leehy and Carla's friend Sherry Wright. Both were dog handlers, part of Central Lakes Search and Rescue, an organization outside of Bertha, Minnesota, that uses dogs to search for people— dead or alive. For the weekend course she also enlisted the assistance of her old friend Wendy Deane, of Northstar Dogs. Wendy and her dog Cassie demonstrated how trailing dogs work in the field.

As soon as John and BJ walk in the door, she listens to her messages. Before her bags are unpacked she is on the phone, inquiring about the search status. It is 8:00 PM and IC—Incident Command—conveys the troubling message: the day has yielded nothing.

"What's being done tonight?" she asks.

"As far as I know, nothing." Dispatch explains that Jim Williams is up on the trail, sleeping in the van in case Rasmussen walks out on his own. But they fear the worst. The whole area is quiet as stone.

BJ is eager to put her learning to work. In some areas searchers will only go into woods during the day, but BJ knows there is plenty that can be done at night. Not only planning the next day's searches, but also performing other hasty searches in nearby woods. Some searchers prefer the woods at night, when their lights are prominent, they can see a fire a long way off, and the woods are quiet—sound seems to travel farther in the dark. She also remembers, from her friends with the dogs, that the dogs prefer going out at night. They work better in the dark: scent settles in the night.

But she has just returned from a trip, and she needs to unpack and get ready for the morning. She tells IC she will be at the trailhead parking lot by first light, ready to lend a hand. She volunteers her husband John to go with her. He doesn't take much persuading. Then she signs off and hurries her chores, knowing she should get some sleep.

If Jason altered his expected route, or took a wrong turn, he could have ended up near Isabella Lake, or south along one of the other routes out of old Forest Center. Just after dawn BJ and her husband are hiking through the nearby woods and along Isabella's shoreline, looking for signs. Rebecca Francis and Jim Williams are back at it, assigning pairs to hit other areas that haven't been crossed.

Sunday morning dawns clear and warm—at least warm for this time of year. The relative warmth feels good but intensifies the melt. Hiking through wet snow is like slogging through sand. Williams knows they won't be able to get to the western side of the trail. He is particularly interested in sending a team up Superstition Spur, since Jason mentioned to his mother he might hike up that trail if he had the time.

Williams enlists the Forest Service plane to fly two pairs of searchers into Lake Three near the northwestern corner of the trail. Brad Johnson gets in, with Richard DeRosier, a Lake County deputy out of the Silver Bay squad, Ron VanBergen from DNR Fisheries, and USFS Forester Terry Olson. Johnson and Olson will hike due east over the trail, as far as they can, given their time constraints. DeRosier and VanBergen will head south toward the Superstition Spur.

It is almost noon. In the plane, Deputy Milkovich and pilot Dean Lee explain their strategy. While the searchers hike, they will be taking advantage of the good weather, doing more flyovers of the area, hoping for some kind of break.

"If you don't want to spend the night in these woods," Milkovich warns, "make sure you're back at the pickup point no later than 4:00."

The two teams are clear about it. They have no intention of spending a cold winter night in these woods.

The trail is almost impossible to follow. But both pairs of searchers are experienced, and they manage to pick their way along the east-west and north-south quadrants. Once DeRosier and VanBergen get out of the blowdown, they make good time south. They radio in every half hour, but there is not much to tell. The open parts of the trail are beautiful. Apart from wet, cold feet, they are enjoying a great day hiking in the woods. Their exertions, combined with the day's moderating temperatures, actually make them sweat. But they don't find any tracks, tent, or any other sign Jason has stepped through these woods. And they don't have enough time to make it up the Superstition Spur.

Another pair of searchers head in the direction Jason said he would take, moving along the trail counterclockwise. But instead of turning to Pose Lake they keep heading north, taking the Lake Insula portage trail. This is the juncture that first lured Jason off the Pow Wow. Midway to Lake Insula the pair of searchers pass Jason's camp and fire pit. But it is still blanketed with snow and they find nothing. They keep heading north, exploring the old portage all the way to Lake Insula. Then they turn around and start back, radioing in their coordinates, conveying the absence of any signs.

Throughout this day Jason, too, has enjoyed the sunshine. His fever broke before dawn. He crawled out of his tree feeling tired and weak, but better. Throughout the day he has witnessed several flyovers, summoning the strength to wave and whistle each time they pass. But he knows they don't seen him.

At midday he walks to a nearby clearing. He finds an open log to sit on. It is warm enough in the forest opening to doff his boots. He tries to warm his feet in the sun and dry his boots. He pulls out the liners and replaces them with dry grass and small spruce sprigs, hoping they'll make better insulation. He still cannot feel his toes. Later in the day he returns to the tree.

The plane has crossed over him so many times he wonders why they haven't seen him. For perhaps the first time, he wonders if he will ever be found. He thinks about it abstractly at first, as though it couldn't possibly be this incident's conclusion, the expiration of his life. He doesn't want to be found months, maybe years later—withered in this distant spot—stumbled over by a moose hunter or some other bushwhacking hiker. He thinks he understands death, that he is equal to wherever death will take him. But when he considers the possibility of not being found, waves of love and concern for his family—his sister, his mom and dad—crash over him. He doesn't want to disappear without at least some final communication to them.

He has a pen. He forages the woods for some adequate birch bark and begins writing a goodbye letter to his folks and his sister. He considers his words carefully. He is still writing by the time night forces him to suspend his effort and return to his tree.

He was able to melt about one good cup of water in the sunlight. It was sweet and delicious, but barely enough to keep him going. He has packed his water bottle again and brought it into his hovel. The bottle full of snow is cold comfort through the night.

Back at the communications van, there is plenty of activity that evening. The searchers have all reported in. There is nothing south of the trail from Lake Three. The east-west team made it all the way to South Wilder, but the trail was untouched. Another team heading west on the northern part of the trail got to South Wilder, so the entire northern stretch of the trail has been searched. Nothing.

The two remote search teams were picked up by 4:00 PM. There was nothing along their distant stretches of trail: no tracks, no signs anyone had hiked that way since the snowstorm.

The typical post-search process involves debriefing incident commanders on where search pairs have been and what they've seen. The pair who passed over Ahmoo Creek report the same results—nothing. They are wet and tired, ready to head home. It is a sentiment everyone shares. In forty-eight hours the ground-pounders have exhausted the trail and found zilch. Back at the parking lot, a pall settles over the remaining searchers.

The Rasmussens have returned to the Cities. They believe the search is continuing—they just have to return and let their employers and neighbors know what's happening. To date, Steve Van Kekerix has done an excellent job keeping the effort out of the press. The last thing any of them wants is reporters on the scene, bird-dogging their efforts.

The searchers are unsure about where else they should search. They feel as though they have exhausted all the obvious possibilities, and then pursued the most unlikely. Everyone is wet and tired. Finally, not ready to give up, but too tired to continue, they decide to call off the ground search. For now. At least for now.

That evening, when Steve Van Kekerix phones the Rasmussens to let them know the ground search has been suspended, he is quick to mention the continuation of the air search.

"The plane will be back up at first light," Van Kekerix says. "If Jason is moving," he repeats, in a phrase the Rasmussens have heard before, "we'll find him. And the Minnesota Department of Transportation has an Air Wing helicopter that can make overhead scans of large tracts of wilderness for thermal signatures," Van Kekerix explains. He has scheduled the chopper out of Cloquet. It should be reviewing the entire area overnight. "If Jason is out there," he repeats, "the Air Wing should pick him up."

Back home the Rasmussens return the phone to its receiver. This news is devastating. They understand it, and they are thankful for all that has already been done, but while searchers were still combing the area there was hope. More hope, they know, than if the air search continues alone. And what if the Air Wing chopper finds no heat trace of Jason?

Now the only thing connecting them to Jason is an infrared thermal device and a Beaver plane with two spotters. They cannot properly absorb this recent shift in events. Since Jason's absence their sleep has been scant and fitful. Now they turn to their bed in silence, unable to speak, knowing it will be another long night.

After dark, up in the trailhead parking lot, the place is empty—except for Jason's patient Saturn, still sitting, waiting in the cold and dark.

After a late supper, BJ Kohlstedt is restless, unable to go to bed—though she is exhausted from the day's search. She is nagged by a recollection from her recent search management class about statistics on lost people. People with Jason's experience, fitness level, and background almost never get lost because they fall and hurt themselves. They are too fit. It makes her suspect he may still be out there. Statistically, the Jasons of the world lose themselves by taking a wrong turn and continuing in error. Widen the search area? Reconsider the maps, looking for obvious points to go astray? Finally, she phones Pete Walsh, the current captain of Finland Search and Rescue.

Coincidentally, this weekend—October 27–28—is one of two weekends a year Pete is required to work. Usually he is laboring Monday through Friday, helping maintain Lutsen Resort. "The oldest resort in Minnesota," he claims. He has been around long enough so no one questions the assertion.

Pete was one of Finland Search & Rescue's charter members. Twenty-five years ago he helped formalize the volunteer squad, and over the years he has spent as much time fund raising and investing in the squad's equipment as he has in the field. It was he and some fellow volunteers who gutted and refurbished the old emergency vehicle, setting it up with communications equipment, a table, a bunk, and other necessary supplies. It is old, but operational—and just one of the efforts that gives him pride.

This evening he is just about ready to turn in from a

long work weekend at the resort when the phone interrupts him. It is BJ, one of his favorite volunteers. He has heard about a search for someone up on the Pow Wow. Although he has lived on the North Shore his entire life, he's not that familiar with the old Forest Center or the trails thereabouts.

"Any luck?" he wonders.

"Not yet," BJ says. "They've called off the ground search, at least for now."

BJ spends a few minutes explaining what they've done, bringing him up to date. Then she starts talking about statistics. She explains that she would like to re-open the ground search. She has some ideas, and she thinks this might be a good place to search with dogs. They can call in dogs from Central Lakes and other dog squads around the state. Since Two Harbors has gone back to their garage, the Finland squad could take the lead. She knows Pete worked the weekend and has Monday and Tuesday off. Pete's fresh. He hasn't yet set foot in the woods, so he's an easy sell.

"Call Van Kekerix and make sure he's okay with it," Walsh suggests—though he already knows Steve's answer. "Make sure dispatch sends out another call for volunteers to meet us there at first light. Just to be sure, I'll make some calls tonight."

Pete Walsh has a list of friends almost as thick as the Finland phone book. And those he doesn't know personally are at the very least friends of friends, friends of relatives, or relatives of friends.

This evening, before he turns in and settles down to sleep, Pete Walsh has wrung agreements out of several searchers. They'll meet him at first light, up in the trailhead parking lot. Some from Finland, Captain Swede Larson and four others from the Silver Bay Squad, and still others coming in from Two Harbors. With any luck they'll snag a couple of DNR conservation officers—Kipp Duncan out of Two Harbors and Marty Stage out of Babbitt. He's got a good crew for the morning. Before he turns off his light, he sets his alarm.

Back at home BJ starts to re-examine all the maps. Van Kekerix thought her idea was excellent, and he asked dispatch to put out another call for volunteers. He also told her to call out the dogs—literally. She would have her people and their dogs' superb noses. He'd be up, too, later in the morning, when he could spare the time.

Before Steve Van Kekerix turns in for the evening, he makes a late-night call to the Rasmussens. They're up. He knew they would be. He tells them the search is starting afresh, and this time they are bringing in dogs. They will find him, he reassures them. He hopes it won't be recovery, but that's a thought he keeps to himself. Some of these dogs are trained to smell death. He only tells the Rasmussens about the ones who are trained to find Jason alive.

Back in bed, before BJ drops off to sleep, she thinks she has an idea of where else to search. And there will be dogs, she knows. The dogs are coming.

18

Bushwhacking the Quetico Woods

Quetico Provincial Park, Thursday, August 7, 1998

Every hour and a half Dan Stephens checks his watch, stopping to drink water, rest, and reevaluate his position. At his first stop he stumbles across a patch of arrowroot. Its large spiked leaves flow down to the water's edge.

He grabs one of the plants by the base of its stem and pulls it up, as though he's harvesting radishes. He cuts off the bottom white root, discards the leaves, and swishes the root in water, cleaning off dirt. It looks like a small white carrot. He recollects the taste of a carrot, its gritty sweetness. He hopes the arrowroot measures up.

He snaps it in half, places the small half in his mouth, and starts chewing. There is an immediate taste of bitterness. He is hungry and hopes it will pass, but after a couple more chews the bitterness intensifies, like the taste of hard, black rubber, and he spits it across the water. He cannot believe people eat this. He wonders if he made a mistake, but the long spiked leaves, wide like arrowheads, reaffirm his choice.

He is still spitting, trying to get the taste of acrid rubber out of his mouth. He takes a drink of water and swishes. He spits, but the taste has penetrated the inner lining of his mouth. He drinks again, swishes, but the rinse does little to diminish the awful bitterness. He knows some plants are edible at different times of the year. *Maybe in the spring,* he thinks. He suspects he tried arrowroot at its worst time.

Throughout the day Stephens pushes his way south in a near-straight line. He uses a navigational technique he recollects from scouting texts: the two-stick method. He finds a straight stick, plants it in the ground so that it points directly into the sun without casting a shadow. Then he waits twenty minutes for the sun to shift. The shadow the stick casts from the sun's movement points due east. He uses another stick, laying it perpendicular to the shadow, marking the direction south. He takes his bearings along a long line southward, whenever possible marking them against a distant landmark—a crest of hill, or a towering white pine—and then keeps walking, keeping his navigable landmark in sight.

All morning he repeats the two-stick method. Whenever possible, he hikes the ridges, walking along the rocky outcrops until he is forced to leave them and turn south. Then he crosses another valley of bogs and thick brush. The sharp trees and brush cut his legs. He struggles to make the next ridge, following it south as long as it holds, then repeating his boggy amble.

Twice he hears a plane in the distance. He suspects they are looking for him. Once in mid-morning a helicopter thunders by within eyeshot. He is on a slightly forested hillside, heading down to cross another section of swamp. He jumps and shouts, waving his arms and his long walking stick in the air. But Dan knows that even if they were right on top of him, he would be difficult to see. It would be better if he were in the middle of the lowland in front of him. But even there the brush is too high and overgrown. His efforts to alert the aircraft are futile, and he reaffirms his belief that the only way out is to continue hiking south.

He maintains his direction. Now that he has recovered his clarity, his will, he doesn't make mistakes. He is familiar with the rule of dominant handedness. His right side has always been stronger than his left. He knows how to compensate. He is careful to stop every ninety minutes to take a drink and recheck his position.

By this reckoning he crosses more lowland swamp and intermittent ridges, trying to keep to the high points, only walking down into the thick brush long enough to make the next ridge.

By late afternoon he is satisfied with his progress, knows he must find someplace to bed down for the night. The next ridge is a clear promontory, better than the previous night's site. He struggles up the high escarpment. At its top he is rewarded by an old blueberry patch and another widow-maker birch. A handful of succulent fruit clings to a few remaining bushes. He forages the hillside and devours the meager supper. The berries are sweeter than anything he has ever tasted. He lingers over each tiny berry, savoring its flavor, sucking down its sweetness. He reflects on some of his past meals. Nothing, not the finest restaurants he can recall, hold a candle to the tiny blue berries cradled in his fist.

While the light is still strong he approaches the birch. The tree is huge—one of the largest he has come across. He revels at his good fortune, sinking his knife into the thick trunk. He cuts off three large coils of waterproof bark, repeating the process from the night before. He crosses over the ridge top. The eastern side is clear, a fitting place to reconnoiter and warm himself in tomorrow's dawn. Now he re-crosses the crest line, finding an open place where the sun's last rays will warm him. He scours the hillside for broadleaf. In his forage he hasn't seen any bear scat. He fashions his makeshift shelter and lies down as the evening darkens.

Back at the OPP base camp the ERT crew settles in for the evening. They built a large fire pit in front of the crowded cedars. The blaze is an excellent way to keep the bugs at bay. Here the trick is to follow the smoke, to stay just to the side of it so the mosquitoes won't hound or hinder. The men have hats with netting, and someone had the prescience to pack in suitable refreshment. After dining on pork chops they sit back and enjoy the evening.

The helicopter rests on the makeshift pad. The tents are set up near the fire. They are all tired from the last twenty-four hours. Most of them have made long bushwhacks through the nearby woods. The dogs rest beside the firelight. There is nothing to do but wait for first light.

The group is hopeful about tomorrow. They've already crossed much of the grid, and by the end of tomorrow they suspect they will have their man. In the close darkness they finish their drinks and plot the morning's efforts. More of them will turn south. Some will cross the lake and hike further north—just in case. Scott Moore and the pilot will rise at first light and fire up the copter, crisscrossing north and south. They are in the right place to be searching. They are confident that if Dan Stephens is still alive, they will find him.

In the waning hours of the day Sergeant Lacey makes one last call to Jim and Mary Ann Stephens. Lacey has been true to her word, periodically phoning Dan's parents with updates. She tells them not to worry, to try to get some sleep. The OPP is on it. They have plenty of men, dogs, and supplies. They are going to find their son. Tomorrow, she says. Tomorrow she is certain their boy will be found.

Back at the Prairie Portage station, Cathy Antle and Carrie Frechette have been busy with the day's travelers. They waited until Jerry Wills returned from his copter ride. He informed them about the ERT and the swarm of constables searching the bush. He was hopeful about their search, increasingly confident that his and Tim Jones's decision to paddle for help had been a good one.

Tomorrow is Cathy Antle's day off. She will make the long trip to Sommers in the morning. Sommers is only twenty miles up the road from Ely, where the Scout group is headed and where she needs to go for some badly needed supplies. She will try to hook up with the fathers then, and give them any news of the search and rescue progress.

The previous day, Joe Mattson and the chaplain had ferried the boys and canoes back to base camp, speeding down the length of Moose Lake in the only section of the Boundary Waters where motorized vehicles were allowed. The Scouts took over one of the camp's vacant barracks.

Now Jerry Wills and Tim Jones take the remaining canoe and paddle the distance down Moose Lake to Sommers. Over supper they are happy to be reunited with their troop. In the evening they bed down in the relative ease of the base barracks. They all turn in early, exhausted from their ordeal. Before bed they gather inside the small room, where Jerry Wills leads them in a prayer for their guide, entreating God for his safe passage.

In the night, on his remote escarpment, Dan Stephens drifts into a troubled sleep. The map dream reappears to him. The familiar yellow-and-blue chart is spread out before him. He searches for the dot signifying "you are here." But across the wide table he can find nothing. He recollects the northwest-southeast drainage he is traversing, determines—in his dream—to remember the message. And then he slips into a shallow and fitful sleep.

FOUND

I had stopped at night, and being unable to make a camp, or kindle a fire, I was endeavoring to reconcile myself to the immediate approach of death which I thought inevitable, when these people unexpectedly found me, and helped me to return to camp.

JOHN TANNER
A Narrative of the Captivity and Adventures of John Tanner

A great thirst is a great joy when quenched in time.

EDWARD ABBEY
Desert Solitaire

19

Searchers Find a Clue

Pow Wow Trail region, BWCAW, Monday, October 29, 2001

By 9:30 AM, BJ Kohlstedt is on the phone to the Search and Rescue Dog Associations (SARDA). Central Lakes Search and Rescue, the dog group BJ met in her October seminar, is one group among a half-dozen located throughout the state. None of them resides in Lake County. The call goes out to the network, and several of the statewide groups respond. It will take them time to gear up. According to Carla Leehy at Central Lakes, BJ should expect at least two dog teams, probably more, by 6:00 PM.

Pete Walsh acts as incident commander, stationed in the Finland Search and Rescue communications vehicle. At times BJ shares the center, or heads out to make another foray into the woods. There are several paired parties making numerous excursions throughout the area—both nearby and much farther up the trail.

Kipp Duncan and Marty Stage, DNR conservation officers, have both heard the radio chatter and added their own legs to the effort. They are sent off south on the trail, motoring over the old path on ATVs. The airplane is back up. Nick Milkovich and pilot Dean Lee are crisscrossing the region.

The previous night's thermal search turned up nothing. The Transportation Department's chopper pilot assures Van Kekerix that if Jason was alive and giving off heat, breathing, or stumbling through the cold terrain, his heat signature would give off a glow as distinct as a camp lantern. They would have found him. When Van Kekerix makes the call to update the Rasmussens, he leaves out the pilot's certitude. "If he's hunkered down in some kind of shelter," Steve suggests, "he's probably not giving off much of a thermal signature. At least not something you can easily see from that high." Before signing off he reminds the Rasmussens the dogs are coming.

At 11:30 the plane takes a low swing over the northwestern corner of Isabella Lake. Nick Milkovich thinks he sees something. In the warmer weather the heavy accumulation of wet snow has begun to melt so that in patches the ground is now clear. The woods are wet and muddy.

Milkovich and Lee take another spin over the area and spot a small orange swatch near the lakeshore. It looks like a piece of tent. Jason, they know, had an orange tent fly. They hone in on the coordinates, circling the spot long enough to get firm GPS readings. Then they radio the location to base camp and tell BJ and Pete Walsh they think they have something.

For three days, an intensive air and ground search has come up empty. Suddenly they may have their first clue. The location doesn't make any sense, but the orange color draws them like a beacon. Pete and BJ re-route the two conservation officers. They send them north on the ATVs to a close point on the trail. Then the two COS turn into the woods on foot.

From the air the region looks impenetrable. The simplest approach appears to be by boat. Pete and BJ also dispatch a runabout. The boat leaves at the same time as the COS. In the wake of excitement generated by their first potential clue, the two teams race toward the orange swatch.

Down in the Cities, Ken Anderson gets a call. One of the dog teams has asked for his assistance. Ken is president of Emergency Support Services (ESS), a company he established to teach rescue skills to volunteer and civic groups. Because Ken is familiar with search and rescue and knows how to work with dogs, he is more than happy to head north.

Ken calls his friend Jeff Hasse, another experienced rescue person and dog handler. Jeff works as a paramedic in Chanhassen, but he often goes out with canine units on search and rescue, or recovery. Jeff is president of Midwest Technical Rescue Training Associates (MTRTA), a company he founded to teach rescue skills to groups like Lake County Search and Rescue and the dog teams.

Over the last few years Ken and Jeff have come to understand and rely on each other's strengths. Jeff is a paramedic with excellent climbing, field, and communications experience. Ken is a master cartographer with a laptop and a load of radio gear. Together these two have teamed up to work on a variety of searches, with dogs and without, as ground-pounders or in leadership positions.

Jeff is at work when he gets the call at 1:00 PM. He has to

find someone to take his shift, but he's in. They haven't been told much about the effort—only that it has been on-going, and this is the fourth day. Together, they pack their copious gear into the back of Ken's reinforced pickup. They start out of the Cities around dinnertime, heading north, Ken's truck riding low from the weight.

Back near Isabella Lake, the pilots report the orange swatch, and everyone in the field takes a collective breath. Then radio chatter swells to a cacophony. Once the COS and a boat are dispatched, the other ground-pounders continue their current searches, but they keep an inquisitive ear bent toward their radios.

It takes an hour and forty minutes for the COS and the boat to converge on the orange object. By the time the COS crash through the woods, the boat crew has already recovered the material, a rectangular piece of heavy, orange nylon. It could be part of a tent. But it appears to have been *cut* and torn into a long rectangle. And it doesn't match the lightweight material of any tents the searchers know.

They begin circling the area, but there are no tracks or other signs of movement or habitation. The fabric could have been packed in over the winter ice.

The boat crew is careful to mark the spot. Everyone has the GPS coordinates locked in. The boat begins patrolling up and down the extensive Isabella shoreline, looking for clues. The COS, already in the woods near the site, begin making broad circles in the trees near the shoreline, looking for other signs of Jason's passing. Other searchers are pulled from nearby bushwhacks and sent in to assist the officers. Pushing through the heavy, difficult terrain makes for a strenuous afternoon. By the end of it neither the boat nor the ground-pounders have turned up anything. It appears the orange swatch fell out of the sky.

Just a few miles from the scene of converging searchers Jason Rasmussen tries to moisten his lips. His mouth is parched and his tongue and throat are dry. Despite the area's ample snow, this is the third day Jason has tried to sate his thirst with one cup of melted water. He is weary and discouraged, and throughout the day, he is often seized with the urge to lie down and doze. But the repeated droning of an airplane convinces him to stay awake, against the remote chance the pilot flies directly overhead, and, by some divine miracle, looks down the exact moment he raises a weary arm.

He is tired. He cannot remember feeling this weak. His left foot is numb clear up to the arch. He tries to wiggle his toes, but if they move he cannot feel it.

He doesn't want to stand. He wants to lie down and sleep. But somewhere in the back of his mind he knows "sleep" is a metaphor for death. Sleep—the sleep he contemplates, the one in which he lays down his burden and puts it finally to rest—is not what he wants. Not now. There is too much left for him, too much to do.

Overhead he hears the plane, further south now, well out of view. The wind picks up in the trees, and he listens. Somewhere over the ridge he thinks he hears people talking. He is startled. He is certain there are voices, but he cannot discern their words.

"Down here!" Jason yells. His voice is not much louder than a sparrow's squawk. He hasn't uttered a vowel in more than a day. "Here," he manages, with more emphasis.

And then he listens closely and notices it is only the

wind. The wind in the trees is soughing mischief. He listens intently, just to be sure. But there are no voices, only a faint breeze presaging more gray weather.

Later in the day he pulls out his birch-bark letters. He reviews what he wrote to his folks and to Heidi. They are reasonable starts, but they are only beginnings. He needs to say more. He must tell them things. He knows he cannot lie down and sleep—lie down for that final rest in his pine chamber until he has finished these letters.

By the time the day turns dark he is still working on his words. Tired as he is, he knows he must survive another evening. He has to finish the epistles to his family. There is so much to say. He has chosen to begin with the practical— explaining about passwords and accounts, the necessary business of life we take for granted. And then he begins to pick up the reins of his most difficult challenge.

Jason Rasmussen has always been a quiet, private person, but he loves his parents, his little sister, his life. On reflection he knows he has been blessed. In the waning light of the day Jason is overcome with gratitude. He sits on the edge of his log, his feet frozen, his body slowly starving, thirst scratching his throat. He is more tired than he can remember. And he shivers. Shivering has become periodic, routine. He knows his body is slowly growing colder, freezing. But before he lays down his bark, placing the letters out of harm's way, Jason feels a kind of grace he cannot recall. He tells his parents he has had a good life, a great life.

By early evening several of the searchers have decided to call it a day. A few decide to wait for the dogs. Search and rescue episodes have a life of their own. This one has already far exceeded the ordinary span devoted to most of these undertakings. But Jason's car sits in the lot, a constant reminder that he is out there—somewhere. And in spite of their poor luck, they have a clear sense of where he went into the woods and his intended route. He is still out there. The knowledge has sustained them long beyond a normal search and rescue. Finding the orange swatch blew momentary life into their efforts, gave them hope. Though it proved to be nothing, it had re-energized them. Now the dogs—new searchers with fresh perspectives and hounds—are about to have the same effect. People are looking forward to working with the dogs.

After an early dinner BJ and John, still pursuing their single dubious clue, decide to canoe along the southern Isabella shoreline and take a spin up Perent River and Pow Wow Creek, all the way to the Ferne Lake portage.

They set off at 4:00, just about the time the sun is hanging low above the western horizon. It is a cold, three-mile paddle. The map shows no easy traverse to the portage area, at least on foot. But it's an open waterway, and Jason could have changed his mind. If he hiked toward Isabella, then around the southern shore, or through the southern woods, he may have been able to bushwhack to the location. It's doubtful, but in the last three days they have checked all the obvious places. They have hiked the entire trail. They haven't yet been up Superstition Spur, but they've scheduled a crew to get in tomorrow. They have examined all the areas around the trail. Now they are waiting for the dogs.

John and BJ are gone until well after dark. Throughout

the day the temperature—mild in the morning and midday—has taken a cold plunge. The canoeing pair notices the drop. The edges of Perent River start to crystallize. But they make the Ferne Lake portage by dusk and decide to hike the 252 rods into the lake, just to be certain. But there is nothing. And by the time they return to their canoe, it is dark.

Back in the communications center, Pete Walsh is worried about the couple. He checks in by radio every ten to fifteen minutes. By the time the couple has paddled down the length of the Perent River, the water is starting to freeze. They have to break their way through the ice with paddles and the aluminum canoe bow.

At around 6:30 PM, Pete Walsh calls the canoeing couple for a regular checkup.

"This is IC, calling John and BJ. How's that paddle coming?" he asks.

He waits several moments for a response, but there is none. He waits a little longer before repeating, "This is IC, calling John and BJ. Give us a call back, eh?"

But there is still no response. Pete starts to worry, counting the minutes between calls.

Search and rescue personnel often count the highest incidence of lost or hurt people among their own. And with so many searchers on this case—already over forty, Pete guesses, and there are going to be more—it is practically inevitable that one of them will be hurt, stranded or lost. He is already thinking about who he can send out after them.

Then the radio crackles back. "We're still here," BJ says. "Must have hit a low spot. We lost your signal for a second."

Pete Walsh is elated to hear her voice. "Those are about the sweetest words I've heard today," he says. There is a collective chuckle over the air waves.

"It's tough going," BJ explains. "The ice is thickening up fast. But we should be back within a half hour, I expect."

At around 7:00 PM, just about the time BJ and John return, Central Lakes Search and Rescue is on the scene. They have three teams, and one communication support person. Their three dogs are certified: one for tracking, and two air-scenting dogs. BJ remembers from her discussions with the handlers that search and rescue dogs come in three types: trackers, air scenters, and cadaver dogs. The trackers are the animals most people imagine, when they think of dogs. Trackers take a person's specific scent and follow it through the woods. Air scenters, instead of relying on tangible ground crossing, pick up scent molecules in the air, finding anyone who might be in the area. Trackers are sometimes more certain, but air scenters are often easier to work with.

"It depends on the terrain," Carla Leehy is quick to point out.

Earlier, BJ Kohlstedt (who was given a key to Jason's car by Steve Van Kekerix) used rubber gloves to open Jason's trunk and extract one of his shoes. The dogs are given the shoe to pick up Jason's scent.

"In this country," Carla continues, "I'd almost rather have an air scenter." She explains that you follow trackers on their trail, wherever it leads. Dogs, she points out, can often fit through brush holes and thickets a human has to hack through—or crawl through on all fours. The areas around the Pow Wow have thickets that even in early winter form a weave as impenetrable as a Georgia swamp.

BJ and Pete Walsh explain what has already been done. They want one of the crews to head into the area where the orange swatch was found. The other two—the tracker and the air scenter—should start up the trail and see if they can pick up anything. The time is perfect, Carla knows. She and Dale, her husband and the one who is taking their air scenter to Isabella Lake, prefer working at night. So do the dogs. Sherry Wright, the group's communications person, sets up in the van with Pete and BJ.

Throughout the late evening other dog handlers come on the scene: Wendy Deane with Cassie, a tracker, and Jim Couch with Tanner, who is both a tracker and air scenter. They are both sent out to cover more parts of the trail.

At 11:30 PM, Ken Anderson and Jeff Hasse finally roll into the trailhead parking lot with their truck full of gear. Neither has ever been to the old Forest Center parking lot. Unless you are a local, it is not an easy place to find. This far north and on the edge of the BWCAW there are few road signs, and the fact that Hasse and Anderson locate the lot in the dark, on their first try, is a testament to the pair's navigational skills.

Pete Walsh, Pete Smerud, and Sherry are in the communications vehicle. BJ has gone out in the field to assist with one of the dog teams. Ken and Jeff introduce themselves and begin to explain why they've arrived and what they can do. The two Petes bring the recent recruits up to date, describing Jason, the search and rescue, and the areas that have already been searched. By this time the entire trail has been covered, and many areas around it, including the northwestern corner of Isabella Lake. Clues are starting to turn as cold as the weather.

Ken and Jeff look at the swatch. Neither of them believes it is from a tent fly. The fabric is too heavy and they have never seen any tents of that particular hue—more of a burnt orange, or orange-red, than the kind of orange you see in the field.

From experience the two search and rescue profession-als know coming onto an active scene can be a threat. De-pending upon the personalities of those heading up the ef-fort, they can feel welcome, or practically shunned. If welcomed, they are more than ready to take a lead role, helping with theories, communications, cartography, and whatever else the search demands. If shunned, they are happy to serve as ground-pounders in the field.

The two Petes have been on enough of these efforts to know every extra hand is invaluable. The more experi-enced, the better. When Jeff and Ken begin asking ques-tions about maps and communications, the efforts to date, the overall plan and where the search is heading from here, the two on-site commanders begin to realize these urban-ites may not know much about the Pow Wow or its sur-rounding woods, but they are plenty informed about search and rescue.

The command center vehicle has a laptop with a map-ping program hooked to a printer. Pete Smerud is operat-ing the equipment. But when Smerud begins demonstrat-ing its capabilities to Ken Anderson, the hard disk fails. There is a collective gasp in the van. These maps help guide the search and track the areas already covered. Fortunately, Ken Anderson has come prepared. He hooks up his laptop and begins displaying USGS aerial photos of the Pow Wow and surrounding country. He has other mapping pro-grams. The application has the flexibility to focus in close, or from far away. And he can create custom subsections of these maps, writing on them, or highlighting trails and the locations of search teams.

Not long after Anderson gets started, two or three cus-tomized maps spit out of the printer. One of them lays out the entire area, highlighting the current Pow Wow Trail and sections of the old trail that they label the North Loop and East Loop. The map joins others on the wall of the incident command center. The cartographers are back in business.

Throughout the night IC is in constant radio contact with the dog teams. They have moved far up the trail and into the woods, but neither the tracking dog nor the air scenters have located any trace of Jason Rasmussen. Around dawn, the teams make their way to pickup points on the trail. They are tired, hungry, and cold, and the ATVs are going to come in and meet them, then ferry them back to home base.

Carla Leehy lets IC know she is at the pickup point. The team sent to fetch her reports that they are at the juncture, but Carla is nowhere to be found. IC begins querying both groups about their surroundings. The juncture at which the Pow Wow begins its circular path is clear and familiar to the ATV folks. Carla Leehy and her team, unfamiliar with the trail or the terrain, only know they are at another juncture in the trail where the main trail seems to connect up with a second path.

Both teams radio in their GPS coordinates, and after Ken Anderson plots them on one of his maps, they see Carla's position is about a half mile south of the pickup team. Within fifteen minutes the two groups have connected. IC is happy they have been able to solve the problem. But the mishap plants a thought.

Before dawn more ground-pounders have shown up. They are sent off in a multitude of directions. Some up the trail. Some head to the juncture and turn west in a clockwise fashion, searching for signs along the southern border of the loop.

Carla Leehy and the other dog handlers feed their hardworking animals, then have something to eat themselves and lie down in their vehicles to warm themselves and get some badly needed rest.

Crowded into or near IC are Pete Smerud, Ken Anderson, BJ, Pete Walsh, Rebecca Francis, Jeff Hasse, and Sherry Wright. They have worked through possible scenarios for where Jason might have gone. Now that the maps are up on the wall, one of the most likely appears to be along the eastern and northern trails—identified on the map as the Northern Loop and Eastern Loop. In both instances sucker trails lead away from the correct Pow Wow Trail. They surmise it was at one of these sucker trail junctures that, hours earlier, Carla Leehy's team went astray. And she was sure she was at the right location—the juncture where the trail starts its circular march.

The mistake hasn't gone unnoticed, and the new theory—the one being mulled over when the radio crackles with a call from the plane—is that Jason was suckered off the main trail by a phantom path.

20

Stephens Finds His Way

Knife Lake, international border, Friday, August 8, 1998

In the first gray light of dawn, Dan Stephens peels back the birch-bark covering and rises in pain to the day. It has been another troubling night. There was the dream, whose details he now recalls as though the map lay on a table in front of him, illumined with a halogen lamp. His legs are painful. His feet burn. And the goddamn carpenter ants have made another meal of him. His scratched eye is taut and bleary.

He's starting to shiver from the early morning cold, knowing he should get over the crest of his hill. And he has back pain from lying coiled in birch bark and broadleaf on hard ground. Otherwise, he reflects, remembering his plan and yesterday's solid southern progress, he feels pretty good. He is comforted by his agenda and his ability to adhere to it.

He crosses the ridge, hoping to warm himself in the sun that breaks over the sea of trees. He moves around, trying to warm himself, considering his day and the long trek ahead of him.

After he is fully awake he re-crosses the ridgeline and checks his markers. They are all aligned in the early morning light. He looks out across the lowland in front of him, to where the land bellies up to a distant rise. He looks down at his southern pointing stick, double-checking it with the other sticks he meticulously laid out the previous evening, and in the middle of the night, when he rose to piss under the North Star. Their corroboration gives him confidence.

He looks off in the direction of the southern pointer, sighting a high white pine on the distant ridgeline, knowing he will be able to keep it in sight. Then he strikes off down the hillside and starts pushing through more brush.

At first light the OPP rises on the no-name lakeshore. Even before the sun breaks, the members have breakfasted and are in the woods. One team works its way north of camp. Three others spread southward in a fan. Scott Moore climbs into the copter and starts crossing coordinates plotted on the map, methodically searching for any sign. Throughout the morning the ERT covers its grid.

By mid-morning Dan Stephens is ravenous. In a patch of shaded saw grass he finds a lethargic hopper. Between his fingers it is sluggish in its struggle, still cold in the grass. He pops it into his mouth. He chews quickly and swallows, washing it down with water.

It passes so quickly over his tongue that it has the flavor of water with the continued bitter aftertaste of the previous day's arrowroot. He can feel his body absorb the morsel, and he appreciates the tiny addition to his diet. He knows he is slowly starving, knows he has to find more food. But he has reserves. He will hike today. Tomorrow he will forage and feed. He returns to the shaded grass, walking south. Over the next hour he finds seven more hoppers and pops them into his mouth, washing them down with water.

By noon he climbs to the top of his next rise—a very high ridge—and looks south. There, at the base of the slope, lies a lake that appears to feed into a longer lake. He smiles, believing the longer lake must be Ottertrack. If he is right, there should be a portage trail from this lake into Ottertrack. That means an open place where he might encounter canoeists. He is exhausted, but pleased. He has made better time than he expected.

He spends the next hour hiking down the steep slope through the woods. He comes down to the water's edge, happy to be here, pleased to have hiked under his own power through such difficult terrain, and found his own way out. The bank is open and warm. He drinks heavily of the lake. He sits back, thinking again of food.

He has avoided crayfish and snails. At times he has thought about them, and all the other possible edible things. Under his shadow the small crustaceans scurry for cover. He has avoided raw meat, particularly something that lives in fresh water, because he is afraid of bacteria, or parasitic giardia. A parasite could slow his process considerably, weaken him with dangerous fits of diarrhea or vomiting. But now hunger drives him to sit on the bank and await the return of the crayfish.

He looks up. His grazed eye is bleary. It weeps, and he

frequently closes it, relying on his other eye to see the trail. Now he looks out over the lake's placid blue surface and is startled by a silver flash.

He looks down, starting to feel weak. He waits. He continues looking down for a full minute before rising to squint again across the water. The streak has moved. The goddamn silver object has moved. But it is still there, across the water in plain sight.

"Hey," he finally yells. His voice cracks. He has not spoken in almost twenty-four hours, and his larynx squeaks like a rusted hinge. "Hey," he clears his throat. He calls again. But there is no answer. Dan Stephens sits down, wondering if he is mistaken, if his longing to see a canoe has prompted his imagination to conjure one.

But the day is beautiful. There is a light breeze across the water. The sky is open, a deep azure. He sits quietly and listens. He believes he sees two people in the canoe. He can barely hear them talk. He doesn't understand what they're saying, but he hears words, and the jangling their lures make when they cast.

"Hey," he yells again. "I'm lost! I need help! Do you have any food? Where's your camp?"

Amazingly, the canoe remains stationary, quiet, as though they haven't seen or heard him. Except for occasional words and the flinging of their lures, the canoeists remain still. He knows they are near enough to hear him. He calls for several more minutes before one of them finally turns and asks, "How do we know you won't rob us?" in a thick New Jersey accent.

Stephens is so happy to hear another voice he is stunned by the question. He starts laughing. "We're twenty miles from nowhere. What am I going to steal, your hat and fishing pole?"

"Maybe," the word comes back, petulant, young, and nervous.

The canoe glides close enough for Stephens to discern the Sommers Canoe Base insignia. They're Scouts out of his own camp!

"I'm a leader out of the Sommers Canoe Base," he explains. "I've been lost three days." He tells them everything. The brief outline of his odyssey tumbles out of his mouth. When they refuse to come closer, he recites the Boy Scout creed. He explains the different levels of scouting and what it takes to advance.

"Why don't you swim out to us?" one of the boys finally asks.

Until now Dan has been more than patient. In his summer of guiding he has met young Scouts from all over the country. Most of them he has appreciated. A very few have been spoiled, morose, mean-spirited, or obviously forced to come on an adventure they didn't appreciate. For these young Scouts he has felt empathy, then the need to administer discipline. He has mastered the authority voice—the one to use when dealing with kids who buck the system, or his leadership. From the sounds of it these kids are from Jersey, maybe the inner city. But today he doesn't have time or patience to coax them. His temper is razor-thin, and that kind of empathy is a luxury of the well-fed.

In the midday light, Stephens's eyes narrow. "Get in here and pick me up," he says, in a voice with unmistakable steel in it, a resolve not to be ignored. "Now," he adds, in a way that leaves no doubt about his meaning.

The voice works. There is movement across the water. The two Jersey Scouts turn and call to another canoe

Stephens hasn't seen. The other canoe rounds a point and together they both paddle in for a closer look. When they are close enough to see Stephens's condition—long hair gnarled and matted, straggly beard growth, torn and filthy shorts and shirt, legs badly abraded—they can see the truth and paddle in to get him.

Dan Stephens is stunned by his good fortune. He quickly forgives the boys' truculence, happy to be talking again, particularly to people. Questions tumble out of him, inane and unabated.

"How's the fishing?"

"How long have you been out?"

"Where are you headed?"

"When are you going back?"

They answer his questions, incredulous at what they've found. Stephens climbs into the second canoe. Skinny as a tall pine trunk, with legs that look as though their outer layer has been stripped, the Eagle Scout jabbers on. He is happy to be talking again. He is pleased to be back in a canoe, traveling easy. He doesn't notice the way they look at him, as though he's alien. They cannot quite believe his story, but the legs don't lie. They are as raw as a third-degree burn, and they glisten in the midday light with a moist layer of fresh blood.

The paddlers dig in and ferry Stephens to their camp, which lies around a far point, nestled below a stand of cathedral pines. To the right of the pines a brook rushes over boulders into the lake.

Once in camp the others who were sitting around the fire ring, or casting for fish from the shore, crowd around

Stephens. He repeats his story, takes his turn to answer questions. Cameras come out, and the kids and adults start snapping photos. Suddenly he's a rock star. A ravenous rock star.

One of the adults is a Jersey cop. Shortly after Stephens is out of the canoe, the policeman is on the radio with the Sommers Canoe Base. From the base the call relays up to the OPP. The OPP radios the ERT and within minutes Scott Moore, who is piloting the helicopter on yet another swing south, hears that Stephens has been found.

The pilot takes down the coordinates, and Scott Moore knows the place. Little Knife Lake, adjoining Ottertrack and Knife Lakes, on the Canadian side not too far northeast of Prairie Portage. The helicopter angles west-southwest in the midday sun. Scott Moore is anxious to see if it is their man.

Within fifteen minutes Moore is hovering over the campsite. He and the pilot can see canoes on the shore and bits of camp under the trees. There is no clear place to land. The only open place near the camp is at the stream's mouth, where the water rushes into the lake. Fifty yards to the right of camp a large boulder sits at the edge of the stream. Moore points toward the boulder. The pilot nods and angles the bird in.

"I think I can touch down one of her legs on that boulder," he yells, pointing at the rock.

Moore nods. "Take her in and I'll go fetch him."

They've already talked with the group by relayed radio. They know Stephens is ambulatory. He has wolfed down several granola bars and a sandwich, warding off the early stages of starvation, and has painfully sore feet and legs,

Dan Stephens on his way to the OPP helicopter, soon after being found by a group of Scouts from New Jersey, being assisted by unidentified New Jersey policeman (courtesy Constable Scott Moore, OPP-ERT)

but they're pretty certain he can make it into the chopper under his own power.

Back in Fayetteville, Jim and Mary Ann Stephens are hanging, awaiting word. It has been a difficult three days. Their old house in Monroe, and the new one in Fayetteville, have operated as central communications centers, keeping their network of family and friends apprised of any new developments—though there have been few.

Dan's parents have wondered how people get through an ordeal like this without the fellowship of a church and a powerful faith. The last three days have been absorbed by the move, the closing on the Monroe home (the only time they have been away), a blur of phone calls, and more prayer, more entreaties for divine intervention than either of them can ever remember making. At 3:30 PM the phone rings.

"We've got him," Doug Hirdler says. "And he's fine. I guess he's a little scraped up, but otherwise okay."

Jim's eyes fill with sudden tears. Mary Ann's throat closes with the rush of emotion. Both of them are mute while Hirdler gives them more details, though there aren't many. When they are able to speak, they pepper him with questions, especially, "Can we talk to him?" Hirdler explains that he hasn't actually spoken with their son; Dan is still in the woods. But they should hear from him soon.

Ten minutes later Sergeant Heather Lacey is on the phone to Jim and Mary Ann, confirming Hirdler's phone message. "We've found him and he's okay," she blurts. She explains that none of the searchers has yet seen Dan, but who else would walk out of the woods on the edge of wilderness, scratched up and starving, and claim to be Dan?

Lacey has never met Jim or Mary Ann, but over the last

forty-eight hours she has grown familiar with the parents' worry. She is happy to finally have something that offers them solace. Over the wires from Georgia, the tired, ecstatic silence is followed by more weeping and questions.

At the Sommers Canoe Base the Chattanooga Scouts have been bored and shunned—at least by some of the other scouting troops. The word of their predicament spread the day the Scouts returned. Some of the Sommers groups have been critical of their decision to leave their guide. The boys sense occasional blame by those who have no idea how the incident unfolded.

Tired of the glances and unspoken accusations, they have come into Ely to kill time and visit outfitters. Ely has a four- or five-block main street where outfitters, stores, and restaurants compete for the tourist trade. Cathy Antle, in to pick up supplies on her day off, runs into the Scouts on Main Street.

She tells them there is no word of Dan, that the opp is still searching. Then she watches them turn in to one of the town's biggest outfitters, where the Chattanooga group loses itself perusing top-of-the-line equipment. Some of the best canoes and gear in the world hang from ceilings and shelves, and these Scouts ogle the assemblage.

Back at her truck Cathy Antle has to check in with the station. Carrie Frechette gives her the excited word on Dan's appearance. Cathy rushes back to the store.

The troop of eight are still mulling over equipment. She sees Tim Jones and blurts, "They've found Dan! He's fine!" The others gather around the ranger, doubting they heard right. "He walked out on his own and was picked up by the opp less than an hour ago. Dan Stephens is safe!"

People walking along Main Street hear the scream go

up. A block away, heads turn toward the collective yell. Cathy hugs Tim Jones and he holds on. Tears well in Jerry Wills's eyes. Dan Stephens is alive. He is safe. For the first time in three long days Tim Jones, Jerry Wills and the teenagers feel a full measure of relief.

With minimal assistance Dan manages the brief hike to the helicopter. Scott Moore helps him through the door. Flying over the wilderness through which he struggled for the last three days—using the sun, stars, and his own dead reckoning—he is stunned at the speed with which they close the distance from the border to Atikokan. At the hospital he has his first opportunity to see a doctor and get cleaned up. Not long after his examination and shower, he gets a dose of penicillin.

Dan is exhausted, but restless. He needs to call Fayetteville.

At around 5:30 PM the Stephens's phone rings. Jim picks it up and hears, "Dad, it's Dan." Again, Jim is speechless, struck mute by the familiar sound of his son's voice.

Dan spends the next several minutes describing his ordeal. There is too much to tell, but he can sense his parents' relief. He tells them he is sure he'll be home soon. Given the condition of his legs, he doesn't expect to be finishing out his term as a guide. After the call he feels elated, like an athlete who has just given an amazing performance. He is jocular in the hospital room—but still polite and respectful, in the manner in which he was raised. When Constable Jim McGill comes through his door, Dan Stephens is ready to tell his story.

21

The Tent

Northeast of the Pow Wow Trail, BWCAW, Tuesday, October 30, 2001

By 8:40 AM, Nick Milkovich and pilot Dean Lee are focusing their air search on a large triangle of woods marked by Isabella Lake in the north-northeast, Ferne Lake in the east, and Pose Lake in the northwest. Although the previous evening turned cold, freezing some of the water along the shorelines, the weather is again moderating.

Sometime in the early morning the thermometer rises above freezing. In the last five days of freeze and thaw, the heavy snow blanket covering the area has gradually thinned. The warmth finally has its way with the thick white cover over Jason's tent. With little fanfare and the sound of a broom brushing nylon, the snow slides to either side of the orange fly. Now the tent sits atop the moss covered hump like a preternatural beacon.

At 9:20, barely into their customary routine, Milkovich and Lee spot something on a clear rise west of Arrow Lake. They have flown over the spot more than twenty times and seen nothing but a big hill covered in white with a long beaver pond south of it, and a swampy bog to the north. Now they see what appears to be an orange tent! They are dumbfounded.

"I think we found a tent," Nick stammers across the radio to IC. "But I know it wasn't there yesterday."

Back at IC they ask for a repeat, wanting to be sure they've heard him correctly.

"A tent," Milkovich repeats. "We are pretty sure we found a tent. Only thing is, I know it wasn't there yesterday."

At IC, BJ and Pete Smerud talk it over with Rebecca Francis, Ken Anderson, and Sherry Wright. Did they send any searchers into that area to spend the night? Would any of them set up camp on their own? Could any winter campers have slipped down the trail without their knowing?

Not a chance, they reason. For the last five days there has been perpetual occupation of the parking lot. There is no way seasonal backpackers could have gotten around them unnoticed. And there is virtually no other way into that region. It doesn't make sense.

"It's an orange tent?" BJ radios for clarification.

"An orange tent!" Milkovich repeats. He's excited by the find. The plane is turning circles over the spot. Others on the radio frequency, out in the field, have picked up on the discovery. The airwave chatter is starting to increase. Questions start flying.

"Only thing is," Milkovich manages to get out through the din, "there is no way to get there from the trail!" He sounds incredulous.

It doesn't make sense. BJ radios back for more clarification. "There is an orange tent," she repeats. "It is on a rise west of Arrow Lake, but there is no way in or out?"

"Affirmative," Nick rockets back. "Not that I can see. Bogs and swamp between it and the trail—which appears to be a good two miles to the west."

The plane circles over the spot to determine the GPS coordinates and looks for more signs.

Before Milkovich and Lee started their triangular air search, Conservation Officers Kipp Duncan and Marty Stage decided to take the ATVs up the trail, just to have another look around. IC gave them the okay, and by 8:30 AM they were throttling north, sliding and splashing through the muddy terrain. They've come up to the circular juncture and turned counterclockwise. At the point where the new Pow Wow Trail makes a ninety-degree turn to the left, they keep heading straight on the Old Pow Wow Trail.

They hear the plane making tight circles in the sky, and they know something's up. By the time their radio picks up Milkovich's chatter, they are much closer to the plane than to IC. They hear Milkovich clarify the tent's position. Then they check it on their own GPS devices, which is when they realize they are within a mile of the location.

From this particular point, radio transmission back to IC is static-ridden and garbled. They can hear Milkovich, but he cannot hear them.

"We are heading in to take a look," Marty Stage finally says, hoping IC will pick it up. He explains their location and estimates that they should be able to reach the tent within the hour.

"I'm not sure you can get there from where you're at,"

they manage to pick up from IC. They're not sure they've heard Milkovich correctly.

"We've got good enough coordinates," Stage repeats. "We'll get there."

Stage and Duncan have traversed their share of rough country. It is wet and cold, but not impassable. The day is moderating nicely. The sky is overcast, but it is bright and the clouds are high enough so they can follow the plane's tight circular flying pattern through the brush and trees. They park their ATVs beside the old Pow Wow Trail and start bushwhacking.

Far to the southwest, Deputy DeRosier, Ron VanBergen, Dan Spina, and Terry Olson are somewhere along the southwestern end of the trail, heading toward the Superstition Spur. As soon as they lock in on the tent's coordinates, they turn around and start back toward the area where the two COs dropped off their ATVs.

IC dispatches two dog crews with support to the area. Carla and Dale Leehy are also approaching the drop-off point with their dogs. Jeff Hasse and a couple of others are with the group. Even with ATVs it is a slow migration. Now everyone in the field struggles to converge on the tent.

As soon as the tent is spotted, Steve Van Kekerix is notified. For the first time in days he has something positive to tell the Rasmussens, who are back in the Cities, updating family, neighbors, and friends. The news raises a dizzying swirl of emotions. On the one hand, they are elated to know the searchers have found his tent. On the other, it sounds like there is no movement, no tracks. They are damned anxious—and would hardly have believed it was possible that the anxiety and dread they had endured for the past five days could deepen even further.

And the undersheriff can tell them little. Rescuers are converging on the point. Apparently, it is remote. He will contact them as soon as he knows anything more.

The Rasmussens ring off. In the house on Quinn Road, they feel reasonably certain they will know Jason's fate within a matter of two to three hours. They feel their last hope of seeing their son alive start to waver.

Deputy Milkovich explains that in order to reach the site all crews will have to go over some nasty swamp, bog, maybe even a river. But they will keep circling, giving them a good idea of the location. In the chaos of radio blather, Milkovich and Lee don't even know that Kipp Duncan and Marty Stage are slogging across the heavy terrain.

For the next hour the two cos struggle through bog and swamp. In places they are almost hip-deep in muck. It is hard going. Their feet and calves grow numb in the icy waters. But their goal keeps them focused.

Back at ic, the group in command doesn't know what to tell the two officers. They are having trouble keeping contact, and they begin to worry about corrupting the tent scene for the dogs. At one point they try to tell everyone to pull back to the staging area, where they will reconnoiter and figure out the next step. But by now the two officers are well on their way.

Marty Stage hears the order to return to ic. He is shocked. "Don't they want to see if the kid's in there?" he asks Kipp Duncan.

Kipp has been a co for less than a year. He is over a decade younger than the seasoned Marty Stage. "Maybe we should wait," he suggests.

"Wait for what?" Stage wants to know. "We're not walking all the way back. That's crazy."

They have heard the talk about marring what may be a crime scene. But they are officers, for Christ's sake. They have the training to deal with a crime scene, if it comes to that. "Let 'em jabber," Stage finally says. "We'll be careful, and we'll find out if the kid's in there."

Over the next half hour they make slow progress through three swamps. They are careful to flag their trail, leaving an obvious path for everyone to follow—at least those who can get there.

By now, IC has radio contact with the two officers and approves their actions. Milkovich and Lee, still circling over the spot, cannot see them from the air, even though they're wearing burnt-orange coats. It isn't until they are within 170 yards of the tent that Milkovich finally catches a glimpse of the two. Dean Lee swings the plane down over the men, turns it around, and indicates by flight path the trail they should take, such as it is.

Other than the occasional drone of the overhead plane and the diminishing radio cackle, the world is eerily still. The rising temperature has filled the air with moisture. It is not fog, but it seems thick, and there is little wind. To Kipp Duncan it looks as though no one has ever passed through this country. It is as though they've entered an ancient burial ground, and the spooky stillness makes them pause.

It takes the pair another ten minutes to close the distance to the tent. By now they are both heated by their effort, heavy with perspiration. When they finally approach the tent through a rise of trees along the western side of the long beaver pond, they aren't thinking about the cold. They are calling out for Jason Rasmussen. They yell his name, but off the surrounding ring of trees their cries echo back unanswered. They push forward.

Overhead, Milkovich and Lee keep circling, but there is no radio chatter. The silence around the two cos is intensified by the sudden absence of talk and static. Everyone is holding a breath, waiting for the two men to reach the tent and look inside. The entire area is quiet as a grave. And that's what the two men believe they will find here. Jason Rasmussen's grave.

They push up through the last small stand of pines and come out near the top of the rise, yards away from the tent. Both of them stop, examining the surrounding area for anything—prints, wrappers, a charred ring of stones.

The tent is sagging on the rise. There are no tracks in the snow around it. Down in front of it, the slope to the long beaver pond—practically a lake, now that they are on the rise above it—is steep and treacherous.

But right now the two men focus on the tent opening. The front of it is clear, uncovered in the snow. Beneath the orange overhang, the green tent entrance is closed.

"We're at the tent," Kipp Duncan radios back to ic. "Request permission to open it."

Back at ic, Pete Smerud, Pete Walsh, Rebecca Francis, BJ Kohlstedt, Steve Van Kekerix, and the others consider the officers' request. None of them can think of a single reason not to open the tent. They have already warned the officers to be careful about disturbing or contaminating the scene, and they know the cos are well trained to handle the situation.

Finally the two Petes nod, and BJ gives the okay. "You have permission to look in the tent," she says. "But don't enter it. Repeat," she says, "do not enter the tent."

"That's a 10–4," Kipp Duncan echoes back. "Open, but do not enter."

The officers are certain that Jason's body lies inside the tent. They smell none of the fetid, cloying odor of death, but then they wouldn't—given the temperatures over the last eight days, cool as a morgue.

Kipp Duncan moves forward, carefully stepping over the ten feet in front of him. He reaches down in the wet air. The sound of the zipper cuts through the late morning air. Kipp holds his breath and parts the flaps.

There, lying inside the tent, are the neat, well organized contents of Jason's pack, sleeping mattress, and down bag. Kipp looks it over, stunned. His heart is pounding and he can hear the rush of blood in his ears.

"Nothing," he manages to call back to Marty Stage. "Nothing but his supplies," he adds.

He hears Marty Stage radio back to IC. "The tent is empty," Stage reports. "Repeat. Jason Rasmussen not found in tent. Over."

Kipp looks through the opening. The tent's contents are neat, straight, put away, and laid out as though their owner had a penchant for order. But where in the hell is Jason? And at this point they don't even know if the tent is his. But who else could it belong to? The place is as stale as a burial crypt.

The two COs know the routine. Secure the potential crime scene and wait for backup. But at this point they can't see anything that remotely suggests a crime.

Still, they zip up the tent and back away from it the same way they approached.

"The site is secure," Marty Stage reports.

"The dogs and Deputy DeRosier's party are on their

way," BJ radios back. "Keep the scene clear and wait for the other teams."

"10–4," Stage confirms.

The two cos are beginning to feel the effects of their struggle through three swamps, the bogs, and the marsh. Now that they're not moving, the cold is starting to settle on them. After several minutes they decide to move well away from the tent. They hike over fifty yards south-southeast, to an area they know the other teams will have to pass in order to get to the tent. Then they build a fire and wait.

In the Cities, Jason's parents are waiting for Steve Van Kekerix's call. When it finally comes, Lee answers the phone. He nods into the receiver. Linda senses bad news. There are other cursory comments, but she knows she is not ready to hear the worst. She will never be ready. She feels a dull panic, an anxious mania rising inside her. She doesn't want to know, but she has to listen. She closes her eyes and prays.

When Lee signs off he turns to her. "It's his tent, but Jason's not in it," he repeats. They don't speak. The days have taken their toll. And now, when they were so close to an answer, confounding it is a calamity they aren't certain they can endure.

Later, when Lee is coherent enough to think, he places a call to Jason's sister, Heidi, in Washington, DC. "I think you'd better come home," he says.

More than three hours later, a little after 2:00 PM, the cos hear the dog teams and the others approach from the southeast. The teams are happy to come up out of the area to a warm blaze. Deputy DeRosier, Jeff Hasse, Carla and Dale Leehy and their dogs, Jim Couch and his dog Tanner, another air scenter—they are all wet, tired, and ready to take a break. It is a convivial gathering, though everyone complains about the effort it took to get here.

They quickly formulate a plan. The handlers will take the dogs to the tent and see what they can pick up. Then Deputy DeRosier and the cos will examine and catalog the tent's contents. They will begin searching the area in concentric circles, starting close in and widening the distance from the tent as they work their way outward. They are all to keep a sharp eye out for any signs of Jason's passing.

By the time the dogs begin working, the skies are beginning to thicken and the wind starts to rise. The dogs whine over the area. One of them picks up a scent and goes down to the water. The other follows a meandering trail to the northeast. Jim Couch works with Tanner to the south.

Inside the tent, DeRosier makes a careful inventory of the contents. Jeff Hasse is behind him, radioing back DeRosier's list. They are struck by what they find. First, the contents are neat and orderly. He didn't leave in a panic. Second, there are no personal items to confirm that this is Jason's tent, though from the parents' recollection of what was packed, there is little question that it is. Third, Jason is an excellent environmentalist. They locate his trash bag, and a quick survey of its contents yields an exact accounting of his meals. They determine he probably left his tent last Wednesday, meaning he has been away from his tent with almost nothing—and apparently no matches—for almost a week.

Their last two observations are perhaps their most disconcerting. The parents described Jason as an expert backpacker. But Jeff Hasse notes several equipment details that contradict that notion. "His tent is in okay shape, but it's old and worn. It's a Eureka Timberline—blaze orange—

from the late seventies. His backpack is really more of a travel pack. And he has a full-sized bow saw and a stove." Hasse shakes his head at the size and heft of it. "Rather than waterproof matches, he's got one of those grill lighters. Rather than a good-quality sleeping pad he has an air mattress. For a backpacking trip, he has lots of clothes. He has clean pants and a couple of shirts folded in his gear. He's carrying ten times the weight he needs to carry."

He may have been experienced, but not in this particular kind of camping. Their quick survey of Jason's equipment suggests that Jason may have known park camping, but not true wilderness.

And finally, the book *Wilderness Survival,* leaning against the side of his pack, has one dog-eared page. Officer DeRosier opens it and starts perusing the section on hypothermia. It makes everyone wonder if Jason may have contemplated suicide. That might explain why he walked off into the woods with no equipment, food, or matches. The dog-eared page is a bad sign.

They are careful to document all the contents in the tent, radioing their list back to the staging area. DeRosier and Hasse conclude Jason voluntarily left his camp and for some unknown reason didn't return. They cannot imagine any good scenarios. When they finally step back from their tent inventory, the dogs are still working the immediate area.

At 3:20 Ken Anderson radios Jeff Hasse and tells him there is a bad front moving in. Ken has been monitoring the plane traffic and Nick Milkovich and Dean Lee corroborate Ken's weather report. They have seen dark clouds building in the north-northwest, clouds that are coming in fast. The weather report from the hangar is bad. A nasty freezing rainstorm is moving in. The plane has to return to

Shagawa Lake, and they suggest the searchers contemplate getting back to the staging area.

Back beside the fire, the searchers hold a general meeting. The dogs are still searching, but don't seem to be picking up anything definite. They believe, from their animals' behavior, Jason was definitely here, but the dogs don't seem to be identifying a particular direction. One of them repeatedly works the shoreline of the small lake, making some of them suspect Jason is somewhere underwater, anchored in its muddy bottom.

As they stand and sit around the fire, one of the searchers—dressed in hunting gear—reaches into his backpack and pulls a sandwich out of a zippered pouch. Jeff Hasse admires the gesture. He surveys the group, and notices that everyone here is properly equipped and clothed for the expedition, carrying plenty of survival gear should any one of them get lost in the woods. He cannot ever remember being on a search with a better equipped and more experienced crowd.

But only one or two have brought the proper equipment to spend the night. IC orders everyone back to the staging area. They will reconnoiter, let the storm pass, and return at first light.

Reluctantly, the searchers begin to clear the scene. Everyone, including the dogs, starts back through the bogs and swamps. It's going to be a long haul out. They probably won't reach IC until well after dark. And from the looks of it, they will be bone cold and covered with rime ice.

Less than a half mile away, it has been another tiring, long day. Jason has heard the plane overhead, to the southeast, almost the entire morning and afternoon. Earlier it passed overhead twice, but he was too tired to climb to the top of his stump and wave. From his perch on his log home he simply waved, exhausted, and then blew his whistle.

The previous night wasn't good for his feet and legs. The cold settled into his feet and began working its way up his legs. By morning he was numb to his lower calf. And now he doesn't have the energy to get up and move around, working the circulation back into his limbs. He is exhausted. He has one more cup of water and manages to fill up his bottle with snow, to bring it into his hovel for the night. But he is cold. Throughout the day his shivering rarely abates, and the periodic bone-rattling contributes to his misery and fatigue.

Jason knows he is freezing.

Now and then, he hears things in the woods. Ravens appear in the nearby trees, and he tries to speak with them. Later, he thinks he hears wolves. He talks to the wolves, tells them how wonderful they are, how much he admires their cunning.

Finally, in late afternoon, he turns to complete his letters. Once he finishes with his lists of usernames, passwords, accounts, he starts to let his parents know he loves them and does not want them to suffer. He wants to let them know he has been happy with his life, fulfilled. He writes about how deeply he cares for them, how lucky he has been. He loves them all more than he can possibly convey with a pen and a stretch of bark. The lunacy of writing this on birch bark makes him smile. And then he feels a surge of emotion he cannot contain. He begins weeping in the woods. He is not ready to die. He doesn't know if he's going to awaken. After he crawls into his hollowed-out tree, he is not certain he will have the strength to crawl out.

The notion that this may be his final night, at least his

last night sitting upright, brings a deep melancholy that weighs on him like a pile of stones. He is surprised he has tears, given his meager intake of water. And then he says out loud, as the dusk light is overcome by clouds, "I love you. I love you all."

The wind picks up in the branches. Up on the rise to the west of his tree he swears he hears the distant strains of Mexican music. It's faint, but reminiscent of the music he sometimes heard in southern California. He smiles now to recall it. He knows it is impossible that a mariachi band could be playing in the darkening north woods. But he appreciates the minor hallucination.

His disposable camera has twenty-four pictures. He has saved the last one. He wants to wave goodbye, to give his parents and his sister one last glimpse of him on the evening of his last day.

Near dusk, with storm clouds moving in fast, he holds the camera at arm's length and positions the lens. He doesn't have the strength to hold the camera long. He summons the best face he can muster. He tries to smile. His large blue eyes try to convey to his family that he's okay, he loves them, and that he will be okay. He is ready to accept whatever comes.

He raises his right hand and waves, then snaps the picture. The flash goes off, and he thinks it probably worked. Now, though, he's just too tired to care.

For one more night he crawls into his hollowed-out tree.

Jason has never experienced this kind of fatigue. He pulls the branches over his head, sealing the hollow tree opening. Not long after he huddles inside he hears the rain begin. Throughout the night the steady rainfall seeps into his shelter, its icy fingers wetting his shoulder, hip, and leg. The cold grip rattles his body with shivers and shakes,

Jason Rasmussen's last picture (courtesy Jason Rasmussen)

though some time after dark, consciousness lapses into a place where he can no longer feel the cold—where for a brief time he can no longer feel anything.

On their way out across the swamps, leaving the tent behind, no one talks about Jason's fate. But Kipp Duncan is certain about one thing: there's no way Jason Rasmussen is alive. No one knows what happened to him, but everyone agrees that he is dead. For obvious reasons they will continue as though it is search and rescue, but now everyone feels the words no one utters: it is *recovery,* recovery of Jason's body.

Back at IC, waiting for the teams to come out of the field, BJ makes a call. She contacts SARDA and requests cadaver dogs. She knows there are several in the state. She's not sure where Jason is, but she suspects he's at the bottom of that lake. Cadaver dogs are trained to scent corpses in wilderness and water. She suspects this one will be found in water. She's already thinking ahead, knowing the recovery could be much faster with as many cadaver dogs in the field as possible.

In the Cities, Mark Haskins and DeeDee Grant, Mary McCormick, and Kathy Newman—all trained dog handlers with excellent cadaver dogs—are summoned. They start the journey north, expecting to be at the IC staging area by first light.

Everyone in the field makes it back after dark. They are covered with rime ice. They hike to their ATVs, and then ride out of the dark like frozen zombies. They struggle to thaw themselves beside a fire. For Jeff Hasse, cold and numb to his inner core, it is the one last bit of physical evidence he needs to know for certain Jason is no longer alive. No one could survive a night like this one—particularly after six days without food or shelter.

Rebecca Francis has arranged for everyone to stay in the Isabella Community Center. A local bar and restaurant supplies pizza and drinks. The searchers and dog handlers change into dry clothes. Rebecca hands out garbage bags and instructs everyone to fill them with their soaking clothes. She'll get them dry.

Steve Van Kekerix, Pete Smerud, Pete Walsh, BJ Kohlstedt, Jeff Hasse, and Ken Anderson contemplate tomorrow's efforts. After some time they realize the recovery could involve water, rock climbing, cutting through thick brush, ATVs—the list of possible equipment needs is staggering. Pete Smerud heads off to begin sorting out equipment and placing it in color-coded, waterproof bags.

Finally, late that night, exhausted, the teams find open spaces on the community center floor to spread their mats and bags. Soon everyone is asleep.

Steve Van Kekerix makes a late night call to the Rasmussens. He informs them of their progress, and their plans for the morning. Lee listens to the undersheriff, thankful for the update. But he hears the tone in Steve's voice.

Back at Rebecca Francis's house the living room is closest to the laundry. She has a good night's work in front of her. In order to get everyone's clothes washed, dried, and sorted, she's going to have to run several loads. She puts in the first batch and retires to her living room couch. At least from here, she thinks, she will be able to hear when the buzzer sounds the end of a wash or dry cycle. She lies down and closes her eyes, hoping for a little shuteye. Every twenty minutes, her sleep is interrupted by a buzzer.

22

Finding Jason Rasmussen

Northeast of the Pow Wow Trail, BWCAW, Wednesday, October 31, 2001

Before dawn the crowd at the Isabella Center has been fed, coffeed, and given fresh, clean clothes. They head back to the IC communications van, where everyone gathers before first light. Mary McCormick, Mark Haskins, DeeDee Grant, and Kathy Newman have arrived with their three cadaver dogs. The dogs are all handsome, large German shepherds, striking with their low-slung hips, big heads, and massive chests. Before entering the field, they are fitted with orange canine search-and-rescue vests.

Jeff Hasse will accompany the group with three ATVs and support from Finland Search and Rescue. Earlier in the morning he had had one of his migraines, and he didn't relish the idea of returning for another nasty slog through those woods. But his migraine finally dissipated, and now he accepts the challenge.

IC is prepared. BJ is incident commander. Pete Smerud is in charge of operations. Steve Van Kekerix is the chief liaison and information officer, and he is also in charge of the purse—should they need another pizza lunch, dinner, or more gasoline. Rebecca Francis is in charge of planning. And Swede Larson manages logistics.

Larson is the Silver Bay commander. Unfortunately, he is preparing for a hip replacement, so he hasn't been able to enter the field. But every time the propane is exhausted, the generators die, or the volunteers' fire wants wood—Swede is on it. Whatever this day brings, IC is ready for it.

They plan to send one team with dogs in from the south, following yesterday's slog to the tent site, and one up the northern stretch of trail, veering due north on the old portage trail to Lake Insula, turning due east somewhere around Ahmoo Creek, seeing if they can find an easier way in. Deputy Milkovich and Pilot Dean Lee will continue doing flyovers of the area.

The team on the trail needs to blaze an ATV trail to the tent. They will need to haul in recovery supplies and to haul out Jason's tent and equipment, as well as to extract their own equipment from the field. And though no one says it, they expect that they will need an ATV with its accompanying pod to haul out his body.

Hasse, McCormick, Haskins, Grant, and Newman will work in to the site from the north. They get ATV assistance from Finland Search and Rescue support people. These guys are young and expert at clearing trail. They live in this country, and know how to wheel through rough terrain. By the time both teams get started, it is 8:40 in the morning.

The dogs and people take turns on the ATV and the trailers. The column makes slow progress up the trail. After a two-mile slog to the circular Pow Wow Trail juncture, both teams turn northeast, following the Pow Wow counter-clockwise for another couple of miles. At the point where the trail turns ninety degrees due northwest, the southern team continues another mile onto the old Pow Wow Trail, where they are finally forced to park their vehicles and head into the swamps on foot.

From this location the distance to the tent is about a mile, but the difficult path crosses three swamps, several beaver dams, and some nasty marsh and bog. Those who went yesterday remember the search, and they know it will take at least a couple of hours to find the simplest route through the muck.

Hasse and the northbound crew turn northwest on the trail, moving ahead with ATVs almost another two miles to the Lake Insula portage juncture. Here the Pow Wow Trail turns due west, but it is not the clear choice. The eight members of the northbound team reflect on how easily the Lake Insula portage could sucker people off the Pow Wow. By comparison, the western Pow Wow Trail looks like a narrow game path. The Lake Insula portage is wide and clear. The rock cairn someone set up to mark the spot is covered over by brush and snow. There is no way for the group to know they are traversing Jason's exact path.

They turn north, making slow headway up the portage.

About two miles to the east, Jason Rasmussen has managed one more climb out of his hollowed-out home. The temperature is moderating. He cannot feel his feet, and his lower legs are numb to mid-calf, but he doesn't have the energy to move around and re-establish circulation and warmth. Instead his body continues its periodic bouts of shivering.

Jason is no longer hungry. He is thirsty, and he manages to trickle down the cup of melted snow from his water bottle. More than satisfying, the brief hydration raises his spirits. But his normal buoyancy is so far diminished now he can only sit and watch the cold forest around him. With his morning draught, something else has entered him. Calm. He sits near his log and feels an unusual stillness. Almost an egoless letting go.

Yesterday he was sure he heard wolves. They were south of him. But he's been hearing plenty, these last few days. He feels as though the woods are playing tricks. More than they've already played on him. Now he is beginning to hallucinate. Not full-fledged hallucinations, but minor alterations in perception. People talking over the hill. The Mexican music. The wolves. He wonders about it all. This much isolation under these kinds of circumstances, where his death seems inevitable, can have a noticeable effect on a mind and the body's ability to perceive.

The air is heavy with moisture. It is cold, but already over forty degrees. The day feels as if it is going to warm, but the wet will keep Jason cold. He continues to shiver.

He is tired now. He thinks he will sit outside awhile. He feels relatively certain the next time he settles into his shelter he won't be getting up. *It is a nice pine log*, he thinks. *It's a fine coffin, if it comes to that*. He feels pretty certain that sometime within the next two or three days—certainly no more—his body will succumb to its regimen of no calories, little water, unremitting cold, and sleeplessness. But for now he feels good about being outside. He likes being in the overcast, misty mid-morning, listening to the trees and brush. He watches them out of eyes sharpened by a sense of impending death. He has stopped thinking, and he lets the world flow in. It is almost as though he is seeing it for the first time. He is haunted by the rhythm of trees. He is mesmerized by the perfect illumination of the muted morning light.

And then as if he hasn't been taunted enough, the plane comes over. In the past it has come close enough for Jason to see the face of the pilot. But it's as though he is invisible. This time, he barely rises, stammers to his feet, manages to wave and then raise the whistle to his lips. He blows, but it is an anemic whistle. Still, it is much louder than he could project with his own voice. But he knows he only acts from habit. Something about blowing the whistle after the fly-overs is comforting. He doesn't want to give up. Not just yet. Not while he still has the energy to raise the whistle to his lips.

He sits down and awaits another flyover, though for what he cannot say.

The eight members of the northern team keep following the trail north over Ahmoo Creek. After a short hike they come to a place where another trail section turns east. They hike onto it, still able to move through the trees with the ATVs, but not for long. After a half mile, the ATVs can go no farther. The group is heading into heavy terrain, and the trail—while still partially apparent—is impassable, except afoot.

Hasse radios their progress at 11:22. The three ATV operators are going to hang back and try to clear a wide enough path for the vehicles to reach Jason's tent.

Hasse, Haskins, Grant, Newman, and McCormick continue east and then south toward the tent, the cadaver dogs accompanying them. They are to work their way down toward the tent and at some point intersect the crew that just now—if Hasse has heard it correctly via his radio—made it to Jason's last camp.

Jim Couch and Carla Leehy are at the tent with their dogs Tanner and Bear. The two dogs begin milling around the tent, trying to pick up scent.

The northern group continues east. The trail becomes harder to find through the thick cover. They continue along it, then lose it, then recover it. Near noon they come to a blowdown area. Much of it appears fresh—perhaps from the same storm that dropped all this snow. Some of it is very old, probably from the July 1999 storm. But at 12:35 Jeff Hasse radios out to IC and the southern group that they have lost the trail.

"It's just disappeared," he declares.

Hasse knows that if they want to make a relatively straight path to the tent they will have to do some serious orienteering. His hands are full with the radio.

"Who wants to work the compass?" he asks, but there are no takers. The handlers are worried about their dogs. The blowdown area is like a sea of pongee sticks, and a careless step on one of the upturned sharpened points could skewer a paw. They need to keep an eye on their animals. So Hasse continues with the compass, moving very slowly through and over the trees.

Mary McCormick and her cadaver dog Elle move out ahead, then down a rise. Elle likes to be in front, and Mary has trouble putting brakes on her.

To the south, near Jason's tent, Tanner and Bear have picked up a scent and are heading north along the long lakeshore, turning into the woods. Mary McCormick calls out to Elle and then hears something. She pauses, leaning into the sound, wanting to be sure she has heard it. Then she turns and looks back at the others, approaching from behind.

"I think I just heard a whistle," she says.

The others stop and listen. No one hears anything.

Jeff Hasse radios in to IC. "We think we heard a whistle," he repeats. He is on the air waves. It is 1:18. The drone of the plane approaching from the west, drowns out all other sounds. DeeDee Grant wonders if they are hearing some kind of harmonic resonance from the plane, or a whistle from the southern group moving north. Hasse asks the plane to circle out of the area. He radios to the southern crew and asks them if anyone whistled.

The northern group pauses while they wait for a response.

"Negative," the answer comes back. "No one's whistled out of our group."

The southern group is still moving through the woods, but everyone is together, and they are over a mile from Hasse and the others.

DeeDee Grant gets on a log and blows hard on her whistle, but there is no response.

"I'm sure I heard a whistle," Mary McCormick reaffirms.

Jeff Hasse radios back to IC and asks if everyone came in out of the rain yesterday. He wonders if they left someone stranded, and the searcher is in the area. Then Hasse hears the whistle.

"Did anyone hear *that?*" McCormick asks.

"That was a whistle," Hasse confirms. Kathy Newman agrees.

DeeDee Grant whistles again, but there is no response. Now Hasse is certain they are dealing with a searcher left in the woods. But IC has double-checked its head count. They can account for everyone in the woods and back at Forest

Center. From their estimation the only people in the woods are those on the teams that went in this morning.

The northern team is confident they have heard something. They decide to work with the dogs. They begin heading south, spreading out in a line through the fallen trees. The plane has been out of the area for over five minutes. The crew makes slow progress through the blowdown.

Jason thinks he hears a wolf bark to the south. He's unsure, though. Then thinks he hears one from the north.

South of Jason, Tanner is angry with Jim Couch, his owner. He is on the trail of something. Over a thousand yards from Jason, Tanner smells him, and Bear does, too. The rescuers are having trouble keeping up. Tanner voices his impatience with a brief series of anxious barks.

To the north, the team with cadaver dogs pauses. Elle gets into some kind of territorial dispute with one of the other dogs. She growls, then barks a warning.

Jason is certain it is a wolf. He stands up and listens. Then he calls out through the woods, in the direction of the northern rescue team.

"Hi, wolfies," he calls. It is odd for them to be out in the early afternoon, but he feels good to know he is not alone. He would like to see the wolf pack. But he knows he is not safe in his weakened condition.

Then he hears a voice. It's a question, and he wonders if it's real.

"What's your name?" comes drifting over the rise.

"Jason Rasmussen," he yells.

But back at the northern group all they can hear is a voice. The words are too muffled to be understood.

Jeff Hasse still believes it is a lost searcher. No one—not the two groups in the field or the congregation back at IC—considers that it could be Jason. They gave up on finding Jason alive before last night's deadly ice storm. Today, with their cadaver dogs, their search through the woods is all about recovery, locating and returning with Jason's body.

And then they hear a plaintive voice, almost a wail. "I'm lost!" Somewhere over the hill.

"Hello," three members of the group call out. "Whistle," one of them instructs. "Keep whistling. Who are you?" they yell.

Jason pauses, manages the strength to climb up on his vertical stump, and hears the last question. He is struck by its strangeness. Who in the hell else is lost in these woods?

"Jason!" he screams back. "I'm Jason Rasmussen!"

All of the searchers hear it clearly.

The entire northern team races through the blowdown, trying to keep up with their dogs. Mark Haskins is the first to come over the rise, following the intermittent blasts of Jason's whistle. He sees Jason on top of the stump and he is stunned.

Jeff Hasse is behind Mark, the others following closely. Hasse cannot believe it. None of them believes it. Hasse's radio is working as he strides forward. They hear Jason's voice at 1:24. It takes two minutes to cross through the woods to his location. At 1:26 Jeff Hasse radios back to IC, and to the southern group, and the overhead search plane, that they have found Jason Rasmussen—alive.

Back at IC, Steve Van Kekerix, BJ, and Pete Smerud ask for clarification. They think they have heard it right, but they are incredulous.

"It's Jason," Hasse repeats. "And he's standing."

Jason Rasmussen, minutes after he was rescued (photo by Jeff Hasse, courtesy Ken Anderson)

The Rasmussen household is all but in mourning. Heidi has returned on an early morning flight. Lee and Linda take her to Lee's mother's house, where they try to eat lunch.

For the Rasmussens, it is almost as though Jason's body is in the next room. They believe he is up there somewhere, and he will be found. Lee has learned more about wilderness survival than he ever expected, certainly more than he ever wanted to know. He knows, for instance, that the likelihood of finding Jason alive is virtually nil. No one has ever existed that many days alone in those temperatures and lived to tell the story. No one. They all know.

What guides Lee now are the words that have guided him since Jason's failure to return. "Pray for the best," he

On the scene of Jason's rescue. From left to right: Kathy Newman, Mark Haskins, Jason Rasmussen, Pat Peterson, Mary McComick, Ed Judkins, and DeeDee Grant (photo by Jeff Hasse, courtesy Mary McCormick)

thinks, "but prepare for the worst." In the beginning, it was easier to lean toward the start of that sentence. Increasingly, he resigns himself to the unimaginable worst.

Later, in an aside to Jason's grandmother, Lee talks to her about burying their son in the family plot.

The Rasmussens' cupboards are as barren as a January field. The search for Jason has been going on for almost a week. During that time, their lives have been everything but routine. Now their refrigerator contains condiments and stale cheese. Heidi is home now, and they know they will have to stop and buy something to replenish their supplies. They have no appetites, but know they must continue, move forward. Maybe buying groceries will at least give them something else to think about.

Inside Jason's tree, reinforced and lined with pine boughs
(courtesy Mary McCormick)

There is a Costco near their house. On the way home
from Grandma's, they swing by the Costco to pick up a few
items.

For the brief few seasons Steve Van Kekerix has been Lake
County undersheriff, he has had to make some difficult
calls. Usually, it is over traffic accidents. It's about the worst
part of his job.

When Jeff Hasse's radio call comes in to IC, Van Kekerix is standing with BJ, Pete Smerud, Rebecca Francis, Swede Larson, and the others. Everyone in IC, everyone on the search, everyone in the field, assumed the cadaver dogs would be the ones to find Jason, not their handlers. The news that Jason is alive, that he is standing, that he appears to be—at least from the first frenetic accounts flooding into IC—in remarkable shape, is incomprehensible. No one has ever survived this long in the forest without food, water, or shelter. And at this point they know nothing about Jason's remarkable story, how he kept himself alive.

For six days Steve Van Kekerix has been the county official in charge of the search and rescue. Everyone turned to him for permission and assistance, and he was the primary voice between the search area and the family. He kept the Rasmussens informed, being honest without sharing all the negative perspectives. But he pulled no punches. He let the Rasmussens know, and they were grateful.

Lee, Linda and Heidi, standing near their car in the Costco parking lot, don't want to answer the call coming into Lee's cell phone. He can see from the display it's Van Kekerix. It is 1:35 PM, and he knows the searchers have been in the field all morning with dogs. He knows the call. He wasn't expecting it so soon. But he thinks he knows the words he is going to hear. For a brief moment he considers not answering.

After flipping open his phone, about all he can manage is a hoarse "Hello." The wind is out of his diaphragm. He feels lightheaded, not entirely present. He hears the familiar voice.

"Jason's found," Van Kekerix yells. "He's alive. He's well!"

* * *

There are no words for how news of Jason's survival and condition—after so long alone in the woods, in the heart of one large tree, after so many people have been searching for him for so long—is heard by Jason's parents, and his sister. This is one of the times in people's lives when prayers are answered, resoundingly and with undiminished affirmation.

In the brief time it takes to speed home, Lee, Linda, and Heidi rock the inside of their car with the remarkable news. "He's found," they repeat, screaming it. "He's alive! He's well!"

They spend less than five minutes tossing clothes into bags. On their way out of town, heading north, they give Jason's grandmother the good news and ask her to spread the word. They know there is no better emissary for conveying rapid news to the wide family network and the wider world than Jason's grandmother.

Van Kekerix has told them it will probably be at least two hours before Jason is out of the woods. Then he'll be taken to some local hospital to be examined. The Rasmussens will find out where on their way north.

Jason was discovered at 1:26. Less than ten minutes later, Van Kekerix phoned the Rasmussens with the miraculous news. But it takes a team of searchers, ATV drivers, trail makers, and communications people another three and a half hours to get him out of the woods. During the long wait, a crowd containing almost everyone who participated in the search begins to form.

Yesterday, Kipp Duncan, the CO who first opened Jason's tent to discover it vacant, was happy he had work the next day in Two Harbors. He felt certain Jason could never be found alive. His work in Two Harbors was preferable to searching for Jason's body in these difficult woods. Now, on his radio, he picks up the incredible news. In less than an hour he pulls in to the IC.

Joe Linneman, the deputy who verified the presence of Jason's car six long nights ago, is back on duty after several days off. On special occasions, Joe plays bagpipes. Today he tosses them into his truck and heads down to the trailhead.

Over fifty people and an ambulance wait in the trailhead lot. When Jason comes out of the woods, a cry goes up unlike anything he has ever heard. They take him to Miller Dwan Medical Center in Duluth, where he will be treated for severe frostbite, and where he is finally reunited with his parents and sister. And where he can finally give each of them the birch-bark letters he wrote during the darkest days of his life.

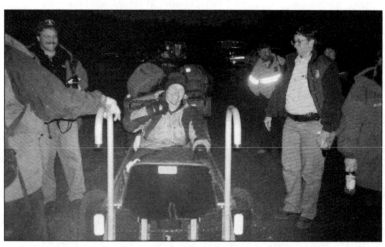

Arrival in Pow Wow Trailhead parking lot. Left to right: Steve Van Kekerix, Jason Rasmussen, Ken Anderson, Rebecca Francis (courtesy Jeff Hasse)

EPILOGUE

Jason Rasmussen lost two toes and the tips of all the others to frostbite and spent a long convalescence at his parents' house, during which he briefly endured a form of post-traumatic stress disorder. He was featured in several news stories and local news programs, and even on National Geographic's *This Week*, Corbin Bernsen's *Wild Survival*, and the *Oprah Winfrey Show*. When Winfrey asked Jason if the experience changed the way he lived or experienced life, he replied, "Sometimes I will be walking down the street and the wind will blow through the trees and I'm overcome by the beauty of that moment. And also there's a feeling of real peace. I don't know what that is, but I've never felt it before, and it's great." Several media outlets tried to obtain exclusive rights to Jason's story, but he refused, considering his misadventure an opportunity to instruct so that others might avoid the pain of his ordeal. When he was well enough, he presented the details of his survival at REI and elsewhere. His parents thanked Minnesota's volunteer search and rescue community by hosting a weekend conference at which many of the state's volunteer groups shared strategies for coordinating future rescue efforts.

Jason Rasmussen returned to medical school after the first of the year. Today he is an emergency room surgeon-in-residence in Sacramento, California, where he continues to repay the altruism of Minnesota's volunteers by saving others' lives.

Dan Stephens had a chance to see the group from Chattanooga before they returned home. He assured them they had done the right thing and congratulated them on their one-day sprint across the lakes. Soon afterwards, he returned home to Georgia, cutting his guiding season short. His parents had local doctors examine his lacerated legs. They removed the bandages and were shocked at his condition. Fortunately, with further treatment, his legs and his eye healed. He became an expert at creating fire without matches, demonstrating and teaching the technique to Scouts and others interested in wilderness survival.

When he was finding his way through wilderness, Stephens could tell that he had a phenomenally heightened awareness and a deep internal focus: it was "the highest degree of concentration in my life. I was in this zone that I don't think I'll ever be in again. . . . I had a lot more capacity than I expected." After being ferried across the water by the New Jersey Scouts, he says, "I wasn't the same person. That's when I felt the pain." The experience also made him re-evaluate his perspective on life. "All of this is temporary," he says, describing his everyday encounters with family, friends, and other experiences. "We really should take advantage of it."

Today Dan Stephens is a hydrologic technician with the U.S. Geological Survey in Atlanta, Georgia. He still loves to spend time in the wild, for pleasure and for work.

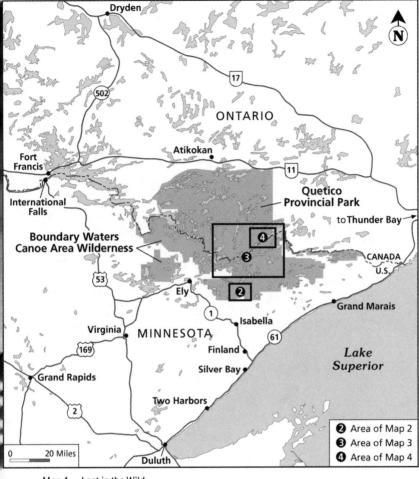

Map 1   Lost in the Wild

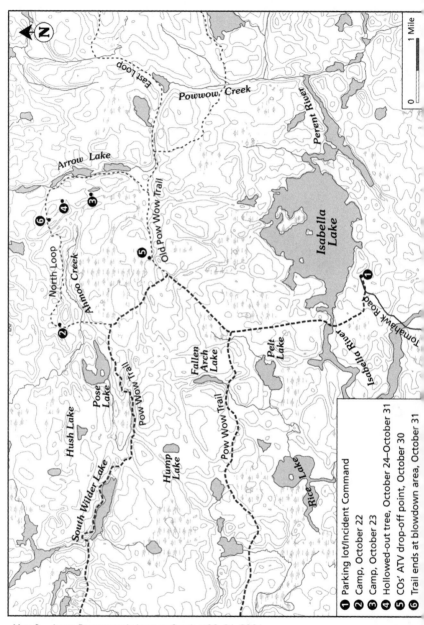

Map 2   Jason Rasmussen's Journey, October 22–31, 2001
Information courtesy Ken Anderson and Jeff Hasse

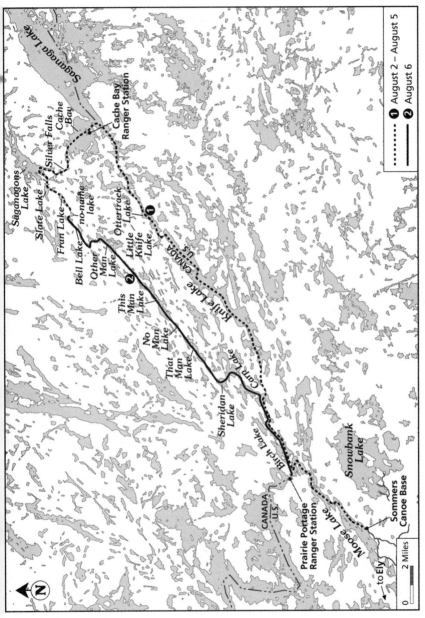

Map 3   The Route of the Scouts, August 2–6, 1998

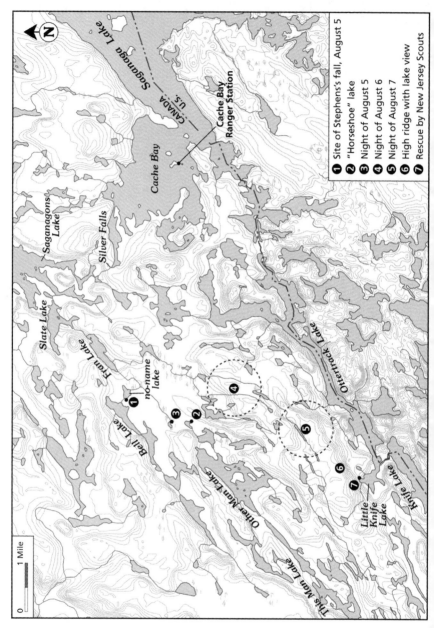

Map 4   Dan Stephens's Journey, August 5–8, 1998

ACKNOWLEDGEMENTS

Writing a book of this type involves a veritable village of volunteers, officials, and witnesses, all of whom deserve mention.

For starters, thanks to Kathleen Weflen, the managing editor of *Minnesota Conservation Volunteer,* and Mary Hoff and Cathy Mix—also from the *Volunteer*—for thinking a story on the subject "Lost in the Woods" would be right for their magazine (January/February 2004 issue). The research for that article introduced me to a half-dozen remarkable stories of people who became lost.

If you're embarking on the journey of writing a book, it's good to have a guide like Ann Regan, editor in chief at Borealis Books. Her early interest in the project provided the necessary energy to give it life, and her suggestions and guidance along the way transformed the work from a sheaf of pages to the book you hold today. I can't speak for its quality, but I can tell you she made it better.

Jason Rasmussen was kind enough to take time away from his colossally hectic schedule as a surgeon-in-residence in Sacramento—on more than one occasion—to be interviewed. He was remarkably forthcoming with all aspects of his experience. His parents, Lee and Linda Rasmussen, were not only generous with their time, but also provided contact lists, pictures, videos, and a variety of other invaluable resources. There were over sixty volunteers and officials who participated in the six-day search for Jason. I interviewed almost half of them, gaining detailed recollections and perspectives. Some of the key volunteer leaders included BJ Kohlstedt, Jim Williams, Pete Smerud, Pete Walsh, and Swede Larson. Key officials included Lake County Undersheriff Steve Van Kekerix, Lake County Deputies Joe Linneman, Nick Milkovich, and Richard DeRosier, and U.S. Forest Service Law Enforcement Officer Rebecca Francis. Minnesota DNR Conservation Officers Kipp Duncan, Marty Stage, and Brad Johnson assisted in the effort. Other officials who participated in the search included Forest Service pilots Pat Loe, Dean Lee, and Wayne Ericson; Ron Van Bergen from DNR Fisheries; and Lake County Foresters Dan Spina and Terry Olson. Volunteer dog handlers included Carla and Dale Leehy, Mark Haskins, Mary McCormick, Kathy Newman, and Jim Couch. Jeff Hasse and Ken Anderson provided logistical, communications, and cartography support for the last two and a half days of the search, and they were particularly helpful in piecing together the last hours of Jason's rescue. And then there are those whom I did not interview, but whose efforts helped find Jason and make the story possible: the ground-pounders who did the heavy lifting, the Lake County Search and Rescue Volunteers who provided indispensable ATV support, and other volunteer dog handlers. Their efforts were appreciated.

Sam Cook of the *Duluth News Tribune* first told me about Dan Stephens and his lone walk in the woods. I read Sam's newspaper story of the encounter and was intrigued.

Once I finally tracked Dan down in Georgia, he was particularly helpful in detailing his ordeal. He drew maps and submitted to numerous interviews, follow-up emails, and phone calls. His parents, Jim and Mary Ann Stephens, were also helpful in describing their perspective regarding Dan's lone odyssey through the Quetico woods. Jerry Wills and Tim Jones, the two fathers with the Chattanooga Scout troop, were extremely helpful and forthcoming about their ordeal. One of the first people I spoke with regarding Dan Stephens's disappearance was Doug Hirdler, general manager of Northern Tier High Adventure, the scouting outfit where Dan was working when he disappeared. He and Joe Mattson, Northern Tier's program director, were both helpful. I cannot say enough about the informative assistance of the Ontario Provincial Police (OPP), Quetico Park Rangers, and other Canadian officials. Once they understood I wasn't muckraking, they openly shared their account of the OPP's search and rescue efforts. People who were interviewed or in some other way offered assistance included Provincial Coordinator for all OPP Emergency Rescue Teams Tim Charlevois; Constables James McGill, Jeff Moline, and Scott Moore (who provided the only photos of Dan's experience); Sergeants Heather Lacey, Phil Donaldson, Norm Mitchell, Paul Michpish, and Terry Blace; and Quetico Park Rangers Kathy Antle and Carrie Frechette.

And finally, many thanks to my family and friends. My family heard countless stories about my interviews during the writing of this book; without their support and occasional readings, I could never have written it. My friends Steve Sauerbry, Drew Skogman, and Mike Reeve taught me at eighteen that if you're going to get lost on a seven-mile-long island in the northern woods, it's good to have someone along who knows what he's doing. And my friends

Doug Johnson, Ron Solyntjes, and Eli Nemer whom have each, at varying times, in one form or another, been lost with me.

To honor Minnesota's volunteers, ten percent of the royalties on this book will be donated to Lake County Volunteer Search and Rescue, who will put the money to good use in Lake County and beyond. Without their remarkable altruism and sacrifice, people like Jason Rasmussen would not be alive.